From Here to Maturity
One Man's Walk with Christ

James P. Lareva

From Here to Maturity

Copyright © 2015 by James P. Lareva

Tri-Pillar Publishing
Anaheim Hills, California
Website: www.TriPillarPublishing.com
e-mail: tripillarpublishing@cox.net

ALL RIGHTS RESERVED. This book or parts thereof may not be reproduced in any form without prior written permission of the publisher.

International Standard Book Number --13:	978-1-942654-01-8

International Standard Book Number --10:	1-942654-01-4

Library of Congress Control Number:	2015948014

All Scripture quotations, unless otherwise indicated, are taken from the Holy Bible, New International Version®, NIV®. Copyright ©1973, 1978, 1984, 2011 by Biblica, Inc.™ Used by permission of Zondervan. All rights reserved worldwide. www.zondervan.com The "NIV" and "New International Version" are trademarks registered in the United States Patent and Trademark Office by Biblica, Inc.™

The Scripture quotation marked (ESV) is from The Holy Bible, English Standard Version® (ESV®), copyright © 2001 by Crossway, a publishing ministry of Good News Publishers. Used by permission. All rights reserved.

Front cover photos:
- Top row, from left:
  - Jim as a boy with his favorite toy rabbit (Muskegon, MI, age 2)
  - Playing baseball (Muskegon, MI, age 10)
  - In the Navy (Camp Lejeune, NC, age 20)
- Bottom row, from left:
  - Concordia Seminary graduation, with Rev. Bill Scheer (Springfield, IL, 1961)
  - Retired but still preaching (2008, Orange County)

Back cover photos:
- Top row, from left:
  - Jim and brother Dave (Arcadia, MI)
  - Concordia Seminary graduation photo (Springfield, IL, 1961)
- Bottom row, from left:
  - Jim and brother Dave (Twin Lake, MI, 1960s)
  - Baptizing grandson Greg (Moorpark, CA, 2007)

Cover design by Peter Dibble, Wilsonville, OR

First edition, July, 2015
Printed in the United States of America

To my oldest son, Mark, 1958-2013

Contents

Preface	7
Timeline of My Life – Jim Lareva	8
Chapter 1: Remembrances, Reminiscences, and History of My Early Life (1927-1945)	11
Chapter 2: My Mother ("Mom")	53
Chapter 3: U.S. Navy (1945-1949)	71
Chapter 4: My Valpo Years (1950-1953)	103
Chapter 5: My Life as a High School Teacher and Coach	121
Chapter 6: My Life in Sports (Mostly Baseball)	139
Chapter 7: The Women in My Life	159
Chapter 8: Seminary Years (1957-1961)	201
Chapter 9: My Three Sons	213
Chapter 10: Congregations I Served in My Ministry	225

Preface

Early in my marriage to Nancy, I heard her voice clearly: "Jim! Why don't you write down these stories from your life that you keep telling me? They are very interesting and worth being recorded so others might enjoy reading them." I kind of shrugged off her suggestion with the words, "I've written hundreds of sermons, delivered academic papers, and addressed many groups of people. Why would I take on such a task now?" Little more thought was given to the idea for a while. Then, one day Nancy showed me an article in our local newspaper about some special classes for seniors at the local Senior Center in the city of Orange, California. One class was entitled, "It's time to write your own life-story." In deference to Nancy's urging more than any real interest on my part, I signed up for the six-week, once-a-week class. Our instructor immediately put our little class of eight people at ease by saying, "Don't be self-conscious about using 'I' and 'me' in such writing because you're not writing so much for yourself as for those who will read it, especially your friends and family, including grandkids for years to come, as well as anyone who is curious."

Every week, each one of the class members presented a brief story about some incident, event, or happening in their life. From that time on, I began my "first person" account of my life. I am indebted to Andy and Josephine Dibble; when I showed them some of my "chapters," they enthusiastically encouraged and supported me to put it all together in book form through their own successful Tri-Pillar Publishing company. This resulted in many long nights of writing and re-writing, including a great deal of excellent correcting, revising, and additions by Andy and Josephine. I am calling my story *From Here to Maturity*, based on Ephesians 4:13 – "until we all reach unity in the faith and in the knowledge of the Son of God and become mature, attaining to the whole measure of the fullness of Christ."

Rev. James P. Lareva
Orange, California
July, 2015

Timeline of My Life – Jim Lareva

September 7, 1927_____Born in Madison, WI to Dano and Alvina Lang Lareva

September 20, 1927 – 1931_____Lived in Roosevelt Park, Muskegon, MI

1931 – 1935_____Lived on 8th St., Muskegon Heights, MI

1935 – 1936_____Lived on Peck St., Muskegon Heights, MI

1936 – 1938_____Lived on Williams St., Muskegon, MI (parents divorced late 1936 or early 1937)

1938 – 1945___Lived on Isabella Ave., Muskegon, MI (joined by stepfather and stepbrother)

1945 – 1949_____Served in U.S. Navy (Great Lakes, IL; San Diego, CA; Long Island, NY; Camp Lejeune, NC with the Fleet Marines; cruises on three troop ships on maneuvers and the line ships: USS Midway, USS Huntington, and USS Philippine Sea)

Fall 1949_____Home in Muskegon, MI (Isabella Ave.) after discharge

1950 – 1953_____Student at Valparaiso University, Valparaiso, IN

1953 – 1957_____Social studies teacher and athletic coach at Lutheran High School, Cleveland, OH

August 25, 1956_____Married Betty Brasch in Pittsburgh, PA

1957 – 1959_____Student at Concordia Theological Seminary, Springfield, IL (birth of son Mark on December 3, 1958)

1959 – 1960___Vicar in campus ministry at USC and UCLA, Los Angeles, CA

1960 – 1961 _____ Student at Concordia Theological Seminary, Springfield, IL

1961 – 1966 ___ Pastor at Trinity Lutheran Church and campus pastor at Cornell University, Ithaca, NY, and one and a half years part-time at Christ Lutheran Church, Interlaken, NY (birth of son Daniel on November 10, 1961; birth of son David on January 18, 1963)

1966 – 1968 _____ Pastor at Our Redeemer Lutheran Church, Solon, OH

1968 – 1985 _____ Pastor at Redeemer Lutheran Church and campus pastor at California Lutheran University, Thousand Oaks, CA

1985 – 1994 _____ Pastor at First Lutheran Church, Ventura, CA (mother died September 19, 1985; Betty died December 19, 1991)

June 30, 1994 _____ Retired from the active pastoral ministry

July 10, 1994 _____ Married Nancy Precker Kilian at Concordia University Chapel, Irvine, CA (Nancy had been widowed with three sons: Joel, Jason, and Nathan)

1994 – present _____ Living on Fern St., Orange CA (son Mark died November 30, 2013)

Chapter 1

Remembrances, Reminiscences, and History of My Early Life (1927-1945)

The First Day of the Rest of My Life (as Told and Retold by My Mother Years Later)

It has been (and still is!) an interesting, exciting, and fulfilling life for me. Maybe my beginning was a tip-off of what was ahead for me. My father Dano was 40 years old and my mother Alvina was 25 years old when they got married in 1926 at Trinity Lutheran Church in Muskegon, Michigan. My dad was a factory worker and my mom was a public school teacher. In those days, school boards didn't like their female teachers to be married, and if they were married, they were not supposed to teach if they had children.

Within the first year of marriage, my mom got pregnant with me, and even though my dad didn't want children, my mom continued to carry me. As near as I can guess, she must have become pregnant during Christmas vacation of 1926, which would make me due sometime in September. (Aren't most September births the result of Christmas vacation?) This posed a problem for my mom, since she could not continue teaching in the fall of 1927 if she had a child. She was able to "hide" her pregnancy until the end of the school year in June (she was a tall, athletic, graceful woman), but what about in September? Since it was very important for her to keep her job (both because she really wanted to and my dad insisted on it), she went to relatives in Madison, Wisconsin, in late summer of 1927, with the idea of giving birth there and then returning across Lake Michigan to Muskegon in time for the beginning of school (which didn't start until the middle of September). Since I was due around the 21st of September, there could have been a bit of a problem. But that's where I came in and played my first important role in life. Here's how it happened.

In May, 1927, Charles Lindbergh made his historic solo flight across the Atlantic Ocean to Paris, France. He was America's "instant hero" when he returned. He spent the late summer and early fall of 1927 touring all 48 states of the Union. On September 7th, 1927, there was a parade in his honor in Madison, Wisconsin, in which he would personally participate. The afternoon of the parade, my mom and her relatives were seated comfortably in their car right along the parade route. Everyone was excited and full of anticipation to see "Lucky Lindy." However, after the parade began, I decided that I wanted to join the parade, so I began to "make my move!" Since it became an emergency situation to get my mom and the car to the hospital, the parade was stopped briefly while they got us out of there! Mom thought it was very exciting, but she was disappointed because she didn't get to see Lindbergh! It was a good thing we left when we did, because I came into the world only a couple of hours later. How many people can say that they held up a parade to be born? To this day, there is "confusion" about my birth in Madison County Hospital because my mom, in order to more thoroughly "cover her tracks," only used part of her real name, but she did use my dad's full name! What an exciting and event-filled life it has been for 80+ years since then! I wouldn't trade it for anything!

My life in Muskegon, Michigan began about two weeks after I was born in Madison, Wisconsin, and my mom returned to Muskegon to resume her teaching career and married life with my father. For the next 17+ years, I was raised in Muskegon, and have always considered it my hometown, even though I was born in Madison.

~

Muskegon

Muskegon is a seaport city on the eastern side of Lake Michigan, with a natural harbor and channel into Muskegon Lake, the Muskegon River, and the western interior of the state. This makes it great for fishing and water events, with the wonderful beaches and the beauty of the colorful coastline providing a paradise setting for a boy growing up. Besides that, Muskegon has always been an important industrial city.

From early in the 19th century, Muskegon was a natural location for the logging industry of Michigan, providing excellent access from the timberlines and rivers to the building of the great cities in the Great Lakes: Chicago, Cleveland, Detroit, Milwaukee, as well as reaching out to the Minneapolis-St. Paul area of Minnesota and the eastern cities of Buffalo and Toronto. This economic boom in Muskegon was spurred on by the entrepreneurship of Charles Hackley (a localized version of Andrew Carnegie), whose memory and contributions are still recalled, recognized, and revered in many ways to this day. They include a library, educational arts center, hospital, art museum, a main street, park and statues, vocational school, endowments, and a special day of the year (September 25th) when he is particularly remembered and honored in and around Muskegon for his impact, influence, and philanthropic efforts.

Before the end of the 19th century, the Michigan timberland had been decimated by the logging industry, and Muskegon was left in a serious economic recession. Fortunately, with resources provided by Hackley and others, the city and community of Muskegon survived and began a successful transition to the mechanical, industrial automotive industry. During the early 20th century, Muskegon emerged as a vital industrial adjunct to the industrial dominance of Detroit, along with Flint, and other areas of the state. Muskegon continued this way during World War II as it became a major contributor to our national defense.

Because of its natural harbors, many small lakes, great beaches and sand dunes, and easy accessibility, Muskegon was a great place in which to grow up and in which to live. Growing up in those years, I had the advantage of wonderful swimming and water activities, a year-round variety of sports such as skiing, ice-skating, baseball, football, hockey, basketball – and additional things like fishing, hunting, dune-scooting, and tobogganing.

All in all, Muskegon was a great place in which to grow up, attend school, experience many cultural and community opportunities, and know the feeling of "small town life" at its best, even though Muskegon's population was around 100,000. My return visits to Muskegon are always filled with clear-pictured images, nostalgic memories, and gripping emotional feelings. I will always feel a deep attachment to my hometown of Muskegon, Michigan, where my life really begins and goes on for more than 17 years.

The best way for me to trace my history of those years is to follow my "migration" year by year, from house to house, from 1927 to 1945.

~

Roosevelt Park, 1927-1931

Every house that I ever lived in was more than a house. It was always a home, and I enjoyed every house/home I lived in, no matter what the circumstances of the times. I remember my first home, which was in Roosevelt Park, a section of Muskegon that was a bit "upscale" but not pretentious. It was and still is a very well-built house, two-story, with a nice yard, front and back, and a small front porch. Although it was a "company house" (through the large manufacturing company my dad worked for and which provided a good payment plan for workers), it probably was not considered a great location, except to a small boy. Behind the house, some distance away, was the company – Campbell, Wyant, and Cannon. We were separated by dozens of railroad tracks with a lot of busy traffic during the years before the Depression. I loved all the trains, all the switching, and all the busy moving about in the yards! I loved playing in the backyard with my little white dog and the noisy, wonderful trains – the earliest memory of my life. At that time, my parents (my father was 42 and my mother 26) seemed happily married, and they had their own home and seemingly secure jobs. Although I don't really remember it, my mom said later that my favorite toy was a wooden bunny rabbit on wheels that I constantly pulled around the house. Years later, among my mother's many photographs, I found a picture of me with my rabbit on wheels. According to Mom, I was a good boy, always cheerful, and I played easily and seemed to exhibit a happy life. In those days, with my brother and me at home (he was born in 1929), Mom was almost always home with us, except for substitute teaching once in a while. That situation would change dramatically in a few years. In late 1929, the Great Depression hit, although its tentacles of joblessness didn't reach Muskegon until 1930. Then in 1931, my dad lost his job and the house. Legally and technically, the company could not foreclose on him, but he didn't know that until it was too late to do anything about it. So, in 1931, we moved to a small, rented house in Muskegon Heights, sort of the "other side of the tracks."

~

Eighth Street House, 1931-1935

Our house on 8th Street in Muskegon Heights was fairly small, but quite adequate as far as I was concerned. We had a large backyard, which came in handy during the Depression for growing lots of vegetables. I clearly remember going out there often and pulling up carrots or potatoes, or picking beans or corn for supper. Meat became a rarity in those days, but we seemed to eat well enough. Years later, Mom told me that she and Dad made a vow: "You boys would never know hunger as you grew up." And we didn't! Maybe it was in those days that I learned to love eating cold, raw potatoes! And I still do! While we lived in a lower economic neighborhood, I didn't notice any real difference, since we had many kids in the neighborhood to play and be with. For little boys, life seemed pretty good. Years later, my mom showed me a picture of a bunch of us kids sitting on the porch steps eating watermelon, and right next to me was a little black kid. When I asked my mom about him (because I didn't remember him, or any of the other kids), she sounded surprised and told me that he was one of my better friends and that he was over to our house often. Apparently, four- and five-year-olds are color blind (at least, I seemed to be). More about that whole subject later, especially during my high school and Navy days. While we lived on 8th Street, I experienced a strange thing called "death" for the first time. The man next door died quite suddenly, and I clearly recall the deep feelings being expressed and my mom as she told me about it in a very gentle and helpful way.

During those years on 8th Street, I attended kindergarten and 1st grade at a nearby elementary school, only a block away. It was close enough to our house that we often played on its playground with its swings, monkey bars, slides, and merry-go-rounds. Once in a while, for extra excitement we would go over to the school to ride the "tubes." We had figured out a way to climb up to the top of one of the fire escape "tubes" that ran down from the second story to the ground. Great fun, if no one caught us! Essentially, it was a good life, although there were a few older boys around who picked on us once in a while. I don't remember my kindergarten teacher's name, but I remember that my 1st-grade teacher was Miss Lincoln, whom I liked very much. One day I made her laugh when I asked her if she drove a Lincoln car. Imagine asking a teacher during the Depression (or any other time, I suppose) that question! However, like many boys, I had already developed a love for cars. Some of that must have occurred because my dad finally got a job selling cars in the Heights, at Boyd Auto Sales, and he would often bring home "demonstration" cars for a few days. I distinctly remember the day he brought home a 1932 Ford Roadster! It was a beauty! White sidewall tires and all. In my small collection of model cars, that includes what I have admired or owned over the years, I have a model of that very car and keep it in my study at home. One Christmas I received a big red truck, with the newest feature for toy cars and trucks: electric lights on front and back! Wow! That was "big stuff!" I believe it was the only toy I received that Christmas, and I'm not sure how my parents even afforded it. My mom later told me about waking up one night and hearing noises in the dining room; when she checked, she found me busily playing in the dark with my new truck, using its electric lights (battery-powered, of course) to maneuver around the many legs of the dining room table and chairs! Ah, childhood!

Quick-recall moments: eating my favorite before-bed snack of saltine crackers and milk; the many times I combed my mom's long, dark, silky hair as she laid back on the sofa, with her head just over the armrest and her hair hanging over the end of the sofa, and I at the end of the sofa with her big comb (years later she told me how much that meant to her in those dark and difficult days of the Depression); two of the longest weeks in a small boy's life when I had the measles and had to stay inside at home (by quarantine law, the house had to be kept dark, with windows covered and a sign on the door saying that I had the measles, and no one but the family could come in); the long, snowy Michigan winters when we would come into the house almost frozen, take off our outer clothes, and sit right on top of the floor heat register to feel the heat blowing up inside our clothes and warming our little bodies; running from the police in the summertime when there was a water shortage (which we apparently didn't understand) and there were restricted hours when you could have water running in your house and yard – and yet we would be running around with the hose and playing games (the police never caught us, but my parents did!).

Here I must insert a most unlikely but true story that illustrates my imaginative but crazy mind. It took place in our house on 8th Street. This was the second home of my childhood and I was about five or six years old, and my brother two years younger. It was a rented house after my father had lost his job and our first home. He did get a job as a car salesman for Ford – and as I said earlier, how well I remember the 1932 demonstrator Ford Roadster, now considered a classic car, with its rumble seat and sharp design! On this particular day, our dad was home while our mom was substitute teaching somewhere. Apparently, my brother and I had recently seen a stirring movie about castles, kings, knights in shining armor, and thrones, with medieval settings and large halls and many fancily-dressed people. Lighting up the huge halls were tall, flaming torches. Well, I decided to reenact the whole scene with my own embellishments and imagination, down in our low-ceiling basement with open wood beams and wood flooring above us. We set up some boxes for an impressive throne, put a chair at the top of the "throne," and I pretended to be a king. But I realized we were missing the most exciting part of the whole scene: flaming torches! So I decided to solve that situation by finding two straw brooms, lighting them on fire, and stood them on either side of my "throne!" Was I ever a proud king, sitting up there in my majesty! As I sat there, I happened to look up at some point and noticed, to my horror, that the fiery brooms had caught the wood ceiling on fire! My brother ran upstairs and got our dad. He came racing downstairs, grabbed the hose connected to the wash tubs nearby, and quickly put out the fire. Unfortunately, the ceiling was well-blackened by then. Next, my dad hauled me upstairs with one arm while he pulled off his belt with the other. Almost needless to say, you know what happened next!

During our time on 8th Street, I started 2nd grade at Trinity Lutheran Parochial School, on the other side of town in Lakeside. It was a one-room, 35-student, one-teacher, eight-grade school which had been converted from the old church parsonage. My mom really wanted me (and two years later, my brother as well) to have a good education in conjunction with our Christian faith and the Lutheran Church. It was quite an experience for the next seven years of my life. Our teacher, Mr. Herman Birkman, picked up a number of kids each morning and took them back home in the afternoon. He was a young, remarkably talented man, who also played the organ on Sunday mornings as well as directed the church choir! (Years later, when he was principal of Fort Wayne Lutheran High School and I was a teacher at Cleveland Lutheran High School, we had a few wonderful get-togethers at educational conferences.) I was one of the students who rode with Mr. Birkman. We had to meet him at certain specified locations, which required my walking almost two miles to a main corner in Muskegon Heights. This happened to be the same corner where my dad worked as a car salesman, but since he usually didn't go into work that early, I usually walked. I loved watching them bring in the new cars from Detroit on their large car carriers, and then drive the vehicles very carefully off the carriers in the early mornings. Quite often I would go with my dad to his work and "play around" among all the new cars on the showroom floor, sitting in the driver's seat and making believe I was actually driving them! What fun for a little kid!

Here I want to write about two wonderful experiences my brother and I had during those years before my parents divorced in late 1936 or early 1937. Our dad's family was from Hesperia, Michigan, only 20 miles or so from Muskegon. My grandmother didn't like the title of "Grandma," so she had us call her "Donnie." I don't know the reason for that name, but she was a wonderful, loving person and quite elderly by that time. I recall my grandfather only very vaguely, with just one brief memory of him before he died. I loved going to Donnie's house, as well as to the homes of Dad's brothers and sisters. My favorite, after Donnie's house, was Uncle Bert's farm, a few miles away. I loved playing with the iron tractors and different farm equipment (which were obsolete even then) and in the barns and hay lofts. One time, I was playing on part of the dirt driveway a little ways away from Uncle Bert's Model T Ford. My brother got in the car and somehow released the parking brake, and suddenly the car came right toward me. I moved in time to avoid the brunt of it. I rolled and moved just enough so that the wheels ran over only my shinbones. The Model T was so lightweight, that it only skinned up my legs but did no other damage, except to scare my parents and Uncle Bert and Aunt Bernice. My Uncle Bert raised the usual farm crops, including fruit. One time while we were there, we all went out to the watermelon patch, with each of us allowed to pick out one watermelon and bring it back to the house to eat later on (and to bring some home to Muskegon). Well, I picked out the biggest watermelon I could carry and went happily ahead of the others back to the house. The watermelon got heavier and heavier as I approached the house, and just as I got to the back steps, I dropped it! It broke into a number of large pieces, so what the rest of them saw as they got back to the house was a little boy fully immersed in eating as much watermelon as he could! And loving it! I have many fond memories of going to Hesperia and being with Dad's family, whom I missed a lot after the divorce when I was only nine and my brother only seven. There are still a number of Lareva family people in Western Michigan, especially around Hesperia and Fremont. Fremont is the home of Gerber® Baby Foods. Incidentally, my dad knew Dan Gerber quite well in the early years of his life and was even given a chance by Dan Gerber to get involved with his new idea of making commercial baby food. But at that time, Dad was more interested in going west as a young man to be a lumberjack in Washington state. Many years later, my dad took me over to meet "old Dan Gerber" (as he called him) at his office in Fremont.

The second great experience along these lines consisted of our visits to my grandmother's house in Arcadia, Michigan, 120 miles north of Muskegon on the coast of Lake Michigan. We called my grandmother "Oma," a typical term from a part of Germany which used such a designation for "Großmutter." Oma's husband, my grandfather, died before my mom got married, so I never got to know him aside from the many wonderful stories I had heard about him. Oma had a large, two-story house with a very big yard in back as well as on the side. It was right across the street from Trinity Lutheran Church, the center of social and religious life in Arcadia for many, many years, and even to this day. It is a beautiful, high-steepled, somewhat ornate building, always painted white with brown trimming. Oma's home included an outhouse for many years, about 30 feet from the back door. Only years later did she get indoor plumbing along with running water and a modern stove to replace the wood and coal stove that I still remember her using, along with a pump for getting water from the well. She also had an ice box, and regularly got big chunks of ice for it as well as for storing food and other perishable items in the basement "cold storage." Her house had a wonderful staircase to the upstairs, which my brother and I loved to race up and down whenever we were there! There was a front room parlor, which we were seldom allowed to spend time in, since it seemed almost sacred, with period furniture and old pictures of family and special items of remembrance. Close by was the home of Oma's sister, my Aunt Hulda, and Uncle Ed, as well as their son Henry, who was much older than me, but fun to be with. Such nice, good people!

The little town of Arcadia has changed very little over the years – it remains a viable community, with a little marina for boats down by the channel to Lake Michigan, and small-town activities and life. The main distinction of Arcadia is the Lutheran Camp, located just outside the main part of town, right on the shore of Lake Michigan. It not only attracts many Lutherans and others during the summer months, but also it is a place where it is common for a well-known Lutheran leader or personality to "hold forth" during the week and then preach at Trinity Lutheran Church on Sunday. The largest and most beautiful house in Arcadia is the Haase House, just a couple of blocks from Oma's house. Built in 1881, it is a large, many-room house, with a long porch/veranda in the back facing the marina/bay and channel to Lake Michigan. It was beautifully structured and painted all white with green shutters and trim. We spent a lot of time at the Haase's, mainly because the two families were close, and Martha (the daughter of the Haase family) was Mom's best friend as they were growing up. In fact, Martha was even taller than Mom, and they were obviously the tallest girls in town – and taller than most of the boys and young men!

Arcadia had at one time prospered as a lumber town with its excellent harbor and small bay. Once the lumber industry "dried up" near the end of the 19th century, Arcadia never got back to its former status, but remained a small town with Camp Arcadia and the marvelous shoreline of Lake Michigan to attract people. Many people from Chicago eventually built summer homes in the area, and that is still true today. One of the most beautiful and memorable times I had with my mom when I visited her in later years, while she could still travel, was to drive her up to Arcadia. We'd walk the streets and she would reminisce about her childhood and tell me stories of the people in each house in town, as a kind of living history of Arcadia. We'd walk all the way out to Camp Arcadia as she told stories about her life and times before she left for college at Central Michigan University in 1920. She told me about how devastated she was when she heard that her father had died in an unusual accident. (He fell out of a car on the way to go fishing with a friend, hit his head on a rock, and died instantly.) Those visits with her to Arcadia are among my most beautiful and emotional memories of the times I spent with my mom in her last few years! To this day, I treasure those times I could be with her and help make her life more enjoyable, and it was from her that I learned how important a sense and knowledge of history is in the lives of people as well as a nation, or even a small town. I especially looked forward to going up to Arcadia with my brother in the last few years before he died, as we'd visit the "family plot," drive around, and I'd share so many memories with him. I realize now how much that must have meant to him. Those were also very precious times with my brother in the last years and months of his life.

During all my early years growing up, summer-long visits and other shorter visits during the year to Oma's house in Arcadia provided many, many wonderful times. As a little boy, what could be a better way to spend warm summer days than on the beach, in the water, or playing with neighborhood kids and a next-door cousin? Oma's house was fairly large, two-storied, with many interesting rooms, especially downstairs. The only thing interesting about the upstairs bedrooms was the beautiful, natural-wood, shiny, double-angled staircase up to the second floor. Oh, how my brother and I loved to run up and down those stairs, probably to the consternation of the adults downstairs. The kitchen was the most interesting place in the house. I still remember the pump handle by the sink with which water was brought up. I remember the old wood-burning stove and the wonderful smells of baking and cooking that seemed to be going on all the time! I remember the wooden icebox (no refrigerators yet) which used 25-pound hunks of ice to keep things cool. I remember the dark, cold cellar where Oma kept her canned goods for long periods of time. I remember the outhouse, about 40 feet from the back door, and what a unique experience it was to use it! I remember the big backyard and big side yard with apple trees and lots of space in which to run around. I remember the delicious ice cream socials on the side lawn of the church every Sunday afternoon and early evening! I remember walking a couple of blocks to Wednesday night "Outdoor Movies" in a large empty lot with a huge wooden screen at one end. People would just gather with their chairs or simply stand and watch *Felix the Cat* or *Popeye* cartoons for an hour or so. I remember going to the quaint, little corner drugstore for a soda, milkshake, or candy. I remember being taken out to the town cemetery where the Mauntler family (my grandmother's maiden name) had a section of the cemetery. There I was told about Oma's "Baby Lang" who died only a few weeks after birth, and Walter, who would have been my Uncle Walter, but died during the great flu epidemic of 1918 at the age of 13. So, Oma lost a baby, a 13-year-old son, and a husband before Mom was 21 years old! Many years later, when I would visit my brother with his Parkinson's disease, I would drive him up north and it was very important for him to visit the cemetery and spend time at the gravestones of the family. That always amazed me because he was not very close to most of the family, including my side of the family (except for me). It was an insight into him which I would later appreciate more and more, especially in my relationship with him, which was not very close for many years. That's a story in itself, which I will tell about later.

    All in all, summers and visits to Oma's house in Arcadia (where Mom grew up) provided some of the best experiences a young boy could possibly have, and I still treasure those memories!

    Along with the visits to Arcadia were the visits to the home of my Uncle Harry and Aunt Aulie in Manistee, about 20 miles south of Arcadia, right on

Lake Michigan. Manistee became famous when huge underground salt deposits were found in the area, which became the starting point for the formation of the largest and most successful salt company in the world – Morton Salt (famous for their motto: "When It Rains It Pours®"!). It's still a very interesting city to visit. My Uncle Harry worked as a salesman for a drug company in Grand Rapids, Michigan. He represented most of Western Michigan for the company, and was what we called a "traveling salesman," a very respected job and one which kept him in good economic straits during the Depression. This turned out to be very important for our own family in Muskegon. Uncle Harry's house in Manistee was a large, two-story house with many rooms and a wonderful front room for large groups of visiting friends and relatives.

Several things happened during the summers when my brother and I spent part of the time in Manistee. I have several vivid memories from those summers. Since Uncle Harry's house was located on a fairly busy main street in Manistee, I would often sit on the front porch with Oma and we would talk and watch all the cars go by. We got into this little game where she would challenge me to name every car that came by as we watched from the porch. She was always amazed that I could name every one. Of course, she didn't know a Model T from a Model A, so I could even fake it (which I only did once!) and she'd believe me. It was during one of those summers that my brother (whom I will refer to as "Aub," rather than "Dave," because there were other Daves coming along in my life) broke his arm when he crawled up onto a large iron casting of a dog on a nearby neighbor's front lawn and fell off. I rescued him from too much embarrassment by contracting two-week chicken pox, which restricted both of us to the house for the next couple of weeks. One of my most vivid memories goes back to one summer when my Uncle Harry was doing some renovation work on the house and had some men working on the house for several weeks. Apparently I listened carefully and watched carefully, and emulated them as they worked. I thought it was great! A day or so later, when my Aunt Aulie entertained a large group of ladies from her church on the large side lawn of their house, I was upstairs on the second floor. As I watched the proceedings below, I somehow decided to "contribute" to the many and loud conversations going on by leaning out of the second story window and demanding in a loud voice, "What in 'ell doing down there?" Even as the ladies titillated with a certain amount of so-called "shock," my mother and Aunt Aulie let me know very quickly that what I had said was very, very inappropriate. Then Mom rushed upstairs and administered the appropriate punishment, all the while chuckling to herself about the incident! Often, during those summers in Arcadia or Manistee, my brother and I would be left with Uncle Harry and Aunt Aulie for a few weeks. They had no children of their own, so we were treated like their own children. And it would continue that way in the years ahead. I probably was closer to them than Aub because I was older and because I was more outgoing and talkative, especially with Uncle Harry. I have one more interesting memory of Manistee. A good friend of the family and his wife (who was distantly related to us) would often come over in the evening and visit. Dorr was the man's name. At the time, I was beginning to get interested in baseball, so we would play catch for a while each time he came over. (By the way, my Uncle Harry had a congenital hip condition which caused him to limp, so he couldn't play sports, but he sure loved them – and in later years he and I would share many times together talking sports.) Whenever Dorr would come over in the early evening while it was still light, the last ball I would try to catch was the most important one. Almost every evening, one of those popcorn-making wagons would roll up the street and stop right in front of the house for some business in that part of the neighborhood. When Dorr and I were finished playing catch, he would tell me with his last throw, "If you catch this one, Jim, I'll buy you a bag of popcorn." Believe me, I can tell you that I never missed his last throw to me on those evenings! All in all, those many summertimes in Arcadia and Manistee in my early years, and also later years, were wonderful for two small boys in the midst of a Depression. We were surrounded by adults in every wonderful way! I'm sure that had many good effects upon my brother and me!

~

Peck Street House, 1935-1936

In 1935, we moved again – this time to the far southern part of Muskegon Heights, a little nicer neighborhood than 8th Street. I don't recall feeling any particular trauma because of the move, and I seemed to adapt quite easily to new surroundings. I had just begun to enjoy baseball, so that helped me join in with other boys in the neighborhood. As I realized many years later, it never was that easy for my brother to make these moves. I do remember my dad taking me to a baseball doubleheader, which almost completely bored me at the time (I was probably only six or seven). Wow, did that change a lot within a year or so! It was while we lived on Peck Street that I first really became interested in sports of all kinds: baseball, football, sledding on the hill at the end of the street two blocks away, skiing on some hills nearby! Absolute fun! While on Peck Street, I learned to ride a bike – adult size – from one of the older boys around. What a thrill! Unfortunately, my brother Aub didn't do so well. He rode a sled down one of the hills and didn't watch too closely where he was going and plowed head-on into a big tree. He was knocked semiconscious and got a big gash on his forehead, which he carried as a scar for the rest of his life. Historically speaking, I can remember playing with lots of little metal toy soldiers in the yard of a boy several doors away, and I distinctly recall our battles with Mussolini and the Italians versus the hopelessly outmanned Ethiopian Army. In our "war games," the Ethiopians always won, because even then we realized how bad Mussolini was.

Our house on Peck Street was a large, two-story home, with many rooms and bedrooms upstairs. My parents rented out rooms to single men, who also had their meals with us. I think my parents thought this arrangement would bring in the extra income they needed to rent the large house. The boarders, usually young men, were always enjoyable and very good to my brother and me. They were always very helpful in many ways, and would often play with us, especially me, since I was really getting into sports by then.

What do I remember particularly? Well, there were the many trips to a little grocery store several blocks away, crossing a field on which we played baseball in the warmer months and had snowball "fights" in the winter. For several years, especially one winter, we had a terrific amount of snowfall, which enabled us to do some wonderful things. We once piled up enough snow on the backside of our sloping garage (which sloped toward an empty lot behind us) that we were able to make a ski run, starting at the top of the garage! What fun! Another time that winter, we actually built a large enough igloo for three or four of us to crawl inside. The boy next door, four years older, even tried to interest a couple of us to try smoking, but in an igloo that didn't work too well! This was the boy I played with a lot, and who was always thinking up "special" things to do. One time, he called me outside to the driveway between our houses. (An all-cement driveway was a "luxury" then.) He had somehow found a real bullet, and decided to see if he could make it "work." He placed it on a brick and then took a hammer and hit the bullet. Well, our driveway was on a plane – level to the street and to the curb across the street. His plan worked, and the bullet exploded and instantly we felt a bullet whiz past our heads and into the open-door garage behind us! It had zoomed across the street, hit the opposite curb, and ricocheted back at us. One of us could have been killed! We decided not to tell our parents! (I wonder why!)

It was during this short time on Peck Street (less than two years) that the marriage of my parents began to fall apart, and separation was soon followed with a divorce. Aub and I never "saw it coming," since my parents took care not to argue or do anything negative in front of us. I have no memory of hostility or acrimony between my parents in those years, and yet it didn't seem to faze me too much when they actually separated. That would lead to moving again.

~

Williams Street House, 1936-1938

Mom, my brother, and I moved clear across town from Muskegon Heights to an area known mostly as East Muskegon, having a moderate-to-lower income level. The large, two-story house had a full-sized upstairs apartment, with long, steep outside steps leading up to it. I must have felt some trauma at the sudden change (neither of our parents really explained much, except that the divorce had happened); however, I don't recall any adverse feelings – just a rather casual acceptance of the whole thing and the change that came with it. I think it bothered my brother a lot more than it did me. I was still close to my dad despite the divorce, and got to be with him at least once a week, often spending an overnight with him in his apartment in the Heights. My parents did the two most important things when divorced: neither of them said or indicated anything negative or bad about the other in front of Aub and me in all those years, and they both let us continue to love each parent completely without trying in any way to discourage it or do any harm to our relationship with the other parent. What a gift that was to two young boys who could easily have been traumatized by an outward show of anger, conflict, or hatred. We also continued at Trinity Lutheran School in Lakeside, part of Muskegon on the western edge of town, near the Lake Michigan shore. That meant we were still picked up each school day morning by our teacher, Mr. Herman Birkman.

Our upstairs apartment was really quite nice, and we were allowed to have our spaniel dog named Blackie (which my mom always called "Beauty"). There were alleyways and empty lots nearby, so lots of room to roam, including a large playing field as part of a nearby public school. As was to become my habit, I would quickly get acquainted in a new neighborhood by taking my bat, ball, and glove and finding some kids to play with. And I always found plenty of them. My best friend, Al, lived just across the street. He was the one who got me going to the YMCA, where we boys ran around and swam naked in the indoor pool and were not at all self-conscious about it. Of course, there was much more to do at the "Y," and I enjoyed going there all through my high school years. It was a great place for a young person to spend time and energy. But baseball had become my favorite sport (I even had a uniform which my parents bought for my brother and me, and I have pictures to prove it!). I got to know quite a few kids in the area, many of whom I would be in high school with, even after we moved again in a year or so. Besides baseball, we also participated in winter sports (skiing, ice-skating), and kite-flying was very popular at that time. A Saturday or Sunday afternoon would find dozens of kites in the sky from Angel School field near our house. For a young boy, nine years old – almost ten – it was a very good life! I should also mention that at this time, my mom began seeing a divorced man (his wife had walked out on him) by the name of John Sevrey (whose given first name was "Milton," but he preferred to be called John). He had a son four years older than me, whom I got to be good friends with over the next few years, since John was to become my stepfather. I don't remember having any negative feelings about him, as long as he was nice to my mother (which he very definitely was). A couple of specific remembrances: I remember working with several older kids in the neighborhood as they tried to and eventually successfully built a crystal radio; I remember so clearly when Joe Louis became my boxing hero (as he did for most of America) when he knocked out Hitler's favorite, Max Schmeling – who, after World War II, became good friends with Louis. This was somewhat disappointing to many white people (including my future stepfather, who was quite biased that way). I remember one particular incident very well, mainly because it was embarrassing, but the result of a wonderful moment for a ten-year-old boy. Dad brought over a junior-sized bicycle for my birthday! I hadn't ridden a bicycle for several months since we had left Peck Street, but I exuberantly jumped onto it and began to ride. The first few seconds were quite unsteady as the bike veered around a bit as I tried to control it. There was only one thing in front of me that I could possibly run into, and it was a telephone pole. Guess what? I ran smack straight into it! From then on, I did very well on my first bike!

My memory is a little vague about this time of my life in terms of chronology, but sometime in the spring of 1938, John and Mom got married, and once again we were on the move.

~

Isabella Avenue House, 1938-1945

East Isabella Avenue, as the name implies, was on the furthest eastern end of Muskegon, with mostly woods and open land beyond the several dozen houses at that end of town. The streets around us, including ours, were primarily hard dirt roads with few sidewalks and no curbs, even on the sections that had been blacktopped. Our house was set on a small but adequate piece of land, with houses around us but an empty lot on one side. A usually muddy dirt alley ran behind the houses, separating our house from the ones on the next street over, with our backyards adjoining across the alley. The alley itself afforded many hours of play, bike riding and "tricks," and extra space to play lots of games, including basketball, behind our garage (mud and all during the rainy season or winter). Our house was quite adequate for the four of us (with two good-sized bedrooms), but it was a "problem" when Oma came to stay for long periods of time. Then my brother and I slept somewhere else, but I don't remember where! After we moved in, John built another bedroom in the basement for the times when his son, Larry (whom we called "Guy" for a long time), would come and live with us. I spent many nights down there, since I was closer to Guy's age than my brother was, and it was more enjoyable at the time. Our basement was the full size of the one-story house above, so there was room down there for laundry facilities, a coal bin, a big stove, and recreation space for a ping-pong table and other activities. Upstairs consisted of a small kitchen, a dining room and front room of pretty good size, and a small front porch with steps. It was a nice house and a good home for the four of us. The negative part, I remember, was scraping the inside walls of wallpaper and the outside walls to prepare the house for painting. Ugh! It was a somewhat long piece of property, so there was room for a driveway of cement strips, a garage, a fairly good-sized garden, a small dog pen, and a small basketball court behind the garage.

For a ten-year-old boy, the location of the house was almost more important than the house itself. Directly across the street was a fairly new six-acre park, complete with a full-sized baseball field with a hard clay infield and a good grass outfield (large enough for sandlot football in the fall), a high and very effective backstop of mesh wire, and seating on both sides of the infield for baseball teams. Also, there were swings, monkey bars, merry-go-rounds, teeter-totters, and other playground equipment for kids. It was a ten-year-old boy's dream! My mom told me years later that she often knew right where I was because she would hear my voice in the midst of sports games across the street. In my later teens, she once heard me utter a bit of profanity quite loudly, and she certainly made me aware of it by calling across the street to me, "Jimmy, come home this instant!" Uh, oh! I got my punishment, and justifiably! Anyway, Harmon Park, as it was known in those days (but changed to Sheldon Park many years later), was a bonanza for all of us kids in the surrounding neighborhood. We used it for baseball, football, basketball, kite-flying, ice-skating (in the winter, sections of the park would freeze over, ideal for playing hockey), and just about any other outside activity kids enjoyed in open space. In the first couple of years there, Tom Harmon, All-American football player at the University of Michigan, would become my first serious football hero, and this was probably because of my strong kinship with Harmon Park – although the name had nothing to do with him. Fortunately for us, not very many people used the park in those days because it was located on the eastern edge of town. But it would eventually become very popular. The city fathers of Muskegon knew what they were doing when they placed the park where they did and when they did! And we boys were the recipients of their wisdom! (Refer to Chapter 6 – "My Life in Sports (Mostly Baseball).")

Since we lived on the edge of East Muskegon, it meant there were woods, lots of trees, and open space beyond us. I can remember many times when we trekked into the woods to look for different little animals, frogs, snakes, or squirrels. But mostly we just liked to hike in the woods, kick around the leaves, and play in the trees. One of our favorite tricks was to find a young tree that was quite tall, and climb up as high as we could. As we climbed, it would cause the tree to bend down to the ground – slowly at first, and then with increasing speed – with us hanging on like a wild ride at the circus. Sometimes we came down a little faster than we planned, and landed with a jolt and a big laugh! Essentially, it was a boy's paradise and we exploited it with all our might and energy. Our parents never seemed to worry about us or what we were doing. Of course, there was a time or two that we experimented with "smoking," by finding some "Indian tobacco" and rolling it up into a newspaper and lighting up. It didn't work very well because it burned our throats and was not too pleasant a feeling, but we were "smoking!" Those were wonderful, carefree, Tom Sawyer-type days for the many young boys in the area. As you can tell from this narrative, they provided many great memories for me. I thank God for such blessings!

Here I describe another crazy incident in those days. In the summer between 7th and 8th grade, a national motorcycle hill climb was held in Muskegon. For several days before the hill climb, hundreds and hundreds of motorcycles roared through town for the big event. Thousands attended from all over the country to watch guys on special motorcycles try to climb a hill of sand, brush, and dirt. Most of them didn't make it. We boys would emulate the hill climb at new houses where basements were being dug, leaving big mounds of Lake Michigan sand. We did our own hill climb on these mounds of sand with our bicycles. Because the sand was soft, we never made it to the top – except once. With my bicycle going full speed, I climbed the hill to the top and suddenly realized I was going downhill into a great big hole. When I hit bottom, I sprained my left wrist severely. But, of course, I never let on to my parents that I had been hurt. So, for months, I functioned with a bad wrist, a reminder of my victorious hill climb.

I had many boy friends in those days, most of them my age, and we had many good times together. Oh, yes, there were a few girls, too, but mainly we were just boys and acted that way most of the time (for good or for bad!). There was my best friend, Fred – a year younger than me, but just as grown up; his younger brother, Bob; my younger brother, Aub; Art and Rich (brothers); Chuck; Bill (another baseball friend); Andy; Bernie; and a few others who came and went. Always plenty of guys to play with! And, yes, there were a few girls that we began to pay some attention to as we grew into our teens: Dolores, who could run faster than most of us when we played "Kick the Can;" Donna (very nice); and her sisters Alice and Viola, although we really only liked

Donna at the time. There was also Betty, who lived on another street and who fooled me once when I was in 8th grade by calling me and pretending she was Vonnie, my heartthrob at Trinity School, and it really upset me when I found out! Also, there was Shirley, the most attractive of them all, and whom we all came to admire very much later on. And then, there was Mary Ann, the nicest of all of them, and whose brother was a wonderful guy and good friend, who died in WWII near the end of the war. He was a year older than all of us. That's about all of them, except for a large number of friends whom I will talk about later in this chapter when I describe Trinity School, which I attended for seven years. Most of us boys moved back and forth, to and from each other's homes comfortably, and were always treated so kindly by parents (especially mothers!). My favorite was Fred's house (I suppose because he was also my best friend) whose mother was like my own mom, and who always treated me very special. Fred had three younger brothers, Bob, Charley, and Rich, and a younger sister, Patricia – a real cutie who came along too late for any of us boys to get interested in, but who was (and is) a very nice person. I still remember her trying to teach Fred how to dance so he could make out better with the girls. He didn't need any help! Our houses were only two blocks apart, and most of us boys lived within four or five blocks of one another. What a wonderful atmosphere in which to grow up! I also remember all of us going over to Art's house on Sunday evenings and listening breathlessly (and with all the lights out) to *Inner Sanctum* on the radio! It was spooky! I realized what a truly blessed seven years I had on Isabella Avenue! More reasons will follow in my narrative.

During my years on Isabella Avenue, I started a lifelong passion: reading books. In those days it was the *Hardy Boys* series and many others like that. I couldn't get enough of books, and my mother, of course, totally encouraged me, particularly since my brother wasn't that inclined at the time. (Later on in his life, Aub became an avid reader.) I'm sure those early days are when my deep and abiding interest in history began to develop, and hasn't ever slackened! It helped that Mom was a history and geography teacher for many years. Years later, when I became a father, I mused to myself how much joy it must have brought her as I devoured books as a child and wanted to know more and more about history. I'm sure it was a joy to her, which I never realized at the time. How blessed I was!

Life at home on Isabella was very good, and I have many wonderful memories of those seven years. I remember the many parties that my parents had at the house, bringing some of their best friends over for an evening of cards (they played Bridge with a vengeance), a moderate amount of drinks, and some wonderful times of singing. Mom played the piano very well, so she would lead in the singing of many songs that they all knew very well by heart. My brother and I would listen from our bedroom late at night as they sang. Most of all, I remember when they would finally get to the one song that they sang with more gusto and loudness than skill: "On the Road to Mandalay." As they say in show business, they "brought the house down" with that one! One of the things I recall, as I reminisce about these days, is how much trust and responsibility my mom and John gave me in those years. I cannot be more specific, except to say that it's more of an impression or feeling that I have about that time in my life. They always seemed to treat me almost as an adult, but still allowed me to be a boy growing up into his teens. I don't ever remember feeling unsafe or insecure or afraid of anything, although I probably was, but didn't really realize or notice it!

Since we lived in a Dutch/Christian Reformed area of Western Michigan, we therefore had many relationships with the Reformed. And they were always good. The family next door was Dutch Reformed (a bit more strict than Christian Reformed), whose kids went to a Reformed school (much like our Lutheran parochial school). They surprised us one day when we were talking about our school and our Lutheranism. They told us they so greatly admired Luther that they used his Small Catechism in their classes on the Reformation and the period afterward. We saw evidence of their somewhat extreme pietism in several ways. For instance, on Sunday afternoons, the two boys (our age) would come over to our house, mainly to read the comics, because they weren't "allowed" to do that at home! But we were good friends and we appreciated their solid Christian focus on Holy Scripture.

One of my hobbies during those years was building model airplanes, almost from scratch, with thin sticks of balsa wood and lots of glue, and then covered with colored tissue paper and painted. When I'd get tired of a plane after a while, I would get up on the roof of the house at its highest point (never with my parents around!), light the plane on fire with a match, and throw it up as high and as far as I could – and then watch it go burning, spinning, diving, and crashing dramatically into the ground. It must have been the affect of the war news and war movies in those days. But I enjoyed building all kinds of models of different planes: German, American, British, and Japanese. Remember, we had no plastic in those days and it took a lot of skill and time to create these models. There were always two or three of my favorites hanging from the ceiling of our bedroom. My favorites were the P-38, the P-40, the B-17 "Flying Fortress," the British Spitfire, and the German Messerschmidt.

Aub and I continued going to Trinity School through the 8th grade before going on to Muskegon High School. Perhaps this is a good place to describe our little Trinity Lutheran Parochial School in Lakeside, the far western end of Muskegon. Even though Muskegon had a population of 100,000, it was spread out quite a bit, with Muskegon Heights and North Muskegon as adjunct towns. With the many sections called such things as Roosevelt Park, East Muskegon, Lakeside, and Norton Shores, you always had the feeling of a small-town atmosphere. Trinity School was held in the parsonage of Trinity Church, until they bought a better house for the pastors on the other side of the church building. They then converted the old parsonage into a more conventional school by taking down some walls and making one large classroom at the front of the building. Because it had been quite a large house, it easily provided for separate bathrooms for boys and girls, space for clothing and lunch bags or buckets, and a large furnace room where the original kitchen had been. The classroom itself was long, with desks for about 38-40 kids, ranging from 1st grade through 8th. The desks in the front of the class were small and gradually got larger toward the back of the room. The classroom was manned by one teacher – there were no paid assistants or classroom helpers in those days. As you became a 7th- and 8th-grader, you also became a part-time helper with the smaller kids.

My teacher from 2nd through 6th grade was Mr. Herman Birkman, a strong disciplinarian and an excellent teacher. Besides teaching, he was the choir director, one of the church organists, and sometimes the youth leader! Try that on for size! He definitely did not "spare the rod," and many a punishment was administered in the "dungeon" of the furnace room! Yes, I had a few of them myself, and he had a pretty good belt! Of course, several of the boys were "regular customers" to the furnace room, and the rest of us in the large classroom could hear the whelps in their agony as punishment was meted out down the hall. But Mr. Birkman was good, fair, and totally in control. Later on, he eventually became the principal of Fort Wayne Lutheran High School, and I had some conversations with him when our Lutheran high school had annual educational conferences in the 1950s. He had mellowed a bit by that time, and he told me how much those early years in Muskegon helped him become a better teacher and administrator. I always respected and revered him tremendously, even as a young boy in school.

For my 7th grade, we had our pastor's son, Gerhardt Luebke, as our teacher, since that was the only way he could get credit for a required year of vicarage from our Lutheran seminary in St. Louis. He was a kind, friendly, softhearted man whom we students "ran over" the whole year because he exercised very little discipline. He was a pushover for a bunch of obstreperous 7th-grade boys (our grade was mostly boys). Besides, he wasn't a particularly good teacher, mainly because his intellectual and academic levels never came down to ours in terms of teaching. Vicar Gerhardt was a good and nice person who went on to several successful ministries in the church before dying at the age of 55.

The following year (my 8th-grade year) brought a young, energetic, and deeply spiritual man of amazing wisdom and great teaching abilities, with a very compassionate and sensitive heart for people, especially kids. His name was Mr. Bill Scheer. I will spend some time writing about him later on in this narrative because he became for me one of the two most influential male role models in my life, along with my Uncle Harry. At Trinity School, as I've mentioned earlier, a number of kids from outlying areas would be picked up by our teacher, well before school was to start in the morning. Our family always seemed to be "out of the loop" geographically, so Aub and I were picked up all the years we attended Trinity. Mr. Birkman had a 1936 Chevrolet, into which he packed quite a number of kids. (Laws today would never have allowed what we did then!) This custom continued on into my 8th-grade year, when, because of my "seniority" as an 8th-grader, I got to sit in the front seat next to Mr. Scheer – with at least one smaller kid on my lap. The back seat was what one might call a "sardine can," with kids squeezed in together as close as possible. Since Mr. Scheer had to pick up so many kids, mostly from the eastern end of Muskegon, we had to get started early in the morning, and we usually arrived at school before most of the other kids. That gave us time to play for a while, until everyone else got to school.

My first day of 8th grade led to a wonderful sermon illustration years later. We arrived that first day, with new school clothes and all, with a brand new teacher and year ahead. Since we had about 20-25 minutes before classes began, a bunch of us 7th- and 8th-graders began a game of ball in the play yard. Actually, the playground was all dirt and dark sand – no concrete, no blacktop, no hard clay. But we didn't mind. As our little game progressed, I was playing in what would be called "left-center field," alongside the alley that divided our playground from the backyards of a number of houses on the other side of the alley. We weren't "allowed" to hit a ball beyond that part of the field. Well, either Carl or Ben (both good home run hitters) hit one way out toward me. It is important to note that this particular day was garbage pickup day, so the alley was lined with a series of metal garbage cans. As I drifted back to catch this fly ball, I realized that I was close to the alley. Just as I reached up to catch the ball, I ran into and scattered two or three garbage cans. There was garbage all over the place! I skinned my elbow and tore a hole in my pant leg. But, to my great satisfaction, I did hang onto the ball, despite the collision with the garbage cans! When I got home that afternoon, my mom wasn't very happy about the condition of my pants or my skinned elbow. But as I described the incident, she softened her look and then asked me, "Did you hang onto the ball?" I replied that I had, and she simply smiled a bit wanly and said, "That's good!" As an avid sportsperson and athlete herself, she could understand a bit of what I had experienced and could relate to it. Not many mothers could have felt that way or handled it that way. She was my idol!

Life at Trinity School was filled with the usual Three Rs, helping the younger children as we advanced to the upper grades, and singing every day. I wasn't good at singing, and I actually got "kicked out" of music class in the 5th grade for a while because I couldn't sing "2nd voice" (in harmony). Hey, I couldn't even sing "1st voice!" We would sing once in a while for Sunday morning church services, but more often than not we sang for funerals in the church. We never enjoyed that very much, but even then I began to understand more clearly about death and our Christian role here on earth. Recess and the noon hour were spent playing on our soft, black dirt playground. I remember coming home many days with dirty feet and ankles, and having to scrub them good before suppertime. (We took a bath in our tub only once a week in those days – on Saturday night!) I still remember the dark, dirty "ring" around the inside of the tub when we were finished. Of course, I did shower up regularly at the YMCA at least twice a week. When the weather was good, we boys (and a few "selected" girls) played ball, especially during the noon hour. Early on, with our new teacher, Mr. Scheer, I learned a great lesson. I must have been acting up a bit as a "superior" 8th-grader, and finally, one day, he held me in the classroom all noon hour. I was crushed! No ball playing, no running around, no fun? As I sat there all by myself, listening to the joyful shouts of classmates having a good time outside, I decided I had better change my attitude. So, I wrote a note to Mr. Scheer and left it on his desk. The note said (and I remember this very clearly):

> *Dear Mr. Scheer,*
> *I have decided to "turn over a new leaf," and I will try to behave better from now on.*
> *Jim Lareva*

When he came in from the noon hour, I was watching him closely as he looked at the note, read it, and then looked up at me with this look that said, "OK, now show me!" And show him I did, from that time on! I spent more time helping the younger children, and I actually helped one little 1st-grader adapt to life at Trinity School. She was terribly shy, a bit scared, and very much by herself all during recess and the noon hour. I took to looking for her every recess and parts of the noon hour, and would take her for little walks up the alley behind the school playground. I didn't think much of it at the time, but it began to have a good effect on her and she went on to do very well in the years following. To my surprise, at the end of the school year, Mr. Scheer made special mention of what I had done, and I felt very happy about that.

A number of years later, when I was at the seminary and had come home to visit my family in Muskegon, I was invited by the pastor to preach for the two services on a Sunday morning – sort of a "son of the congregation" thing. I still recall the look in some people's eyes and faces as they saw me up there, saying to themselves: *This is Jimmy Lareva, who once hit a ball that broke part of one of our stained glass windows in the church?* Yes, that was me! Anyway, after the service, with many people greeting me at the door, this nice-looking woman, a bit younger than me, came up and said, "Jim, I'm Carol Theiss. You were the boy who helped me so much when I was in 1st grade at Trinity School. Thank you so much for that, because it is still one of my most distinct and fondest memories of school!" You can imagine my thoughts and feelings at the time, as I hugged her and thanked her for telling me her little story. I guess I really must have "turned over a new leaf," as I promised Mr. Scheer. It was a wonderful moment for me in my memories of Trinity School.

I had a lot of friends, mostly boys, of course, at Trinity. They had names like Dave Skelly (who moved to Cleveland during my 7th-grade year, and with whom I reconnected many years later in Cleveland, Ohio, when I went there to teach at the Lutheran high school), Bennie Heiman, Carl Greenert, Louie Newman, George Rhode, "Tubby" Folbrook, and a few others. We were a little "gang," and we continued our friendship well past our days at Trinity School. As for girls, Delores could run faster than any of us, so she was always on our team when we chose up sides. Joanne and Marian were there, Gerda, and Peggy – one grade ahead of me and who reminded me of Shirley Temple, so I liked her very much in the 4th and 5th grades. However, it wasn't until my 8th-grade year that I really "fell in love" for the first time, and it was with Yvonne "Vonnie" Hall, a 7th-grader. Wow! Did I have a "crush!" That spring and summer were some glorious times in the life of this young romantic boy! (For more on this, see the chapter entitled, "The Women in My Life.") That was a wonderful time for a young, 13-year-old boy! Unfortunately, it didn't last, and I kind of "reclused" into a somewhat girl-shy period during my teens. However, that didn't last too long!

At this point, I want to share something about my two groups of friends. I consider attending a school way across town not to be a negative factor in my life, but rather a very positive one. Look at it this way: I had two sets of wonderful friends on both ends of town! I had my terrific neighborhood friends in East Muskegon, with whom I sometimes went to church, and I had my many great friends at Trinity School! In a sense, although I didn't think about it at the time, I was "doubly blessed" (a term I will use later in this book, in a far different sense). I treasure to this day those two sets of very special and important friends in my life!

The culmination of my days at Trinity School was my youth Confirmation on Palm Sunday, 1941. For two years, we had spent an hour once a week in Confirmation study (plus the usual religion that was part of school curriculum).

We had an advantage over the dozen or so non-parochial school kids who received their instruction at the church on Saturday mornings for those two years, and it showed in our pre-Confirmation examination in front of the entire congregation on the Sunday before Palm Sunday. Two aspects of that whole process caused me to be proud – in a bad way and in a good way. In the examination period (during which we were seated in a long, arching shape facing the congregation as the pastor asked the questions), I was given six questions and I answered every one of them correctly. I was "bad" proud! On Confirmation Sunday a week later (after I had chided myself for my pride the week before), the pastor confirmed me with the Bible passage, John 3:16. Sometime later, I heard from his son that he always reserved that passage for the most commendable student in the Confirmation class. So I was "good" proud of that, and have remembered it to this day as a very special moment. It was probably not a tremendously spiritual experience for me at the time, but it became much more meaningful for me over the years, and I tried to impress that on my own Confirmation students during the 33 years of my pastoral ministry later on.

There's not a whole lot more to say about my experiences at Trinity School in Lakeside, except that I was able to continue my many relationships and friendships on both ends of town. Quite a blessing! My years at Trinity School were some of the defining years of my life, especially because of my friends and because of Mr. Birkman and Mr. Scheer. I will treasure those years always!

~

My High School Years, 1941-1945

My high school years included a lot of sports, which I will write about in more detail later in this book (see the chapter entitled, "My Life in Sports"). But those four years were filled with other things, too: the long walks or bicycle rides to Muskegon High School (two miles away), the many neighborhood activities at our home and at the homes of "the guys" (my favorite place was Fred's!), many indoor and outdoor games, and a growing awareness that girls were more than just neighborhood kids to be teased or put up with. At about this time, my straight black hair turned naturally curly and has stayed that way ever since. For the first two years of high school, I had the Muskegon Chronicle newspaper route in my area, including the streets of Isabella, Catherine, and Ada, where many of my friends lived. I delivered 80 papers every day except

Sunday, in all kinds of weather, either on my bike (in good weather) or walking the route (in rain or snow in winter). I kept up with war news as I folded papers, and also got to know a few girls on my route whom I dated later on. It was a good experience in business dealings with people, socializing, and being responsible and accountable in my job. Only when I got into sports more seriously during my last two years of high school (1944 and 1945) did I give up the paper route and pass it on to my brother.

In the summer of 1944, I got a job at West Michigan Cold Storage Plant, right on a dock area on Muskegon Lake. The company provided huge amounts of ice for the refrigerated railroad cars. Throwing big chunks of ice from the second-floor platform into the holds at the end of each refrigerated boxcar was always a challenge, and sometimes a bit dangerous for anyone who happened to be below! We also worked on the Milwaukee Clipper, a cruise ship that also ferried cars between Milwaukee, Chicago, and Muskegon for many years. On weekends, we would help drive cars on and off the ship. Some of the guys were pretty wild, and more than a few dents were sustained during this whole process! It was a great summer job, with better pay than I'd ever had before. I saved my money carefully for a special week in Chicago at the end of summer, before beginning my last year of high school. Late in August, 1944, my mother took my brother and me to Chicago for a week. (She had this wonderful tendency of exposing us to good, new experiences.) We stayed at the Blackstone Hotel in the center of this great city and took in all the sights and great things there: the Museum of Art, the Natural History Museum, the Science Museum, other cultural things, and a lot of fun activities. We rode the "El" (elevated train) all over the place, visited big department stores, and saw the famous "Navy Pier" (but couldn't go onto it, since it was wartime). The high point for me was the day I went, all by myself, to Wrigley Field on the north side of Chicago, and watched the Cubs play a doubleheader – and then quickly grabbed a train up to Evanston to take in the annual College All-Star Football Classic, where a team of star college seniors from the previous year played against the past year's NFL champions. Normally, it was mostly an exhibition, since the College All-Stars couldn't really compete with a professional team. However, that year it turned out to be a very competitive game, with quarterback Glenn Dobbs of Tulsa essentially single-handedly almost beating the Chicago Bears, who won on a last-minute field goal by the score of

24-21. There I was, a 16-year-old kid, bopping all around Chicago to different places, using public transportation he'd never been on before, and doing it successfully and with no real concern that I wouldn't get back to the hotel all right by midnight! All I remember was the wonderful experience of being able to do all that, and a mother who trusted me to make my way around without any real trouble!

That led me into my last year of high school, with no regard for preparing for college. All I could see at the end of my graduation was military service (see my chapter entitled, "U.S. Navy (1945-1949)"). Since I was in a vocational training program to be an Apprentice Printer, I only took a minimum of college prep courses. I was good at my work as a printer and by the late part of my last semester, my teacher got me a job at Earle Press, a local printing press company, where I worked from late spring into the summer before going off to the Navy. I must have done a pretty good job those months, because I was promised a job when I got back out of the Navy.

As far as my high school academics, I was good in history, geography, government, economics, English literature, writing, and music appreciation! Everything else suffered, but I survived. Girlfriends at this time are covered in my chapter entitled, "The Women in My Life." I enjoyed high school, but never felt I was a real integral part of it, since I was from the "Eastside" (something which plagued a few of my athletic friends, including one of the best athletes our high school ever produced – Bob Ludwig). But I had such great neighborhood friends, and I had one other important ingredient in my life: our Trinity Lutheran Church youth group, which was part of the Walther League (named after C.F.W. Walther, who played a major role in the founding of the Lutheran Church – Missouri Synod (LCMS) in 1847, and was the first LCMS president).

It was during those last two years of high school that I was totally involved with Walther League, becoming an officer and a leader. The Walther League became the center of what social life I had in those days. I didn't relate well to most of the "high school crowd" and their upscale and somewhat snobbish approach, even though I got invitations to some of their parties. One girl, Patty, really tried with me (I think she liked me quite a bit) but when I didn't come to her parties, she really froze me out – and I understood right where I stood with that "crowd." No problem, since I had my own "social network" going at

Trinity Lutheran Church. I would describe our dating habits in those days as "round-robin" dating, with different people within the group dating each other at various times. Actually, it was quite successful, with three couples eventually getting married! Not so with me! But there were some truly nice girls in that group, some with whom I reconnected after my Navy years. Incidentally, it was during this time, in my senior year of high school and as president of our Walther League, that my pastor, Rev. W.F. Luebke, suggested to me that I might consider the pastoral ministry. I think it was because he had seen me speak publicly several times in front of a lot of people and was impressed with how well I did. My reaction to his suggestion was a bit of a laugh, and a response of something to effect of: "No way!" Some years later, I responded much the same way when he suggested it again when I got out of the Navy. So you can imagine that it was very, very special to me (and especially to him!) when one day I told him of my plans to attend the seminary to become a pastor in our church. That occurred in early 1957, and he died very soon afterward. I'm sure my decision gave him joy.

Our Walther League group was very active, mostly because of the efforts and leadership of Bill Scheer. He got me active in the Walther League when I wasn't really interested. Our League put on a number of plays in the church, and it was during that time when our group became more closely connected to other congregations and Walther League groups in the area, including the youth in Conklin, Michigan. That's when I first met Harland Reister, who was to become one of my very closest friends – both before, but especially after, my years in the Navy. Some years later, I was his best man at his wedding in February, 1954. (That's quite a story in itself, which I will cover later in this book!) My high school years and youth league experiences were good and helpful to me. It was a great and wonderful growing-up period of my life, and once again, I can say how much I treasure those years in my life's journey!

Basically, that's my story for the first 17-plus years of my life in Muskegon, Michigan. Despite the Depression, moving around a lot, my parents' divorce, and a new family situation on Isabella Avenue, I think I thrived very well those years, thanks to some very, very good people in my life – people whose memories I treasure to this day, especially my mother!

Remembrances, Reminiscences, and History of My Early Life

~

A description of my life on Isabella Avenue and afterward would not be complete without a few words about my stepfather, John Sevrey. He had been turned off by religion and Christianity early in his teens, when his best high school friend broke his leg in a football game, and his Christian Science family kept him in a bedroom for three days, after which he died. John never quite got over that misuse of what he perceived as "Christian faith," and was always at odds with his Christian Science sisters for the rest of his life. And yet, here he was, married to a very committed Christian woman who continued to bring up her boys in the church. To John's credit, he never interfered, he never spoke out to us about his feelings, and he never in any way made us feel any less because of our Christian faith. He even attended church when something special was happening for my brother and me. I respected him a great deal for that, particularly when I learned years later about his high school friend's death and how it happened. My stepfather had a temper, but I never felt it directed at me. He was always reasonable and kind with me in our relationship, which didn't always seem to be the case with my brother, whose temper often got him into trouble. I guess you might say that I liked my stepfather but certainly not in the way that I loved my father, nor did I ever feel that John was trying to supplant my dad in my own relationship with him as my stepfather. What I appreciated most about him was his relationship with, and love for, my mom, and how he expressed it over the years. As a boy growing up during those years, I probably didn't always appreciate fully how much he meant to Mom and how he provided a secure, stable life for her, as well as being a loving husband to her. I do not recall having any negative feelings or attitude about him because he was a stepfather, and there were many times that I valued his advice and counsel. He was good to live with on Isabella Avenue! Some years later, shortly before he died at the somewhat young age of 57, I expressed to him my feelings and gratitude for the way he treated me, but mostly how he had treated my mother so well and lovingly, and I thanked him as sincerely as I could. He rarely expressed or showed a great deal of emotion, but after I spoke to him that way, I noticed a few tears welling up in his eyes. Later, when I said something to my mom about that exchange, she had a few tears too. She explained that John always like me very much. Even though he didn't agree with my decision to go to the seminary, he still accepted it and was kind about the idea. When he died, not too much later, I realized that the Lord had given me a very special moment in his life that brought some happiness to him, and maybe even joy.

~

That was the first of two great lessons I learned as I matured into adulthood. The next great lesson came a few years later. Near the close of my college years, my father suffered a stroke, which left him paralyzed on much of his left side. I still remember playing Canasta with him by the hour, and the long time it sometimes took him to play his cards (nothing wrong with his brain, though!). When I came home from college that last year, and then while I was teaching my first year in Cleveland, I would always spend some time with him in North Muskegon, where he lived for a number of years with my stepmother, Lydia, a good Christian woman. He liked nothing more than going for a car ride into the country, especially because I'd let him drive the car for a few miles out in the open countryside. Oh, how he loved those times of driving! He had always been so involved with cars all his life, and because of his paralysis he wasn't legally allowed to drive anymore. Late in the summer of 1954, as I prepared to leave home for my second year of teaching at Cleveland Lutheran High School, he called me up two days before I was to leave. I had seen him a few days before, so I was surprised to hear his request. He wanted me to drive him around the next day (my last day home), all over the part of Western Michigan that was his old "stomping grounds," so he could visit some of his old buddies and relatives. Inwardly, I groaned, *I really don't have the time for this, just before leaving town.* But, after a few seconds of hesitation, I agreed to do it, even though I realized it might be an all-day job. When I told my mom, she nodded approvingly, as she seemed to understand better than I did what he might have been asking of me. So the next day, I picked him up late in the morning, and we proceeded to drive all over Western Michigan (or so it seemed), visiting every friend and relative of his (many of whom I didn't even know) for the next seven hours. What a joy it was to him! Finally, about 6 P.M., he said, "Jim, I'm tired, it's time to take me home," which I did. I bade him goodbye and finished getting ready to leave for Cleveland the next day. In Cleveland two days later, as we teachers prepared for the beginning of school in a few days, I got a phone call at school from my stepmother, telling me that my father had died suddenly that day. All I could do, besides feeling my natural sorrow, was to thank God that I had not refused my father's request because it was so "inconvenient" for me at the time. For the rest of my life, I have referred to that occasion to advise people to take the opportunities to share some special time with important people in their lives before it's "too late!" What a lesson the Lord taught me!

~

During my first 17 years, two men played an especially important role in my life. They were the two main male role models for those years, and for the rest of my life. My high regard for them in no way diminishes the good relationship I had with my father. Dad was a good man who was decimated emotionally by the Depression at his midlife period, and he never seemed to fully recover. He was a loving, gentle man who seemed like more of a grandfather to me than a father. I loved him very much and we had many, many good times together. I would often go to his home in North Muskegon and mow his lawn, complete some chores around the house, and do other activities with him and for him. We talked a lot, but seldom about really important things, and I could never influence him about my own personal Christian faith and what it meant to me. He was, to me, just a sweet old man to whom I always felt a close attachment all my life. He was, in God's way of doing things, a special gift to me and I cherish every memory of him.

Having said that, let me tell you about my first important male role model, my uncle, Harry Knuth. Uncle Harry was a fairly large, robust man with a keen sense of humor and a disposition that was gregarious, loving, and generous. The one physical limitation he had was a congenital condition with one hip, which caused him to have a pronounced limp. This disability hampered him very much at times, and was sometimes quite painful. In spite of that, I never saw him "down" about it, or not optimistic and upbeat. Maybe I'm seeing him through the eyes of a young boy and then a teenager and then a young man, who felt so very close to him all my life. Only years later did I realize just how influential he was in my life, and how very, very much I adored and appreciated him. He had a kind of slapstick sense of humor, and he put a lot of joy into his own life and the lives of those around him. One of the most important things that happened for me was when he and my Aunt Aulie moved from Manistee to Muskegon Heights about the time my parents divorced. He did not "replace" my father (any more than my stepfather could have), but he did become someone significant in my life in an intimate, close way, which would be a big plus in my life! How God blessed me with my Uncle Harry! Over those years when he and Aunt Aulie were in Muskegon Heights (mainly in a nice home on Peck Street), my brother and I (but mostly I) spent a lot of time in their home. My grandmother, Oma, divided her time between our house on Isabella Avenue and their house on Peck Street. So I was always "at home" in either place. As I grew older, I spent more time with Uncle Harry for two reasons: as the older of the two boys, I was more in touch with him and more mature than my brother; and Uncle Harry and I shared a love of sports, especially baseball. He was a Chicago Cubs fan and I was a Detroit Tigers fan, so we had many interesting conversations – and I also became a Cubs fan for the National League. You can imagine my special delight when the Tigers beat the Cubs in the 1945 World Series! Although I was in the Navy at the time, and wasn't able to share that special time with him in person.

By the way, I want to mention something very important in my life's direction because of Uncle Harry. Sometime during the war years, he told me that since I would probably get drafted as soon as I graduated from high school, I should really think about voluntarily joining the Navy before they drafted me into the Army. I'm not sure why he advised this, since he never did any military service due to his physical handicap. However, because it was my Uncle Harry who made such a suggestion, I never questioned that I would join the Navy after graduation. What a very important decision that was, to which my chapter entitled "U.S. Navy (1945-1949)" will attest. I am so grateful to him for that advice!

During my teen years in particular, I went over to Uncle Harry's house almost every Saturday, and sometimes on Sunday. I found that I could do a lot of yard work for him – mowing the lawn, pulling weeds, raking leaves, burning trash, helping to paint his house, and whatever else I could do over there. I got to know a number of kids in his neighborhood, including kids next door, and that was a real plus for me in those years. Another group of friends during my growing-up years! In the best sense of the words, it was a "home away from home." Both Aub and I really benefited from having Uncle Harry and Aunt Aulie in our lives.

There are many memories I have of Uncle Harry and Aunt Aulie. My Aunt Aulie was almost like a second mother, and she was such a good person! Besides many good memories of her, I probably most remember the time during my years in the Navy when I wanted to get back to Michigan on leave in April of 1947. I was due a couple weeks, and applied for early April. At almost the last minute, they changed my leave time to later in April, which really ticked me off at the time. However, because of how God works things, I was able to be back in Muskegon during Aunt Aulie's last days. She was dying of Hodgkin's disease, and I was able to spend some meaningful time with her in the hospital. I was with her the night before she died, and I know it meant a lot to her, as she expressed very softly before I left that night. My pastor was there that evening, and as we left the hospital, he said she would not live through the night. I didn't accept that at the time, but he was right. As a pastor myself many years later, I realize how often that "extra-pastoral sense" served well in ministering to dying people in my congregations.

While I have diverted briefly to write about Aunt Aulie, let me get back to Uncle Harry. One of my many memories of him was seeing him sitting in his office (a separate room in his Peck Street home that allowed him privacy when he wanted it, to work at his desk). He would often invite me into his office to chat, and to watch him work as I read the Chicago papers. He preferred them to the Detroit papers, probably because of his business in Western Michigan, which had many ties to Chicago. And many times we'd just talk and enjoy each other. Those were always wonderful moments together, even though I probably took them for granted at the time. As a married man without any children of his own, it must have been very special to him, as it was to me.

One of my most wonderful memories of Uncle Harry was when I went fishing with him. Uncle Harry was the type of fisherman who loved fishing so much that he could go out for most of a day, not catch a thing, and come home happy. On the other hand, I was not that way. For me, if the fish didn't come in fast enough or big enough, I wouldn't wait too long to go back home and try again another day. Not Uncle Harry! But I would go fishing with him for hours on end, I guess just to be with him, even though I didn't really realize it at the time. And what I didn't understand then (but which I understand now) is that he loved having me with him. I was his "son!" That's all that mattered. Some days we would sit in a rowboat half a day in the bright sun on Lake Michigan (when it was calm enough) or Muskegon Lake, just fishing and talking. Believe it or not, it was never boring for me, but I really couldn't understand this "fetish with fishing" (as I called it, but never to his face). The most interesting times were in the winter when Muskegon Lake froze over and ice fishing was the big thing. Many "ice shanties" were set up on the lake for those three or four months of winter. Naturally, Uncle Harry had his own ice shanty, and I would spend many a Saturday or Sunday afternoon with him in his little hut, trying to catch some poor fish through a hole in the ice, while we were freezing cold at the same time! Why did I do it? Because I was with my Uncle Harry! Also, I'd bring my rather primitive (by today's standards) ice skates, and when I got too cold or just needed to move around a bit, I'd go outside and skate around for a while. It was a wonderful time with him!

Some of my fondest memories of Uncle Harry were in the summertime. Both Aub and I spent more time at their place during those summers, often staying for days at a time. It was during those summers when I was still fairly young (before and into my early teens) that my Uncle Harry would invite me to come with him for the day as he traveled over his sales route in Western Michigan. He stopped in almost every town, large or small, as he delivered his products and took orders for more. I got to sit in the front seat with him in his big car. (He needed a big car to comfortably accommodate his size and his hip handicap.) In almost every place we stopped, he would talk to the people in the drugstore while I sat at the soda fountain and enjoyed a free Coke®! Then at lunchtime, he would stop at a favorite restaurant of his on the route, and we'd have a wonderful lunch together before doing the afternoon part of his route. I cannot ever remember being bored on those trips, especially since he and I talked a lot while we were riding along. I do recall Aunt Aulie telling me one time how much Uncle Harry enjoyed having me along on those trips. Although I thought it would be the opposite – that it was *my* thrill to be with *him*! Maybe it was the special feeling I had while spending those times with him that influenced me years later to make a very conscious effort to make every Saturday noon available to one of my own sons to have lunch with me, one-on-one, at the restaurant of their choice. What a terrific time that was for me with each one of my sons, and I know it was special for them because they kept close track of whose turn it was each week to have lunch with Dad! All in all, those were some truly wonderful times with Uncle Harry, and I really didn't appreciate how important they were to me until years later.

One great memory I have goes back to about eight months after Aunt Aulie died. By this time, Uncle Harry treated me very much like an adult. I was home on leave from the Navy for a week or two, and he and I got together, as was our way when I came home on leave. This time, he got very confidential and brought me into the most intimate dimensions of his life. He told me that he had met (or already knew) this widow in the congregation. I knew her a bit, simply because she was sometimes the organist at Trinity, but more so because she was the mother of one of the most beautiful young women in the congregation – a knockout redhead! My buddies, Bill and Roger, and I used to "drool" over her when she would come to the Sunday evening worship services at Trinity! (Actually, Bill and Roger were my two best buddies in Walther League, and we did a lot of things together outside of Walther League.) Anyway, Ruth was the name of this widow whom Uncle Harry was interested in and whom he was dating a bit. I realized just how close and important my relationship was with him when he asked me so confidentially, "Jim, what do you think of the idea of my marrying her within a couple of months?" It would be almost a year since Aunt Aulie's death, and in my youthful "brilliance," I thought it was a great idea, and I told him so. Basically, I told him, "Go for it, Uncle Harry!" I don't know why my opinion was important to him, but the fact that he confided in me and took my answer seriously said something about the level of our relationship and trust in each other. It was a great compliment to me, as well as great evidence of the strong relationship we had. Of course, my grandmother, Oma, didn't like the idea at all; she felt it didn't show enough respect for her daughter, Aunt Aulie. My mom was fairly neutral about it, although I could tell she wasn't too enamored with the idea. However, in her usual, kind way, she didn't voice any negative feelings. And she knew Ruth, which I believe helped my mom be more understanding about the situation, which she was sensitive to since she and my Uncle Harry were very close.

Well, Uncle Harry married Ruth, whom I began to call "Aunt Ruth." I had some nice times with her and my uncle the few times I came home on leave in 1948. It seems almost mystical, but somehow I wonder if my uncle knew something about himself that no one else knew. After about eight or nine months of a wonderful marriage, in which every evidence showed that they were immensely happy, my Uncle Harry found out that he had very quick-acting Hodgkin's disease. By February, 1949, the tenth month of their marriage, he was dead. I didn't find out until later because our U.S. Marine outfit was on maneuvers in the Caribbean Sea off Puerto Rico, and we didn't get mail delivery for a couple of weeks. My mom wrote me a long letter and described Uncle Harry's last month or so, and commented, "It's better that you remember him the way he was and looked because he was a shell of the man you last saw, and it wasn't very pleasant." Of course, I was shocked since no one had told me about his sickness. It had happened so fast, and I'm sure they didn't mean to "neglect" me so many miles away. The next time I got home, during the spring of 1949, I visited Aunt Ruth several times and had some long talks with her. One thing she told me several times (and her daughter, June, reiterated it to me in the years following): "We had less than a year together, but it was the best year of my life, and I will never regret it or feel sorry for myself that it was so short. That's what a truly wonderful man your Uncle Harry was for me and to me!" Aunt Ruth and I kept in close touch with each other over the following years until she died. My bond with Ruth's daughter is because of Uncle Harry, whom June loved and admired so much. June was very happy that her mother had that special time with him toward the end of her life. My Uncle Harry was the same age as my Aunt Aulie was when she died in 1947 – only 52 years old!

There is one more thing to share about my Uncle Harry, and I didn't know about this until many years later. My brother Aub, who lived very close to our mother and John in Twin Lake, Michigan, often found out things from Mom that I didn't know about. One of the things he learned was that Uncle Harry (who was economically well-situated during the Depression) often gave money to our parents during the worst years of the Depression, but would never allow them to tell anyone, or to ever pay it back. Uncle Harry and Aunt Aulie knew they were blessed through all those difficult Depression years, and their deep Christian faith and generous spirit expressed itself toward our family. By the way, when Aub told me this some years ago, after Mom had died, he indicated that he found out by accident one day when our mom was talking to him about those Depression years and she let it slip about Uncle Harry's generosity. Because he had sworn her to secrecy, she said, "And please, Aubrey, don't tell Jim." So this is one more reason, among a multitude of reasons, why Uncle Harry and Aunt Aulie were such a major part of my life. I know it is a very human feeling on my part, but one of the major disappointments of my life (and I don't have many of them) is that my uncle didn't live 15 or 20 years longer, so I could have had all those years of my adulthood to enjoy, appreciate, and relish my loving, almost adoring, relationship with my Uncle Harry Knuth! He was my "idol!" At the same time, I am so totally grateful and thankful and blessed to have had him in my life as I did, and for as long as I did. What a blessing!

Before I move on from this period of my life, I must include one more very important person whom I've previously referred to – Bill Scheer. Some of my early "exploits" with him I have already described in some detail. These following lines will delve more deeply into the relationship that developed between us over the years, and why I still consider him one of the two most important and influential male role models in my life.

Rupert "Bill" Scheer came to Trinity Lutheran Church in Muskegon in the early fall of 1940, at the beginning of my 8th-grade year at Trinity School. When he began his teaching career at Trinity, he had recently come out of Concordia Teachers College, Seward, Nebraska, with only one year of teaching at an all-boys school in Kansas. We 8th-grade boys at Trinity were now "Kings of the Hill" at this little eight-grade, one-room, one-teacher parochial school. After "walking all over" the previous teacher (Pastor Luebke's son, Vicar Gerhardt, who was a loving, nice young man who exercised very little discipline or control over a class of 35 children, ages 6-13), we boys figured that we "had it made" with the next new teacher on the scene! Little did we realize what would happen to us for the next nine months of the school year!

I have already described earlier in this chapter my first day of school that 8th-grade year. And I've already recounted that extremely important discipline lesson that Bill Scheer taught me. Let me now share more intimately all that God did to bring about a most amazing and beautiful relationship between Bill Scheer and me that would only grow wonderfully over the years ahead.

First of all, about my 8th-grade year at Trinity: Once I understood that he "meant business" as a teacher, I realized how much I was learning academically. What horizons and vistas he opened up to me and to all of us who were "smart" enough to realize it! I grew so much in that year of preparation for going into a big four-year public high school in Muskegon. More importantly, Bill Scheer exhibited to me the true meaning of my fledgling Christian faith experience, even though I probably didn't really recognize it at the time. However, it would serve me well in the years ahead!

Two years after I finished the 8th grade, on August 14th, 1943, we had the fascinating experience of attending Bill Scheer's wedding to a very pretty young woman, Lois Rechnagel, whose father occasionally dated my mother when they were teenagers in Arcadia, Michigan. Lois was a girl Bill had become close to during his first three years of teaching at Trinity, and whom he kissed during the ceremony (against the pastor's instructions) much to the delight of everyone!

During my first two years of high school, I wasn't involved with my church's youth group, which was part of the Walther League. However, at the beginning of my junior year in high school, Bill called me and suggested that I might like to join some of Trinity's Walther Leaguers in planning and putting on a church play. I was not enthusiastic about the idea, but I couldn't turn him down, especially when he even offered to pick me up that first time. That led to two terrific years in our Walther League, and a growing attachment to Bill Scheer. We played together on the fast-pitch church softball team the summer of 1945, just before I left for the U.S. Navy. He even gave me one of his "looks" when I used a cuss word in one of our games! He didn't say a word, but he didn't have to!

All during my four years in the Navy, my four years at Valparaiso University, and my four years of teaching at Cleveland Lutheran High School, we kept in regular touch and each of us knew generally what was happening in the lives of the other. Much of this was due to my knowing Lois's family quite well (they were on my paper route in Muskegon for two years) and knowing Bill's family, including his teenage sister Vera through Walther League, and his parents and other sister who lived near our home in East Muskegon. After my teaching years in Cleveland, our lives would intersect more closely than ever.

While I was at the sem (I was one of the earlier, married guys at Springfield, since the St. Louis sem didn't yet "allow" married men), I chose to visit Bill and Lois in Grand Haven (a few miles from Muskegon), where Bill was the principal and a teacher at St. John's Lutheran School. Meeting in their home, he and I talked about teaching (he was in his 20th year) and the pastoral ministry in general because he was so supportive of my entering the ministry. During our conversations, with Lois listening (a bit like "Sarah"), Bill asked about the sem and the idea of an older man like himself starting out to prepare for the pastoral ministry at his age. I simply replied that the Springfield sem had lots of married guys in their late 30s and early 40s, and even a few in their 50s. Then he said something about all his children (they had six at the time), but I replied rather casually, "Oh, we have guys with more kids than you." (I was referring to one of my classmates, and also to Morrie Watkins, of future Lutheran Bible Translators renown, who had at least six children at the time). I'm not sure (and it was probably my imagination) but I thought I heard Lois gasp in the background. She told me later that she was sure I would discourage Bill, but instead, I encouraged him!

While I was on my vicarage in 1959-1960 in Los Angeles, Bill, Lois, and family began a special two-year ministerial colloquy program at the Springfield sem. At the same time, Bill was called to be principal at Immanuel Lutheran School near the Springfield sem campus, so they had an income for those two years. When my wife Betty and our one and a half-year-old son Mark returned from California for my last year at the sem, we all became even closer as families, and this only furthered my special relationship with Bill. In fact, Betty and I (and often only myself) would go to the Scheer home, just to be with this wonderful family. Their oldest daughter, Sandra, was our babysitter for Mark a number of times! Those were truly beautiful days of closeness with the Scheer family, and this continued for years afterward. In the years following, Bill and his growing family would carry out pastoral ministry in several places. Bill concluded his formal ministry in Fremont, Michigan, home of Gerber Baby Foods. In his retirement, he assisted at Trinity in Muskegon until his Day of Glory on February 22, 2001. I had the honor and privilege of attending his memorial service.

What best characterized for me those last years of Bill's life here on earth were the wonderful visits to Fremont by Betty and me, and later by Nancy and me. What special times when we'd all meet for breakfast and a couple hours of wonderful, wonderful conversation! After Bill's death, it was so special to get together with Lois in Fremont. In recent years, when Nancy couldn't come with me on my visits to Michigan and up into Canada (Betty's family), Lois and I would get together (if she was in town and not gallivanting all over the country visiting kids and grandkids!) and we would share some warm, loving moments about each other and our memories of Bill. He will always be one of my heroes!

This concludes my special section on the two most important male role models in my life. Their influence on me and their love for me is incalculable to measure, except in heavenly terms. I am so grateful to them, and to God who put them into my life!

~

Whenever I spoke about my mother on Mother's Day, I always closed with these words: "But this is the most important thing my mother did for me: She introduced me to Jesus and everything that would come to mean for me." And the most important thing that Harry Knuth and Bill Scheer did for me was to teach and exemplify what my mother did for me! How blessed I was!

Chapter 2

My Mother ("Mom")

My mother was the single most important human and spiritual influence in my life. She was born on October 15th, 1901, in Arcadia, Michigan, of Herman and Frieda Lang. She was named Alvina Louise, but as she was growing up into her teen years she was often called "Dutch." Later she was called "Al" by friends and acquaintances, which she liked. She had a sister, Hulda, two years older, and a brother, Walter, almost four years younger (who died in 1918 at the age of 13 during the national flu epidemic). She grew up with them in a large home right across the street from Trinity Lutheran Church in Arcadia. It was a totally German-American community, even to the status level of families within a tight-knit, clearly defined infrastructure. I believe that almost from the beginning, my mother rebelled against such a "caste system" (as she would later call it). She expressed this feeling in several obvious ways in the years to come as she grew up. In spite of that, it was a wonderful, caring atmosphere at home and in the community, filled with many of the joys of childhood in a very small town on the shores of beautiful Lake Michigan, north of Grand Rapids and south of Traverse City.

Arcadia was and continues to be the home of the International Lutheran Camp, where she spent many delightful summers with other kids in Arcadia. From very early on, my mother displayed independent characteristics along with her strong religious faith, athletic abilities, and leadership qualities. As she grew, she developed into a tall, dark-eyed, attractive young woman. Already in high school, she was the star basketball player with her height (about 5′ 8″ – very tall for a girl in those days), agility, and leadership. She loved sports of all kinds, but mostly basketball and baseball. This interest was fostered by her father, who was a baseball player and umpire for many years in that area and who always encouraged my mom in athletics as well as academics. My Aunt Hulda (whom my brother and I called "Aunt Aulie") was small, pretty, and very different from my mother in academics and athletics. It is also my strong feeling that my grandfather ("Opa") was so devastated by the death of his only son, Walter, in 1918, that he subconsciously transferred much of his athletic aspirations upon my mom, who already had exhibited much athletic interest and ability. Her love of baseball in later years translated itself into my own "love of the game!" I am sure that my grandfather derived much joy and satisfaction from my mother's many athletic achievements over the years, especially as a basketball star in high school and college.

What makes my mother's accomplishments so amazing in these areas of academics and athletics was the "tenor of the times." Growing up in a small, German-American community with very strict rules and traditions, clear-cut levels of social, economic, and cultural lines, and a male-dominated atmosphere, my mom must have felt inhibited and frustrated in many ways. So, with her father's encouragement, she resisted and finally "broke out" of that atmosphere, even though she treasured it all of her life in remembrance and memory. She taught me that you can love and relish the past, but don't let the past imprison you with too much nostalgia, sentimentality, or even fantasy. That is why, to this day, I can enjoy and appreciate the past and its values and yet not be entrapped by it.

My mom was part of the first class of girls to graduate from high school in Arcadia (up until then, girls only went through the 10th grade), and was the first woman from Arcadia to go on to college! She graduated from Arcadia High School in 1919, and attended Central Michigan University in Mt. Pleasant, where she received her teaching degree. From there she took a high school teaching position in Cass City (in the "thumb" of Michigan) and was also the high school girls' basketball coach for several years from 1921-1925. It was during this period that she received the tragic news of her father's death when he accidentally fell out of a car and hit his head on a rock. He was on his way to go fishing with some friends. To this day, I am convinced that this traumatic event in her life affected her selection of a husband several years later. Let me put it this way. My mother, a most independent and modern woman of the 1920s, who had learned from and grown up with a father who constantly strengthened her resolve to be herself and to be independent and strong, was suddenly and tragically deprived of that source of emotional, spiritual, and familial strength and support. Since she never spoke directly or specifically about it in personal or intimate terms in later years, I cannot presume to interpret her emotional condition at that time of her life and in the immediate years to follow. However, I have some pretty definite thoughts and ideas about what happened to her. Deprived of the strongest and most important male influence in her life, my mother went on with her life but with a different perspective of everything. I don't know what her love life was like at the time, although I know she had a very active one up until then. However, I suspect that when she moved to Muskegon, Michigan sometime in 1925, something struck a chord in her life when she met my dad, Dano Lareva. He was from Hesperia, Michigan, about 20 miles from Muskegon, and was a 39-year-old bachelor who had never been married before he met Mom. My dad had been very independent and had lived a varied life with many jobs. He had been around the country a bit, even working as a forest ranger in the state of Washington at one time. Back in Muskegon, working as a machinist at the largest manufacturing company at the time – Campbell, Wyant, and Cannon (which made parts for automobiles in Detroit) – he somehow met my mother. I never heard any details of how they met or the circumstances. All I know is that they were married in early 1926 and moved into a home which they were able to buy from the company he worked for (a kind of company store – low price and no down payment). During the four years they lived there, both my brother and I were born – me in 1927 and he in 1929. It was a very nice home and my parents were, in a sense, "on top of the world" until the "Crash of 1929!" The fallout from the stock market crash didn't reach that area of Michigan and my dad's company until 1931, when my father lost his job, his home, and his self-esteem. He was never quite the same after that! This is not said in criticism or judgment. It's just the way it was, and it never affected my love or respect for him in the years to follow. He was suddenly and painfully deprived of his job, home, and economic security without any other appreciable gifts or talents with which to cope and handle a radically new situation for a man in his mid-40s with a family to support. In a way, it simply "wiped him out" and he never fully recovered in the next 25 years of his life. More about my father in another section of my story and my life.

Almost needless to say, this was a most difficult time for my parents. When I was around four or five years old, we moved from our nice home in a somewhat upscale area of town known as Roosevelt Park, to a small rental house in a lower-scale economic area on 8th Street. "From Broadway Avenue to 8th Street" says it all! My father got a job as a car salesman with Boyd Ford Auto Sales in Muskegon Heights (not much of a job in those days, but it was a job). My mother continued her teaching career as best she could as a substitute teacher. For them, these years must have been terribly frustrating, immensely stressful, and filled with much anxiety, doubts, and questions. So how did my mother cope? Well, she told me many years later that she and Dad had decided that no matter how bad things got, my brother and I would never know physical or emotional deprivation, or the pangs of being hungry. And we didn't. I don't ever remember feeling hungry, deprived in any way, or even feeling in a "bad way" as a child. Somehow, my brother and I never experienced all of the reality of the thing called The Great Depression. Our childhoods were a series of healthy, good, active, and unthreatening years, with no sense of loss, fear, or trepidation. How my parents did this for us, I don't know. It seems to me that I should have picked up some kinds of neuroses, emotional baggage, or psychological aberrations to last a lifetime. Somehow, my dad and mom made sure that my brother and I had good lives during those troublesome years and we, as two little boys, seemed not to have suffered adversely because of The Depression.

During those several years on 8th Street, when I was five or six years old, I used to do something with and for my mother which I remember very clearly to this day. And now I realize many years later how very much she must have enjoyed and appreciated it. In those days, my mom was a woman in her early 30s who had very long, beautiful black hair, well down below her shoulders. I don't know how it started, but every once in a while she would lie down on the sofa with her head on the end of the sofa and her long hair hanging down over the end. Then I would take a chair, sit down, and comb and brush her hair many, many times. Obviously, she enjoyed it! Thinking back now, they must have been special times of quiet, peaceful moments with her "little Jimmy" in the midst of very trying and difficult times. And I know that I must have enjoyed that time with her, too! For me, those were wonderful years.

But now, back to my mother's ongoing life. After a couple of years on 8th Street, my parents rented a large home in another part of Muskegon Heights. This seemed to work for several years until I was nine years old. During those several years (two or three at the most), my parents' marriage was failing, and by 1936 they were in the process of divorce. I know no details about this situation, and the only thing I remember was a statement by my mother some years later as to why she divorced my dad: "It was to save my family!" I didn't pursue that statement because I sensed that she didn't mean for it to be elaborated upon, in deference to my dad and to my mom's own personal privacy. The only other thing I can recount about that situation is that my pastor in Muskegon during that whole time (he baptized and confirmed me) dealt with Mom particularly and assured her that what was happening to her and her reason(s) for the divorce were not against the Word of Scripture, and she was allowed to keep her church membership in good standing at Trinity Lutheran Church in Muskegon.

Now, for my own "take" on why the divorce occurred. First of all, my mother had lost the strongest and best paternal and loving influence in her life when her father died suddenly when she was only 22 years old. It devastated her! For a tall, dark-haired, dark-eyed, attractive young woman in the prime of her maturing beauty, she would have been a great "catch" for any man! With many boyfriends and suitors along the way, she certainly wasn't "pining away," waiting for that proverbial "knight in shining armor" to come along. My sense is that when she met my dad, who was an older, more mature and seemingly more stable man, her instincts and needs for such a type of man (represented by her own father) took over and she became very much attracted to him and perhaps saw in him the male influence that her father had been to her for so many years. I'm not so sure it was entirely "true love" that drew her to him, as much as it was a need that my mother found so important in her relationship with my father. Of course, my father (at the age of 39 and never married) must have been "swept off his feet" by the loving interest of this young, vibrant, dark-eyed beauty with personality and independence.

That leads me to the second important dimension of that divorce – a spiritual one. My father had been brought up in a very religious, Christian home. However, his mother, so deeply religious herself, never imposed or "forced" religion on his many brothers and sisters in terms of church attendance and Christian education. My dad responded to this by never really becoming part of the religious scene or following in his mother's footsteps. Therefore, when he met my mother, it seemed to him quite comfortable to "go along" with my mother's strong Christian and Lutheran identity and commitment. Without my mother's urging, before they were married he joined the pastor's "Information Class" and quickly became a confirmed member of the LCMS and Trinity Lutheran Church in Muskegon. Then came the great disappointment to my mother: he never again, after their wedding, attended church, even when I was very young and in Sunday School programs or parochial school activities. I can only imagine what this must have done to my mother and her strong, sensitive spiritual feelings. But that didn't keep her from making sure that my brother and I received the best spiritual upbringing possible! How grateful I am for that!

The third important dimension of their divorce that must have deeply affected their relationship is a very personal one for me. When my mother became pregnant with me in late December, 1926, my father's reaction was for her to have an abortion! Somehow or another, they must not have discussed this part of their future life together before they married. For my mother, in the parlance of today's vernacular, she simply said, "No Way!" And so I was allowed to live! Two years later, the same thing happened when she became pregnant with my brother. And she gave my father the same answer! In light of my warm, loving, and very good relationship with my father over the years, especially in the later years of his life, I believe he was happy about my mother's decisions in those days of 1927 and 1929. But, his attitude and feelings about not wanting children must have had a very negative influence in my mother's relationship with him in the years to follow.

Sometime in late 1936 or early 1937, my parents divorced. My life in the large house on Peck Street was suddenly reduced to an upstairs apartment in East Muskegon, all the way across town. I suppose this should have been a negative emotional time in my life (and I think it was for my brother more than for me), but it didn't seem to affect me very much. I went on with my life as it was then for me, and that was mostly school and sports, particularly baseball. My mother's interest, agility, and genes in athletics didn't "kick in" for me until I was about eight or nine years old. But when it did, I just "took off!" From that time on, no matter where we moved to or where we went, I used my baseball interest and agility to integrate myself into my new environment positively and successfully. About that time, another man came into my mother's life, and consequently into my life, too. She met and dated a divorced man named Milton Sevrey, who went by the name John. In the spring of 1938, they were married and we moved to a home in East Muskegon (near the outskirts of what was then the city limits).

Very fortunately for me, the new house we moved into was located right across the street from Harmon Park, a large baseball field and park with large playground areas, ideal for boys who wanted to do sports and athletics. It was in this home that I lived for the next seven years (during my last three years at Trinity Lutheran Parochial School and my four years at Muskegon High School, which was only two miles away).

I don't know how I would describe myself as a son, but I adored my mother and she was the essence of femininity, strength, and spiritual direction for me. My stepfather was a good man, but an avowed atheist who had no room or place for religion in his life. To his credit, he did not seek to impose his beliefs or lack of them on us.

At this point, I must tell about my mother in terms of my spiritual life and development. From the very beginning, she had my brother and I in Sunday School and church. After our move to 8th Street, she enrolled us at Trinity Lutheran Parochial School in Lakeside, Michigan (a part of Muskegon but designated as a community within Muskegon). From 2nd grade through 8th grade, I was a student at Trinity School. I'm not sure how my mom did it, but she somehow managed for my brother and me to be at that school, even though it must have cost something extra at a time when my parents couldn't afford it. Here I was in an eight-grade, one-room, 35-student school with one teacher (Herman Birkman), who also had to pick up some of his students from around town in the morning, and take them back in the afternoon. But my mother was convinced that we needed such a special educational and spiritual atmosphere and training, even though she herself was a public school teacher. I recall that at one time she was an elementary school principal for two years at a local public school. I remember how proud I was to visit her school and walk around with the realization that she was the principal! Sometime later, after she had returned to regular classroom teaching, she told me how much she missed the classroom, in spite of the higher salary as a principal. Years later, I would understand that feeling more than I did at the time.

I don't remember a time in my life when I wasn't extremely proud of my mother! Whenever I was somewhere with her, it was a very special time, whether just driving up to her hometown of Arcadia, or spending a wonderful lunchtime with her in downtown Muskegon, or simply chatting with her on the porch of our home in Twin Lake, Michigan (ten miles from Muskegon) when I was older. I think the best times with her in my young adult years (U.S. Navy, college, and later years in teaching) were the trips up north to her hometown of

Arcadia. We would do lunch together somewhere along the way, have lots of wonderful conversation and many laughs together! She was always a delight to be with! We often talked about church and spiritual matters, which really meant a lot to me at the time, as well as since then. She was always active in church, even though my father and stepfather did not attend or believe in that "stuff!" She often was in the choir and helped out in Sunday School, and she always attended worship services. She was my spiritual anchor for many years, and I am eternally grateful! I know now that it wasn't always easy for her, but her attitude simply was: "Whatever you do about your spiritual, religious life down the road, you will, at least, have a basis for a direction and decision about Christianity when you are older. I owe you that much as a parent!" I hardly need tell you how great she felt when I decided to become a Lutheran high school teacher and then an ordained pastor in the Lutheran Church. Fortunately, we were able to share many thoughts and feelings about that in the years before she died in 1985. I am indebted to her!

My indebtedness to my mother sometimes came at a price – discipline! There was a lot of disciplining and growing to do, and she was right there to make sure of it. She didn't spank my brother or me too often, but when she did, we knew exactly why and learned from it. The spanking I remember the most clearly occurred when I was about eight or nine years old and we were living on Peck Street (shortly before the divorce). My brother and I had identical toy "cash register" piggy banks. Each time you put a coin into the bank, you registered that amount with the register keys. The accumulated amount would then show up, as in a regular store or bank register. Well, I had developed such an obsession with a certain kind of candy and small toy at the time, that I figured out a way to "finance" my obsession! With some clever manipulating, I could open my brother's bank from the bottom and remove coins without it showing on the register amount. I did pretty well for a while, and I was quite popular with a few of my close buddies in the neighborhood with my special treats for them and for me. Then my brother began to figure out that while his registered amount of savings was increasing, the weight of those savings was decreasing! Something was evidently wrong. Finally, my mom figured out what was happening and immediately knew who the culprit was. She took me into my bedroom, laid me across the bed, and gave me a very sound spanking! And I really felt it! Then, to my shocked surprise, she sat there next to me on the bed and began to cry with deep, tearful sobs, all the while crying out quietly, "Oh, Jimmy, you're going to be a thief and a criminal! Oh, Jimmy, how could you?" For an eight-year-old boy who adored his mother, that was an awesome and memorable scene, and it stuck clearly with me ever since. So, I never did become a thief or a criminal. My mom saw to that! One more example: Sometime later, during my teen years when we lived on Isabella Avenue in East Muskegon across the street from Harmon Park, a bunch of us were playing sandlot baseball and, as one might expect, making a lot of noise with our yelling and shouting. Well, I must have used a few expletives (with which I had become familiar during my teen years) and she even heard me from across the street. After a few minutes, I heard her call me to come home for something very important. When I came into the house, she "let me have it" about my language and how ashamed she was of me. Wow! Did that ever make an impression! That cured me of the flagrant mode of cussing that I had developed in my teen years, and held me in good stead during my years in the U.S. Navy. However, I still "let a word fly" once in a while from my lips, and I have to remind myself, even to this day.

Educationally speaking, my mother did several wonderful things for me. When I was in the 9th grade, I made up my senior high school (grades 10-12) academic schedule. I had no intention of stretching myself academically, intellectually, or culturally. So, I scheduled myself for every soft course, every vocational course, and every non-college prep course I could find. My mom took one look at my schedule when I brought it home near the end of 9th grade, and declared it was not acceptable. The next day she marched down to the high school and said the same thing, and demanded a more academic and challenging set of classes for my three years of senior high school. Well, I still didn't have a college prep program, but I did have enough "solid" classes for my three years of senior high school to ultimately qualify for admission to college after my four years in the Navy – thanks to my mom and the G.I. Bill! And my schedule provided me with a very excellent vocational program that allowed me to claim the job designation, "Apprenticed Printer," and thus a possible useful occupation after high school, if I so chose. In my senior year, my mom insisted that I take a full year of typing. "What use is that?" I demanded. And she simply replied, "Someday, but not right now, it will come in handy and to your advantage wherever you go or whatever you do." How very, very right she was, and how very thankful I am to her for insisting that I take typing classes. Smart Mom!

Mom, with her athletic abilities, was an avid golfer for most of her adult life, and was even good enough to beat my stepfather once in a while (much to his dismay and slight embarrassment). But, to my mind, her greatest golfing achievement came late in her life, after my stepfather had died. In her middle 60s, she tripped at the top of some cement steps and plunged forward headfirst to the bottom – six or seven steps. Just before hitting her head on the cement, she managed to cross both of her hands and arms in front of her forehead and face. That quick action saved her from a serious head injury, but the impact of the fall broke both of her wrists severely. You can imagine the almost helpless condition this left her in, along with cumbersome plaster casts up both arms above the elbows. My wife, Betty, a compassionate and gifted nurse, immediately left me with the three boys in Solon, Ohio (my congregation in the mid-60s), and went to be with my mother in her apartment in Muskegon to take care of her for the first two weeks. Quite an undertaking, which Betty handled very well. Within ten days, the right-hand cast was cut down below the elbow, and my very independent mother insisted that she could navigate all right at that point (which she did). What has this to do with her golfing game? Well, she had to go through a lot of painful physical therapy just to get her hands and wrists working adequately again. She once told me that she often would be in tears of pain as she determinedly went through some of those sessions, especially the one where she had to "crawl" up the wall with her fingers and hands over and over again to strengthen them. Her goal? To play golf again! Her doctor said at the outset that it wouldn't be possible. Wrong! She actually was able, within a year or so, to once again swing a golf club successfully. Even I was a bit skeptical as she told us about her remarkable recovery, until she came out to California to visit us a couple of years later (in Thousand Oaks – my congregation from 1968 to 1985). At that time, I was still playing some golf myself, and she suggested that we go out to a par-3 course (shorter than a regulation golf course) and play some golf. My skepticism was soon replaced with amazement, wonder, and admiration! She was terrific! If you were wondering where the dogged determination which I exhibited at times in my own life came from, now you know!

Another aspect of my mother's life was her love of music and her wonderful piano playing ability. It was she who first introduced me to the world and wonders of classical music, with many records (the old 78 RPM's) that we had at home. But most of all, I remember how much she enjoyed playing the piano for parties at our house. Among my clearest and fondest memories are the many times that she and my stepfather had their group of friends over on a Friday or Saturday evening for hours of playing bridge, and then hours of singing and boozing a bit around the piano. My brother and I would listen from our bedroom into the wee hours of the night, and thoroughly enjoyed it (and quickly pretended we were asleep when Mom checked up on us once in a while). The one song I remember the most from those many "musical evenings" is "On the Road to Mandalay." If you know the song at all, you can imagine what it sounded like when about ten or twelve slightly tipsy men and women "took off" with some of the notes in that melody! What a show!

Only years later did I tell my mother about our enjoyment of their singing parties. She wasn't embarrassed but just laughed heartily and told me that it's not only young people who can enjoy themselves! By the way, she tried to teach my brother and me how to play the piano; he wasn't interested at all and I was more interested in sports.

Many later memories of my mom are mostly little vignettes and particular events. I recall how, in later years when she was in a very nice apartment in Muskegon after my stepfather had died at the age of 57, I loved to visit her for a few days from time to time. Such visits were possible for me in the late 70s and early 80s because I was often in the Chicago area (200 miles from Muskegon) for campus pastors' meetings, or in St. Louis (450 miles from Muskegon) for the same kind of campus ministry meetings, representing our Southern California District. I'd just "pop up" and see her, and stay in the other bedroom of her apartment. What good times those were for both of us! Then, after we were in California for a few years, she would come out for 28 days in February (exactly the days between the arrival of her Social Security and retirement checks at the first of the month). The boys in particular needed and enjoyed those times with her! Dave with his basketball, Dan with his writing and stories, and Mark, who would occasionally spend time with Mom in Michigan when the rest of the family was on a long vacation, brought her much enjoyment and fun. We all treasured that one month every year for a number of years in the late 70s and early 80s. We took her to many places of interest out in California, including a Lakers basketball game a couple of times.

I have a distinct memory of several of my visits to see Mom in early summer when I was in Chicago or St. Louis. While visiting her, we would go out to my brother's home in Twin Lake (about ten miles away). Dave and his wife Betty had a big back yard in which they grew many vegetables and some fruit. And they grew the most beautiful and delicious red raspberries in the world! When Mom and I would leave later in the evening to go back to her apartment, we'd take a big bowl of raspberries with us. Just before we'd retire for the night, we would have a big bowl of raspberries, milk, and sugar. Then, the first thing in the morning for breakfast, we'd have another big bowl of raspberries! What enjoyment! And how we'd laugh and "carry on!" Mom was a great conversationalist!

The declining years of her life were also important and memorable. She loved to drive her Buick in those later years, and was always available to help out. Once, when I was visiting her and talking about her driving and how important it was not only for her but also for others, she said to me, "Here I am in my late 70s and before church on Sunday mornings I pick up several of my "little ol' ladies" who are ten years younger than me!" A tough time came for her when she voluntarily gave up her driver's license when she was almost 81. It was difficult, because she had grown up with the automobile – all the way back as a teenager – and she always loved to drive her different Buick models over the years. But she realized, as she told me one day, "I am so afraid with my slowing reflexes that I might cause an accident or hurt someone with my driving." In spite of that, she also said a number of times to me, "Jim, I really miss driving my car!"

As she declined in her later years, she had to leave her apartment and live with my brother and his wife for six months or so in Twin Lake. Most of this happened without my knowledge, since both my brother and his wife, Betty, are not communicators and did not inform me of what was happening to Mom. That included their going through all of Mom's stuff, throwing out most of it (some of it would have meant a lot more to me than to them apparently), and leaving mainly several boxes of old photographs and mementoes of Mom. I wasn't too happy when I heard about all that, but I found out far too late to do anything about it. Subsequently, I heard about some of the "trials and tribulations" while she was at my brother's house, and she must have been somewhat of a burden. The next thing I knew she was in a convalescent home in Muskegon, ten miles from Twin Lake. This shocked me a bit, but I realized that my brother would do the best he could, and he did. Interestingly, in the years prior to this when my mom would visit different people from church in convalescent homes in the area, she made it very clear that if the time ever came for her to go to such a place, she knew exactly which one! And that is where she spent the last year and a half of her life.

During that time, I was in Chicago or St. Louis at least four or five times for meetings. So, I would add four or five days to my trip back there and go up to Michigan to see my mother. I stayed with my brother, but saw no one else but Mom, in spite of many friends I would have liked to visit while back in my old hometown. How do I express or describe what those days meant to me or how important they were for both Mom and me? Let me put it this way. They were some of the most beautiful days and loving experiences of my life! The first time I showed up at her convalescent home was a bit of a shocker. As I went in, I was told it was midday eating time and she would be in the large dining hall. When I went there, I was faced with a sea of gray and white hair! In her later years, Mom had resorted to dyeing her hair a light brown to cover the gray. So that is what I looked for in that dining hall that day. Obviously, I'd never find her that way. But like a parent recognizes his or her own child in the midst of many bodies and heads, I quickly recognized my mother in the midst of that sea of "white heads." Even though I had told my brother that I was coming to see Mom, he may have failed to tell her, or she forgot. Therefore, my appearance at her dining room table was a complete and wonderful shock to her! What a delightful time we had! And that was true every time I went back to Michigan to see her.

My brother saw her once in a while and would even take her out for a ride, but that was about it. My sister-in-law simply could not stand being in such a place as a convalescent home and, therefore, didn't visit her there. I do not judge her in that situation, but I do feel sorry for her that she can't handle such situations, because she is in many ways a sensitive person. Anyway, for the next year and a half, my most precious moments with my mother occurred during those times I visited her. My visit always occasioned many wonderful vignettes of time together.

The last couple of times I was with her, I simply wheeled her around in her wheelchair (which she needed to use by that time) up and down the hallways of the convalescent home, which were filled with many interesting and beautiful paintings and nature scenes. By this time in her life, she had begun to take on a kind of physical trait of letting her head drop quite low as she went about in the wheelchair. When I noticed this happening as I rolled her around in the wheelchair, I'd rather crisply say to her in front of a picture, "Look up at that, Mom! Isn't that beautiful?" And she'd look up and agree with me with a sparkle in her eyes, and we'd continue our "tour" of the hallways and all the pictures and paintings. What enjoyment that was for both of us, even if it took a lot of time.

A somewhat humorous incident took place during one of my last visits with her. I came directly from the airport to see her that first evening of my time back in Muskegon and Twin Lake. I couldn't find her in the dining hall, so I asked where she was eating. They directed me to a smaller area where a number of people (about six or eight) were being fed their supper individually by the staff. When I introduced myself, they took me to my mother who was being fed by a member of the staff. I suggested that I take over and feed her, and they gladly acquiesced. That, too, was a wonderful time with Mom, because she gratefully ate every bit of food on her tray! During that meal, one of the staff came up and introduced herself and told me how much they liked my mother. My mom responded by introducing me to this person. Well, as she got to the part where she was to use my name, she hesitated for a few agonizing seconds, and I quickly interjected, "I'm her son, Jim." At that, she just laughed with a bit of embarrassment and said, "Yes, that's my son!" During the rest of our "journeys" down the many hallways of the home, I would stop once in a while and ask her, "Who am I, Mom?" And she would laugh and grin a bit capriciously and say, "You're Jim!" and then laugh almost uproariously! What a delight she was!

My most endearing and memorable moments with my mom in her last days were not only in the convalescent home, but also in the time we had together before she went to bed at night. When the staff of the home took her to her room for the night, they would have a very specific procedure and routine. It mostly consisted of getting her ready for the night and comfortably settled in bed. When I was there for those times, I would help her and then spend some time with her before she went to sleep. What a very, very special time of prayer, devotions, and blessing that was! There is no way that I can adequately describe what those times with her meant to me. The last time I saw her was just that way. An evening devotion, an intimate time of personal prayer with her, a benediction – and then, a very practical thing of arranging her pillows and blankets so they were comfortable for her. How I treasured those moments of loving service to her!

What more can I say about my mother than what I've already written, except to say that I could have written two or three times more and still not done the job adequately. However, when it comes right down to it, I want these last words of mine about her to be very clear, simple, and laudatory: *She's the best thing that God could have done for me!* That takes nothing away from the many, many wonderful blessings of people in my life since then. There are two very marvelous and important things she did for me as I became a man. First of all, she taught me the supreme essence of womanhood, and whatever deference or special feelings I have about all the terrific women in my life through the years, I give her credit and joyful commendation! Secondly, and most importantly, she did *one* great thing for me, which over the years I have used in my Mother's Day sermons: *My mother introduced me to Jesus!* As the saying goes, "'Nuff said!"

On September 19th, 1985, she died peacefully in her sleep and returned to her homeland with Jesus, her Lord and Savior!

~

My Mother, the Basketball Star

The most obvious way in which my mother expressed her independence and free spirit (besides academically) was in the field of sports and athletics, particularly basketball. Here we have to pause and remember the situation in our country at the time. There was World War I, which ended when she was 17 years old. The flu epidemic of 1918 took her younger brother, age 13, leaving only my mother and her older sister as children in the family. During the teen years of the early 20th century, the Women's Suffrage Movement came into full swing and was a powerful element of American life until the Women's Right to Vote (Nineteenth Amendment) occurred in 1920. A dimension of that whole period of time was the rise of girls in athletics, especially in high school and college. The movement was slow in reaching such out-of-the-way places as

Arcadia, Michigan, but my mother was one of the first to ride the crest of the great Suffrage Movement, and girls' basketball became surprisingly popular.

My mother was tall (nearly 5' 8", which was considered very tall for a girl in those days), athletic, and aggressive, and became a dominant player in high school and college. Sports clippings from those days of her exploits and successes are intriguing, particularly when the newspapers always referred to the women in sports as "Miss." "It was the tall and accurate-shooting *Miss* Lang who dominated the game," or "It was the hard-working *Miss* Lang who outplayed Miss Jones to lead Arcadia to victory," etc. Girls' basketball became so important that the varsity girls' team played their game immediately before the varsity boys' game, and they traveled together for out-of-town games. Since most of the basketball season was during the winter and the snow season in Michigan, they traveled together by horse and sleigh, with a free intermingling of the players to and from the games at night in a glorified hayride. My mother loved those "away" games! One time, many years later, she was telling my three sons (who were teenagers at the time) about those wonderful basketball games and the hayrides with the boys' basketball team, and her snuggling up with one of the players on the way home. As she recounted those late-night rides, my boys' eyes and mouths popped open in wonder, awe, and a bit of shock. When they questioned her further about it, she replied quite honestly, "Listen! I was always a 'good girl,' but remember, those basketball boys were the only ones tall enough for me to go out with. Besides, I liked boys!" After high school, she went on to college at Central Michigan and played there for several years until she received her teaching degree. After teaching and coaching girls' basketball in Cass City, Michigan for several years, she moved to a new teaching position in Muskegon, Michigan where she met my father in 1925 and married him in 1926. And then I was born in 1927 in Madison, Wisconsin.

A bit of a sequel to this whole story took place many years later in Thousand Oaks, California, where I was pastor of Redeemer Lutheran Church. My youngest of three sons turned out to be an outstanding student and athlete, especially in basketball. He was a Ventura County All-Star and Most Valuable Player at Thousand Oaks High School, and then he became a three-time All-Star and two-time Most Valuable Player at California Lutheran University. Since I was quite well-known around the campus of Cal Lutheran, it was very natural that people would say something like this when they heard that my son was attending CLU: "Oh, Dave Lareva? Isn't he Pastor Lareva's son?" But after several years of basketball stardom at Cal Lutheran, there was an interesting change in emphasis: "Oh, Jim Lareva? Isn't he Dave Lareva's father?"

I would like to conclude this way. Sometimes people would come up to me and talk to me about my son's basketball prowess, and then relate it to my own athletic abilities when I was younger. I would usually reply in this manner: "My athletic abilities tended toward football and especially baseball, but Dave's talents are in basketball. Whatever basketball genes he inherited, he received from *"My mother, the basketball star!"*

Chapter 3

U.S. Navy (1945-1949)

All during my high school years, 1941-1945, World War II raged in Europe and Asia. My stepbrother was in the U.S. Navy in the Pacific, and that kept us apprehensive. Since I had a newspaper route for several of those years, I kept up with the war news quite closely, reading the paper as I folded them before beginning my route to 80 customers in East Muskegon. In high school, I excelled primarily in social studies and English, but did a bit poorly in other courses and did not have a particularly good grade point average. I did exceedingly well in one of my manual arts / vocational training courses – professional machine printing. I had no intention of going to college and I had no intention of going to work for very long after high school, except as I waited to join the military. Shortly before I graduated from high school, I got a good job as an "Apprentice Printer" in a local print shop called "Earle Press." But I knew it would be only for as long as it took me to enlist in the military. You need to understand the mentality and feelings of young men at the time. The war had been going on for several years, and we went through high school with the natural assumption and feeling that we would be in the war as soon as we got out of high school. And most of us looked forward to it! Patriotism was very strong and loyalty to our cause was assumed to be right and just, so it was only proper and normal for us to think in terms of joining Uncle Sam and the fight for freedom! The issue was clear and the situation was definite: As soon as school was over, you joined up or waited to get drafted into the Army. And we hoped that our rigorous P.E. (Physical Education) training would have us well-prepared for the military life ahead of us. That's the way we thought and felt in those days. College was not even a serious consideration for the large majority of us, and only the very brightest students (of which I was not one!) contemplated anything other than military life and fighting for our country as soon as we got out of school. With my growing sense of history and my awareness of the momentous events that were occurring in the world then, I somehow realized that I was part of it – whether I liked it or not. And I wanted to be part of it!

During the month or more that it took to process my enlistment that early summer of 1945, I worked hard and successfully at Earle Press, so much so that I was promised a job whenever I came back from my military service. While I fully enjoyed working as an Apprentice Printer, I could hardly wait to get into the U.S. Navy and begin my Navy career. (I joined the Navy before the Army would draft me.) Little did any of us realize that the war would end so abruptly because of the atomic bombs that were dropped on Hiroshima and Nagasaki on August 6th and 9th, 1945. Along with my fellow Americans, I was jubilant at the resulting surrender of the Japanese on August 14th, 1945. But since I was barely out of "Boot Camp," and had no intention of returning to civilian life within a year or less, I continued in the Navy to make it a full four-year enlistment from that point on. Actually, it turned out to be one of the most important and best decisions of my life! God and I used those four-plus years of my life to mature and grow and develop as a person and as a Christian. Those four years gave me some of the most wonderful and meaningful experiences of my life, from which I was able to learn to direct my energies and goals toward life beyond 1949. Many of these special experiences I will relate in the following pages of this part of my life story. However, I have spent these many opening words in this "Introduction" to my life in the U.S. Navy for a good reason: You cannot really understand much of who I am or what happened to me later without this "background check." My little more than four years in the U.S. Navy was one of the great "defining" times of my life, and you need to know about it to understand much of what my life was later on.

In my whole life since my Navy days, I have never in even the smallest sense regretted one minute of that Navy life! That also happens to be the way I have felt about every moment of my life. That, of course, doesn't mean that everything was just great or that I would not have changed a lot of things in my life in the past if I could have. But every moment of my life is what I am today – good, bad, or otherwise. At a recent conference, a young pastor (in his late 30s) asked at our dinner table a form of a question to me in regards to my age and well-lived life up to this point. "Don't you just wish you could blot out or erase some parts of your memory of your life?" I immediately replied, "No! I do not want to lose one moment of my life and memory, no matter what it was about or what happened. Whether it was success or failure, joy or sorrow, calmness or stress, good or bad, even or uneven, faith or doubt, fun or tragedy, love or hate, grace or lostness, healing or hurt, warmth or coldness, in-love or out-of-love, or whatever other contrast in life, I want to remember as much as possible, because it is me, for better or for worse. That's the way it is!" How can one regret any moment of life which God gives a person, even if events and times in that life aren't always so good or exactly what one wants, plans, or expects? For God to be the Ruler of our lives means that He is in every moment and experience of that life! Hallelujah!

Now, on to my naval career!

~

My career in the U.S. Navy began with Boot Camp at the Great Lakes Naval Training Station, just north of Chicago. It lasted from the summer of 1945 until late October. Several things stand out in my memory of Boot Camp. First of all, I realized how fortunate I was to have had a very strong Physical Education program in high school, along with my conditioning as a baseball player in the spring and summer of 1945. The physical demands of Boot Camp (which were devastating to lots of guys) were not difficult for me. In fact, I kind of relished them and did very well. Physically, I had a lot of endurance, and had I not played baseball every spring, I would have been a good half-miler in track – a very demanding event. I liked running and I was in good condition. Two incidents come to mind. The first time occurred when the best-known and most famous mile runner in the world at the time, Lieutenant Glenn Cunningham of the U.S. Navy, came to our camp and led several hundred Navy "Boots" on some multi-mile runs. While he did not run "all-out," he did set a brisk pace that caused a number of guys to either drop out for a while, or give up altogether. But not me! What a challenge! The world's greatest runner – and I kept up with him all the way, and at the end he complimented those of us who had kept up so well!

Along with that incident was another one that tested our endurance and condition. Our company commander, a seasoned Navy veteran, demanded strict obedience and tip-top conditioning. Our particular company CO decided that it was time to separate the "men" from the "boys," physically and attitude-wise. So, shortly after noon chow one day, he had the whole company of nearly 200 men assemble on the parade grounds (about a quarter-mile around, and all blacktop), and he began running/walking us. That is, we ran around the parade grounds once, and then walked very briskly the next time around. This continued on and on all afternoon. Almost needless to say, this really got to most of the guys. And it was exhausting! When I began to realize what he was doing, I made up my mind that he wasn't going to run me into the ground/blacktop! I felt that my personal pride was at stake and I wouldn't give in. Several hours later, almost all the guys had fallen out, either from sheer exhaustion or from sickness (a nice way to describe throwing up all over the grassy areas and simply giving up). A dozen of us were still going around when he called a halt in the late afternoon and rewarded us with a compliment and the next two days off from drills! Along with these dozen guys, I felt very good about the whole thing and we were happy that a lot of guys who were trying to "goof off" had received their just reward!

One other incident impressed itself upon my memory from Boot Camp – my first real encounter with blatant racial prejudice. Near the end of Boot Camp, it was the custom to select or elect from among the "Boots" one guy who seemed to best represent our company and what we had been through as recruits in the Navy. By far and away the one guy who seemed to be the most liked and the best representative of this designation was the "oldie" black man (he was in his late 20s and most of us were still in our teens). He was a really neat guy! One day, while showering and talking with a guy from Mississippi whom I had come to like very much, the subject came up of who we would vote for in this kind of "popularity contest." When I mentioned the obvious choice among the guys in the company, he said he wouldn't vote for him. A bit surprised, I asked him why. He replied very simply and matter-of-factly, "Because he's a nigger." I could hardly believe what I had heard! In my naiveté, I couldn't really comprehend what he meant. I had playmates as a child who were black; I had played football and baseball with blacks; I even had a good friend in high school who was black. Without trying to sound condescending, I never quite understood the "differences" between us, probably because I had been able to know black guys on a personal level, and they with me. That makes a big difference! I didn't associate with that guy from Mississippi after that. In the years to follow, I would come to "understand" a bit where my Mississippi friend was coming from, but I could never accept his attitude or his use of the word "nigger" – a reprehensible word and term.

All in all, however, my Boot Camp experience was great and I never regretted it or looked back on it in a negative way. I enjoyed the camaraderie, the shared goals, the friendships that developed with guys I would never see again and yet who experienced with me a significant segment of my life. So, I can and do treasure those memories as a worthwhile part of my life.

The next step in my naval career involved a most important decision. Near the end of Boot Camp, every man was interviewed concerning the areas of special work, interests, or classification of work that they would like to do or were most qualified to follow. With many options available, I naturally sought to continue my apprenticeship printing career in the Navy, especially since they had me for almost four years. Unfortunately (I thought at the time), there were no openings in that somewhat restricted area of specialization in the Navy. Since I wasn't interested in many of the technical areas of Navy work (electrical, gunnery, radio, etc.), I found myself facing a strange choice – specialize in something besides printing, or just be a "deck swabbie" for four years. In one of the very rare and truly altruistic moments of my life, I thought to myself, *Well, if I can't be what I want to be in the Navy, I might as well choose something in which I can do some good and serve other people in a worthwhile way.* Whether those were the exact words that came to my mind at the time or not, I do remember thinking that way and suggesting to my interviewer that I would like to serve in the medical branch of the Navy and study to be a pharmacist's mate (later changed to hospital corpsman). He was very pleased with my selection, since very few guys wanted to be a "medic" (as they are called in the Army, or "doc" as they are called in the Navy and Marines). A Navy hospital corpsman is something between a registered nurse and an orderly in a regular civilian hospital. It turned out to be one of the very great decisions of my life. I thank God for all He had given me and been to me up to that point in my life, so I would choose something that worthwhile and at the same time that valuable to my total experience in the Navy and my life. After a ten-day leave back home in Muskegon, I was sent to the U.S. Naval Hospital Training Center in Balboa Park, San Diego, California. Again, just as in Boot Camp, it was a good experience and I really enjoyed our camaraderie and the sharing of mutual experiences as young men in the Navy.

One interesting interruption to this eight-week training period was my contracting measles. At the time, it was diagnosed as "three-day measles" but in good safe Navy fashion, they kept me in the U.S. Naval Hospital for two weeks, including the Christmas holidays! But even that was not a negative because I had a good time there for those two weeks, receiving and writing many Christmas cards, including to and from some very nice girls!

Our graduation from Hospital Corps School was very important, and we waited anxiously to see where we would be assigned. (I wanted to be on a ship, but they told me I would need more experience first.) I was sent to the U.S. Naval Hospital in St. Albans, Long Island, New York. St. Albans is situated in the borough of Queens, one of five boroughs in New York City – connected by a series of subways, railways, and wonderful bridges (Brooklyn Bridge is my favorite). And thus began one of the most enjoyable and formative ten months of my life, including what I would call my "romantic coming-of-age" time. It was a great ten months, and it started off very well. As they interviewed each new hospital corpsman who had been sent to St. Albans, they asked one significant question: "Can you type?" Everyone in front of me answered, "No," and they got assignments to be "bedpan jockeys" (as we called them, with the worst jobs on the hospital wards) and other mundane jobs. When it came to me, I answered, "Yes, I can!" and they celebrated (sort of). It turned out that I was a "rare bird" and they needed a typist in the Emergency and Admissions Room of the hospital. Not only did it turn out to be a good job with much better liberty privileges, but also I was "thrown in" with a group of Navy people which included WAVES (Women Accepted for Volunteer Emergency Service) and officer nurses. Tough life! Interestingly enough, officially I wasn't allowed to date nurses, since they were officers and I was an enlisted man. But I really didn't need to be concerned about that since there were many other and better opportunities "outside." However, I remember saying to myself at the time of my typist assignment, *Thank you, Mom!* Several years earlier, as I began my junior year in high school and was setting up my courses for my senior year, my mother suggested quite strongly to take a year of typing – "just because it will do you some good someday, even though you don't realize it now." From that time on, in New York and in several other situations to follow in the Navy, my typing skills saved me from some lousy jobs and allowed me to be needed, since not many guys could type and do hospital work at the same time.

As referred to earlier, my ten months in New York also saw my "coming-of-age" romantically. I dated so much in New York that one time I found myself deciding not to date for a whole two weeks because I was "tired!" But remember, my "policy" with girls at that time and for the years ahead was simple: enjoy the "necking," but no inappropriate touching. I am still convinced to this day that this policy was one of the main reasons why I had such wonderful relationships with so many girls. Please do not mistake these words and my recording of them as some kind of "Jim-piety" or "moral self-promotion" or anything like that. Very honestly, girls trusted me in such a way that neither of us needed to be defensive or uncomfortable in any way. Therefore, we could enjoy each other as real, genuine individuals. What fun! For a further description of the girls in my life in New York, please see my chapter entitled, "The Women in My Life." That chapter will help you understand why I still consider my time in New York as one of the most truly enjoyable and memorable periods of my life!

As for my Navy work at St. Albans, it went very well. Although I worked in the Emergency and Admissions Room doing a lot of yeoman (secretarial) work, it was also the Emergency Room and I was often involved in the medical work, and experienced and learned a lot. Within the first few months, I gained seaman 2nd class rating (comparable to corporal), and before my ten months were over, I had gained my petty officer 3rd class rating (comparable to sergeant). That was unusually fast, but I guess I was also learning fast. The rating would stand me in good stead when I was later assigned to the U.S. Marines and had the status of NCO (non-commissioned officer). Very helpful! It was also necessary for me to take my regular shifts on the wards of the hospital with the rest of the guys. So, it was a well-rounded experience in medical work that was also very useful to me when I was aboard the ships later on.

One of the more interesting aspects of my job was working with nurses. It was official policy for enlisted men and officers not to "fraternize" with each other, and nurses were officers. That meant no dating each other. Actually, that wasn't really much of a problem because most of the nurses were "a bit old" (at least in their early or middle 20s) – and generally not that "attractive" to 18-year-olds! One pretty nurse did have a little fun with me one morning as we were making up a hospital bed together on one of the wards. There was some nice conversation as we worked. Just as we finished, she looked at me and asked very seriously, "Do your eyes bother you?" I quickly answered, "No!" wondering about the strange question. She paused a moment, and then with a very cute smile replied, "Well, they bother me!" And she flounced off, chuckling to herself. Oh well.

Besides lots of dating, the best thing about being in New York in late 1945 and 1946 was the city itself. There were the famous landmarks: Times Square, 5th Avenue, the Statue of Liberty, the Empire State Building, Central Park, and so many other wonderful places! Especially did I enjoy and appreciate the fabulous subway system! For a good understanding of that, read *722 Miles: The Building of the Subways and How They Transformed New York* by Clifton Hood. The Servicemen's Center was right in downtown Manhattan at 95 Park Avenue. We could go there and get free tickets to just about anything in the city: baseball games (I attended around 60 games at Yankee Stadium, Ebbets Field, and the Polo Grounds), football games, musical shows on Broadway, theaters of all kinds, some famous restaurants, symphony concerts, museums, and a host of other areas of entertainment. It was a bonanza for anyone in the military service, especially for a kid from Michigan who had been to the big cities of Chicago and Detroit only once each in his whole life! I don't know how many stage shows/musicals I saw, but they included, *Annie Get Your Gun*, *The Red Mill*, *Carousel*, and many others. My favorite was *Charley's Aunt*, with Ray Bolger in the lead role (Charley). He was absolutely terrific. You might recall that he played the Scarecrow in the movie *The Wizard of Oz*. The best place to see a movie was Radio City Music Hall. They changed their program every three months, and I saw some good movies: *Gilda* (Rita Hayworth), *The Razor's Edge*, *To Each His Own*, and others. However, the best part of going to Radio City Music Hall was the live show that went with the movie. It began with a 12-15 minute classical music presentation by a small symphony orchestra or symphonette. That was followed by an on-stage personality for about ten minutes (a magician, singer, comedian, etc.), and then a dazzling performance by the Rockettes! What a show! As often as we could go, we did – even with the same movie and the same program.

Sometime later, after I had left New York to go to North Carolina, I found myself walking along in a Marine "forced march" in Camp Lejeune and humming a few notes of a completely "unknown" tune. At first, I could not place the tune, until an hour or so later I realized that it was the main theme from the overture to *Tannhäuser*, by Richard Wagner. I first heard it at my first real live symphony concert, with the world-famous NBC Symphony Orchestra, conducted by the greatest conductor of all time: Arturo Toscanini. Later, I heard the overture when it was the classical music presentation at the Radio City Music Hall. To this day, that overture remains as one of my three or four favorite pieces of classical music, and I even "composed" some romantic words to go with the main theme, entitled "Be Mine." Such audacity! Well, anything to impress a girl, right?

Of course, being in the midst of downtown Manhattan, there were movies and live shows of every kind and variety. Most clearly of all, I recall the live programs that went with the first-run movies: The Mills Brothers, The Ink Spots, The Glenn Miller Orchestra (without Glenn Miller, of course), Xavier Cugat, Count Basie, Duke Ellington, Lionel Hampton, Tommy and Jimmy Dorsey, Robert Alda (father of Alan Alda of *M*A*S*H* fame), Spike Jones, Harry James, Stan Kenton, Benny Goodman, Sammy Kaye, Nat King Cole, Burl Ives, Artie Shaw, The Arness Brothers, and various other well-known male and female singers. It was a regular "Who's Who" of the big band era. Of course, there was always the USO right on Times Square if we were hungry for a snack.

For me, however, the sports events were the main attraction. I saw the New York Giants of the NFL play a couple of times. I also went to some good college football games, including Navy vs. Columbia (top teams at the time, with the Navy quarterback being a high school friend of mine, with whom I talked briefly after the game) and Fordham vs. St. Mary's of California (with an All-American running back, "Squirmin' Herman" Wedemeyer). Most memorable and enjoyable to me were the baseball games that summer and early fall of 1946. With free tickets to every game in New York and with my generous liberty schedule, I attended a lot of games, as previously mentioned. There were the New York Giants (now the San Francisco Giants), the Brooklyn Dodgers (now the Los Angeles Dodgers), and the New York Yankees, whom I "hated" but admired immensely. I saw the Giants play only two or three times, and attended mainly because of their player-manager, Mel Ott, one of the really great home run hitters of all time. He was in the late twilight of his career but would get a long and rousing cheer from the fans when he would pinch-hit, even if he struck out! I went to a lot of Yankee games, partly because of the great players who had come back from the war or who were part of the great "Yankee Dynasty" of post-war years, i.e., Joe DiMaggio, Charlie Keller,

Tommy Henrich, Frank Crosetti, Red Rolfe, Joe Gordon, Red Ruffing, Aaron Robinson, and a few more that I don't recall. But my main motivation for attending Yankee games occurred when the Detroit Tigers came to town. In those days, a team played eleven games at home and eleven games on the road against each other each season. By a fortunate circumstance, I got to see nine of the eleven games against Detroit that year at Yankee Stadium, and Detroit won eight of them! You don't believe it? Just look it up!

Detroit also had some great players back from the war, primarily my "idol," Hank Greenberg, and a tremendous left-handed pitcher in Hal Newhouser (who beat the Yankees three times that summer in Yankee Stadium). Both wound up in the baseball Hall of Fame, as did some of the Yankees mentioned above.

But my most impressive experience with baseball in New York that summer, and for some of the following years when I could get up to New York from North Carolina, was my becoming a National League fan of the Brooklyn Dodgers. I thoroughly enjoyed all the young players and returning players who came up with the Dodgers in 1946 and 1947 and became known as "The Boys of Summer" (Gil Hodges, Carl Furillo, Duke Snider, Pee Wee Reese, Dixie Walker, Billy Cox, Bruce Edwards, Carl Erskine, Preacher Roe, Roy Campanella, and many others). But 1947 was the year that Jackie Robinson became the first black player to sign a Major League contract to play baseball! I even got to see him play several times in 1947 and 1948 when I went to New York on leave from the Navy in North Carolina. To this day, even though I had nothing to do with it, I feel that I was a part of history, and I look back on that time with special feelings and great respect for the Dodgers, which remains to this day.

Another great part of my experience in New York was attending "my" church, i.e., congregations in the Lutheran Church – Missouri Synod (LCMS). In Chicago and San Diego, I didn't have much chance to attend church outside of the worship services conducted by Navy chaplains on the bases. The beautiful singing of the then-famous Bluejackets Choir of Naval Station Great Lakes was a very special part of worship there. Sometimes the sermons left something to be desired. I found myself really wanting to get into one of my own churches off the base, which I was able to do a few times in San Diego. In New York, and particularly in St. Albans, I was able to do this and it was very rewarding and pleasant. There was a little congregation, Redeemer Lutheran, just getting started outside the distant side of the Naval Hospital. They were meeting in a house which had been converted into a worship center until they could build a church. Pastor Meyer and his wife lived only a few blocks from the main entrance of the hospital, and I quickly got acquainted with them. The first time I went to their home, they brought out several volumes of cartoons which they had cut out and pasted into a number of albums. Their idea of entertaining a young sailor boy was to let him look at all the cartoons in all the albums while serving him cookies and chatting casually. It's the only time in my life that I got tired of cartoons, so I asked if I could come back another time and finish them! They were very nice to me and I felt at home in their little house-church, which I attended frequently. I kept in contact with Pastor Meyer and his wife for many years afterward, and was always grateful for their care and concern. I did date a girl in New York for a while who was Lutheran, so I attended her church several times too. I don't remember if I ever attended the Protestant services on the base. It always felt so good to hear a familiar liturgy, sing familiar hymns, and sense a kinship with the people and God's Word in sermons in "my" church wherever I went during my Navy years.

Those were wonderful days in New York, highlighted by that newfound treasury of joy: girls! I met them in roller-skating rinks, in Central Park, at bus stops, in movie theaters, in stores, in churches, through buddies, at the beach, and on the New York subway! (More about them in my chapter, "The Women in My Life.") However, those halcyon days in New York ended abruptly in November, 1946. The Navy doctor in charge of the X-ray Department (who was not well-liked and under whom nobody wanted to serve) would routinely go looking for new people for this department. Several of us got on his list, and we were given the option of accepting or rejecting his "invitation." Well, none of us accepted his invitation to join the X-ray Department and within a week all of us had orders to transfer out. I was transferred to the Fleet Marines of the U.S. Marine Corps at Camp Lejeune, North Carolina, built on 166 square miles of pure swamp in Eastern North Carolina. It was considered by most guys in the Navy medical corps as one of the real dregs of naval assignments, but I didn't know this and accepted my new place and work with anticipation and a certain amount of excitement. A new place, new people, new experiences! I was assigned to a regular infantry company – Company B of the 21st Battalion, 8th Regiment, of the famed 2nd Marine Division. Two Navy corpsmen were assigned to each company, with a Sick Bay building nearby where several Navy doctors, a dentist, and several other corpsmen worked. We split our time between duty at the Sick Bay (which also had ten hospital beds for short-stay patients) and with our own Marine company. We did "Sick Call" each morning for the company, sending the more serious cases to the Sick Bay to see a doctor, but we took care of most of the routine cases. The two company corpsmen were literally a part of the U.S. Marine Corps in almost every way, including Marine uniforms, weapons, and sleeping quarters. I enjoyed it all very much and made many good friends in the Marine Corps those years between November 1946 and September 1949, when I was discharged. I had no regrets about the new assignment out of New York, and I eventually was grateful to the X-ray captain who "arranged" my transfer to North Carolina and the Marines.

I got along extremely well with my company commander, Captain Flake (yes, that was his real name, but he definitely was no "flake"). Our good relationship may have begun because of the first "forced march" of three days, right after I got there. The whole battalion went out for those rather rugged three days, since the physical condition of the fighting men was essential in any kind of battle situation in which men marched continually, with very little rest and little opportunity to do anything else but eat and sleep. Of course, since I was part of the company, I was expected to be right up there with the Marines on their march and help out in any situation which demanded medical attention. Before we began, I was kidded quite a bit about being a "soft" Navy guy and that I would be in big trouble as the march continued for those three days. Well, they didn't know two things about me: I was still physically fit and well-prepared for physical endurance, and I have a very competitive nature. During the next three days, I had to stop frequently to help Marines who were "pooped out," or were sick to their stomach, or were having foot problems, or just plain could not keep going. In a gentle, but very clear way, I kidded them about being such tough Marines, most of them just out of the hellish Boot Camp at Parris Island, South Carolina. And remember, when I stopped to give help or aid to someone, the rest of the company kept right on marching and I had to hurry to catch up with them, which I did without a problem. Apparently none of this was lost on my new captain, because I noticed that not only he but also the officers and NCOs treated me well and just like one of them after that!

Life at Camp Lejeune was pretty routine, with morning Sick Call and company activities during the day (marching, inspections, maneuvers, military practices, and work at the regular Sick Bay with other Navy corpsmen in our battalion). For the most part I enjoyed this, partly because much of it was outdoors and partly because I developed a real kinship with the Marines in my company, especially those in the Machine Gun and Mortar Platoon. There were movies on base and even a roller-skating rink. And often in the evenings a few of us would go to the nearby "slop shoot" for some "3-2" beer and lots of talk. Several times I got to play some football with the company, mostly on a battalion level. We also had a good baseball team and that was great, except we missed a lot of games due to our being in the Caribbean Sea on maneuvers or in the Mediterranean Sea with the 6th Fleet, patrolling "our" sea as part of Uncle Sam's "Big Stick" policy to prevent the spread of Communism in that part of the world. Generally speaking, it was good military duty, even though we sometimes felt that we were far away from civilization in North Carolina's Camp Lejeune.

One of the most significant and enjoyable experiences while in North Carolina happened because I went out looking for a "civilian" church – "my" Lutheran Church. Since there weren't (and still aren't) many Lutheran Churches in the South, I had to do some traveling. The nearest town to camp was Jacksonville, or, as we called it, "J-ville." There wasn't much there at the time, but it has grown quite a bit over the years. (Interestingly, a seminary classmate of mine started a congregation in Jacksonville years later and I was able to visit him back in the middle 1960s on a trip down there with Betty and the boys.) Now, back to finding a church. One weekend, I took a Trailways bus all the way to Raleigh (about 120 miles away). By the way, it was in North Carolina that I first discovered something that I didn't like at all but which was part of the "scene" down there. The first time on a Trailways bus, I headed for the back because I liked to sit in the last seat of a bus, or the very front seat. I was quickly informed of the way things were down South, and that was that. But it really ticked me off anyway. Well, I couldn't find the church in Raleigh, so I headed back the next day. On the way home that Sunday evening, our bus stopped for a moment at a corner in the small town of Wilson (about 90 miles from camp). I noticed a beautiful, small, greystone Lutheran Church with the sign "Church of the Lutheran Hour" – a clear indication that it was LCMS. The next weekend I traveled to Wilson, attended church on Sunday morning, was invited by the pastor and his family for dinner, and spent the rest of the day with them. They had a married son living at home with his fairly recent bride, an Italian girl, while he studied for the ministry. His younger brother, about my age, became a good friend and the whole family made me one of "theirs." From then on, I always stayed with them on weekends when I had liberty (usually three out of four weekends, except when I was off on maneuvers or a cruise). Pastor Lineberger was from the old school of "fire and brimstone" but he had a heart for the Gospel and was very loving. He was also a real missionary in the way of going into a place and literally building a church with his own hands, including the one in Wilson. His wife was a most gracious and generous woman who always made me feel "right at home." Even before it was officially allowed for military men to wear civilian clothes off the base, I began to do it on my weekends in Wilson. There were no MPs or SPs in town and it really felt good to be almost a civilian again. My main contribution to Pastor Lineberger and his congregation began late one Saturday evening. I had noticed that his church bulletins were quite poorly organized and typed, as well as rather sloppy-looking and smeared. Because it was a small church and a kind of "one-man operation," he did the Sunday bulletin himself on Saturday evening, using an old A.B. Dick mimeograph machine in his study in the parsonage next door to the church. He was not a very good typist and an even worse mimeograph operator, usually leaving small gobs of mimeo ink all over everything, including his bulletins. When I saw this happening, I offered to do it for him since I was well-experienced in typing and running a mimeo machine. He was extremely relieved and happy to give me the job, and I did turn out some neat, well-balanced, clean-looking bulletins. Later on, members of the congregation told me they always knew when I was in town for the weekend by the way the Sunday bulletin looked! The pastor even let me use his Pontiac several times for dates in town, until I managed to crunch up a fender one evening. After that, it was back to long walks in the park in the center of town! However, it was a marvelous experience for a young man, and to this day I am very grateful to the Linebergers and our Lutheran Church and the state of North Carolina for lots of loving hospitality and genuine care for this kid from Michigan!

During my four years in the Navy, and particularly while I was stationed in North Carolina, I began to give some serious thought to the rest of my life and what to do with it. After a couple of years in the Navy and the Marines, I realized that I still had lots of "wanderlust" – that is, I wanted to move about in life and go to different places and do different things and have a variety of new experiences. It didn't take long before I knew that I didn't want to just go back to Muskegon and pick up my life as an Apprentice Printer. Boring! What I wanted to do or be I didn't know at first. But rather suddenly it came to me. I wanted to be a teacher! Wow! Talk about a turnabout in my thought and life – that was it! Since my mother was a teacher, I had silently vowed to myself that I'd never be a teacher. I knew what it entailed and required in study, sacrifice, and hard work. But while attached to the Marines, I was asked (and in a sense, required) to teach some classes to Marines about battlefield first aid and treatment of wounded comrades, as well as other medical information. The thrill of passing along some useful information and procedures to other people (even though the Marines were a captive audience) gave me a "rush" like few other things in life. It was then, after about three years of military life, that I decided I wanted to be a high school teacher. Nothing else interested me at the time, although I did give some cursory thought to the pastoral ministry of our church (which my home congregation pastor, Rev. Luebke, had strongly suggested several times in the past). I simply wanted to be a teacher. To that end, I began to write to colleges and universities for information and possible entrance. Remember, I did not have a college prep program in high school and I did not have terrific grades (except in social studies, history, and English). I had even changed one of my grades on a report card that came home to my parents, but which I intercepted first. I changed an "F" into a "B" and then back again to an "F" when it was returned to school, and nobody ever knew the difference. My "F" was in a class called "Electricity," but it was really a high-powered math course, taught by a man who had never taught before. He flunked more than half of the class, including me. Incidentally, that was the only year he ever taught – just a last-minute wartime replacement. Well, I was called into the high school office the semester before we were to graduate, and I was told that I was one credit short of graduation because of that "F." But it was not in a major subject, so I could choose just about any elective available. By that time in my life, I had become interested in classical music, often hearing it at home and also listening to the Detroit Symphony late on Saturday nights in my room. I chose to take a course on "Music Appreciation" for the fun of it and because it was a so-called easy class. Well, it was fun! It opened up to me a whole new world of joy, appreciation, and interest, especially since I am not musically talented. When I showed up for the final two-hour exam in music (which I was not required to do as a graduating senior with a satisfactory grade point average), my teacher – Mrs. Luther (with blue/white hair) – just about went berserk and burst her seams in pride and joy that she had infected me with such a joy in classical music! And she announced it loudly and proudly, while the rest of the class looked at me like I was some kind of nut! So flunking that other course turned out to be one of the wonderful blessings in my life! Years later, when I told my mother about my changing that grade, she just laughed and commented, "Well, God turned a negative into a positive, and don't ever forget that He can do that in many ways in the future!" Wow! What a lesson!

Once I had settled on the goal of being a high school teacher, it remained for me to decide where I wanted to go, and who would accept me. I wrote to a number of schools, including Michigan, Central Michigan (my mother's alma mater). The prestigious, nearby Lutheran University, Valparaiso in Indiana, was the one that really attracted me, but was one I was doubtful about being able to enter due to my barely average grades in high school. Well, in those days after World War II, the G.I. Bill allowed many men and women to enter college even though they didn't have the best credentials – one of the wisest things our government ever did for our society for the years ahead. To my great joy and excitement, I was accepted at Valpo! In the meantime, I had to finish up my naval career. The last couple of years were marked by many months in North Carolina and a number of maneuvers in the Caribbean Sea (near Puerto Rico) and two cruises with the U.S. Navy's 6th Fleet in the Mediterranean Sea in the spring and summer of both 1947 and 1948. The maneuvers in the Caribbean were not much to write about (San Juan and Ponce I do not want to visit again), but I want to spend some pages describing our two Mediterranean cruises.

In the spring of 1947, our Marine battalion was assigned to the USS Midway, the most modern ship in the fleet, then over 1,000 feet long. We were headed for a 5-6 month cruise in the Mediterranean Sea. The main reason (although not stated officially) was to establish that the Mediterranean Sea was an "American lake" and the Russians better stay away. It also served as a positive influence on the Mediterranean nations in their fight against the rise of Communism in those countries (especially Italy, France, Greece, and Turkey).

This was graphically portrayed in the great double harbor of Naples. We took our carrier and her fleet of smaller ships into the neck of the two harbors and effectively "blocked" both harbors on election day in Italy, thus indicating where the "Big Stick" was in terms of power. In that election, Italy was barely able to keep the Communist Party from taking over. Maybe we had some affect on the election! Later, we watched the Communist and Greek governments' gunfire in the hills above the coast cities of Greece, where Gen. Van Fleet (later of Korean War fame) got his first real taste of guerrilla warfare. We dropped anchor in many places all around the Mediterranean Sea (both in Southern Europe and in North Africa) so please consult my USS Midway yearbook-type book on the whole cruise. Standing out in my recollection of that cruise were two incidents, related in the following two paragraphs.

The first incident concerned meeting Pope Pius XII at the Vatican. He spoke very good English, and when he came to me and noticed that I didn't bow down or kiss his ring and didn't have a neck full of rosaries and other things to bless, he knew I was a Protestant. Since he didn't have to say a bunch of blessings in Latin (as with the Catholic boys), he asked me about my work in the Navy. We had a brief conversation and then he went on. The same thing happened on my second cruise a year later when we visited the Pope at his summer home in the hills above Rome. Each time we met him, he gave us a medallion with his image on it, about the size of a quarter. Because I had two of them, I gave one of them to a very nice Catholic girl I dated in New York. She was ecstatic and very, very pleased! And so was I, since she was a wonderful Christian girl, and the medallion meant a lot more to her than I'd realized when I decided to give it to her.

The second incident of special note on that USS Midway cruise involved our ship being anchored in the bay outside of the great French naval base at Toulon. On the last night of our stay in Toulon (which included side trips to Nice), they packed more than 100 sailors and Marines into the last "Liberty Launch" which operated between the shore and the ship. Since a Navy Liberty Launch was supposed to hold a maximum of 70 men, it was a disaster waiting to happen. And happen it did! Halfway back to the ship around midnight, in some rough outer bay seas, the Launch capsized, sending 100 men into some very cold water. Rescue efforts began at once, but before it was over, 12 men had drowned. Several of them were never found. Those of us in Sick Bay were roused out of our sleep to attend the ones being brought in, most of them suffering from cold and hypothermia. Out came the blankets, out came the medications, and out came the brandy! One of our guys, well-known for his drinking habits, dispensed the brandy this way: "One for you and one for me!" By early morning we had a few other corpsmen "under the influence" (no, not me – I don't like brandy). At the time, we didn't yet realize how many men had been lost or how serious the whole thing had become. Almost needless to say, it cast on the cruise a pall which lasted quite a while. On the way home across the Atlantic Ocean, we had to go through a hurricane. It sent one of the smaller ships back to port, but a large ship like the Midway sustained very little damage. In fact, one of the big thrills was to stand on the fantail and "ride" it up and down like an out-of-control elevator. Very exciting, and a little dangerous.

The second Mediterranean cruise in 1948 was significant in a number of ways. For this cruise we were assigned to a cruiser, the USS Huntington, a 700-foot ship with more than 800 crew and Marines aboard. I enjoyed it more than the carrier I had been on the year before, probably because it was smaller and it too was a beautiful ship. Basically, we covered the same territory around the Mediterranean as we had the year before, except we visited more places this time. The names of the places we visited ring out with history and antiquity: Rome, Athens, Istanbul, Cairo, Taranto (Italy), Trieste, Venice, Suez Canal, Malta, Crete, cities in North Africa, and other smaller ports where a ship our size could fit into the harbor or dock. This was especially true in Venice, where we were the largest ship to ever traverse the Grand Canal and make the difficult turn-around at the main junction of the canal at the heart of the city, near St. Mark's Square and the Venice tower (St. Mark's Campanile). I loved Venice! We went swimming at Lido Beach on the other side of the city, took numerous trips in gondolas throughout the waterway streets of Venice, and experienced the wonderful ambience of this marvelous, ancient city. We met and dined with an American reporter who had just left Palestine. President Truman and the United Nations had just declared officially that Israel was a nation or state, and the Arab countries nearby were ready to go all-out in war. Later on our cruise, our 6th Fleet would "lay off" the Israeli coast, both to warn the Arabs that Truman meant business, and be prepared for a possible support landing of Marines as a show of force. Anyway, what an interesting tale the reporter had to tell, supplied with a number of alcoholic inducements!

One day at Lido Beach, three of us ran into Orson Welles at the hotel bar. At the time, he was "recovering" from his recent divorce from Rita Hayworth. However, he took an amazing interest in us, probably because he missed the States and liked talking with some Americans for a change. Also, he had just made a movie version of *Macbeth* and was interested in previewing it on our ship while we were anchored in Venice. We relayed this message to our ship's captain, and a couple of days later it was shown on the ship. However, we were too busy in the city to stay aboard for the showing. Besides, it wasn't that good of a movie, as critics told us later. The special thing was having that 2-3 hours with Orson Welles on the beach and his complete naturalness with us as we talked. A good experience! Incidentally, as we talked with him on the beach, he paid no attention to his girlfriend who was there all the time. And she didn't look at all happy!

At this point, I'd like to relate a story about my second visit to Rome. Since I had done the usual "tourist thing" on the previous cruise, I decided to pretty much go on my own for the three days we'd be in Rome this second time. Also, I had a favor to perform for my pastor's family back in Wilson. The oldest son had met and married an Italian girl in Rome after the war was over, and had brought her back to the States. While I was in North Carolina and periodically in Wilson, the young couple was staying with his folks in the parsonage, as I previously mentioned. After telling them that I had been in Rome the previous summer and would probably go there again in 1948, Corley (the son) and his wife, Pina, got very excited. If possible, she would like me to contact her family in Rome, and I agreed to do it. She wrote a long letter in Italian, introducing me and explaining who I was and why I was visiting them. In Rome that first day, I took off to find their apartment. Fortunately, I had a very good street map of Rome and everyone that I asked for help was most cordial. I soon found myself in the outer part of the great city where I suspect an American sailor had never appeared before. It looked a bit dangerous, I suppose, in that part of the crowded city, but I don't remember any feelings of fear – only concern to find the family. Well, at dusk I did find Pina's family in a third floor, large apartment, where about seven family members all lived. Since I spoke no Italian and they spoke no English, my letter from Pina and lots of gesturing and fanciful drawings helped communicate. They were all extremely happy to meet me and were very friendly. After a little while, they decided it was time to celebrate by going to a nearby restaurant for a big spaghetti dinner. As we were dining and struggling to communicate, a man in his 40s came over and in perfect English asked if I'd permit him to help with the language problem since he also spoke perfect Italian. Gratefully, I asked him to join us and then we really had a good, old-fashioned gabfest in English and Italian! After several hours of this, I got ready to go back to my hotel in the heart of the city. After making arrangements to meet Pina's mother the next day for lunch and a tour of Rome which visitors seldom saw, my new friend offered to drive me back into the city in his car. He turned out to be what I would call a "displaced American," since he was a trainer of boxing fighters and had somehow violated some licensing rules back in the States and so left to train boxers in Rome. He had in his stable of boxers the 2nd-ranked middleweight boxer in Europe. (I looked it up later and he was right.) Pina's mother met me for lunch in the city and had Pina's brother with her. However, his only interest in me was his hope that he could pick up a girl with my uniform as the attraction! I wasn't interested, of course, so he soon left us. Pina's mother took me to a wonderful place for lunch and then showed me the backside of Rome (not pleasant, very dirty, and very much neglected by the Vatican nearby), including the "red-light" district right next to the Vatican! She was very nice to me, quite motherly actually, and I enjoyed her immensely. Most of the next two days were spent with my American-Italian friend who took me to his training camp for his boxers. It was just a low-ceilinged basement with the usual boxing equipment and boxers all over the place. He even had his highly-ranked middleweight boxer go a couple of real rounds in the ring, and he was good! My new friend also took me around Rome in his car, which was a marvelous, but scary experience! Crazy driver, but it seemed that all of them were in Rome! All in all, it was an amazing three days! I don't even remember his name, and when we parted, he was happy to have been with me but played down any close identity. Well, whoever he was, he certainly made that time in Rome very special, and for that I am very grateful. Like Orson Welles, he just seemed to like being with an American for a while.

It was aboard the USS Huntington that I gained maturation and skills as a medical person. Our doctor in charge, Dr. William Old III, from Norfolk, Virginia, was both a terrific doctor and a terrific person who had little use or concern for the military or military protocol. Early on during our cruise, he put me in charge of the Treatment and Emergency Room of the ship. He discovered that I had an uncanny ability to do a good job in sewing up (suturing, in medical language) wounds and cuts. That was probably due to my sewing up loose covers on baseballs years before, especially during the war when new baseballs were hard to get and expensive. Also, I seemed to have the facility to determine which cases in the Sick Call line needed a doctor's attention and which ones could be taken care of by our medical corpsmen. That's a great asset with so many men to take care of everyday, and Dr. Old trusted me with that job. As an enlisted man having the confidence of the doctors and staff, and with a lot of good medical knowledge, I thrived on the ship. It also helped to make my last 15 months of Navy duty more interesting and worthwhile. I got so close to my work in the ship's Sick Bay, that I developed the habit of often spending my nights in an extra hospital bed in Sick Bay, instead of returning to my regularly-assigned bunk in another compartment of the ship. It was also during this time that I was often kidded by the guys (sometimes a bit cruelly) about the fact that I was a "male virgin." However, it didn't seem to bother me that much, especially when an older sailor would sometimes catch me alone and encourage me, usually with words like, "I wish I'd done that for my wife," etc.

There was one neat experience which best characterizes, in a rather strange way, a positive spin from this moral resolve of mine. We were in Athens, Greece, for several days. Most of us took advantage of the city: its tremendous history, architecture, and buildings, as well as its pubs – they being the only places to go to at night. The first evening was not that great as we plied ourselves with warm British beer with some of their sailors at the British version of the USO. The second evening found a rather large group of us at a well-known, large pub, replete with the usual assortment of "ladies of the night" and their "invitations" and the watered-down drinks that accompanied their "friendliness." One young woman, almost a girl (probably no older than me at 20 or 21), latched on to me almost immediately with her invitation. I bought her a drink, along with one for me, but politely refused her invitation. We sat and talked a while (she knew some basic English) and she repeated her invitation. I bought drinks again (which she hardly touched, since that was part of the "game"), but I again politely refused her invitation. We talked some more and the sequence was repeated, and again I politely refused her invitation.

At that point, a rather strange but subtle thing began to happen. She softened her approach, seemed to relax comfortably with me, and we just kept on talking. She told me about her family which had been devastated by the war and was still struggling three years later. She talked about these struggles and the financial problems of post-war Europe and her attempts to become independent with a small-paying job in the daytime and "this" work at night. While I do not condone what she was doing at night, I also accepted the reality that I was with a good young person my own age who was willing to forgo whatever money she could make that night to spend those hours with me. We even talked of Church and the Christian faith, but she had been disillusioned by the Greek Orthodox Church and its distance from the people, and she had little use for religion of that sort. I made what was probably a weak personal witness, but she appreciated my attempt. At least she had a person with whom to relate her "lost" Christian faith, and that sometimes helps. Well, we spent that evening together in a unique and unexpected way, and I have only the special satisfaction of helping bring some hours of enjoyment and good feeling to a girl my age in Athens – a girl who in the circumstance of life in our country I might have taken an ongoing liking and interest in, and she likewise. As it was, the whole group of sailors I was with left near midnight for our ship ten miles away. Just as we left and when I gave my young friend a bit of a goodbye hug, I pressed into her hand the monetary equivalent of two or three consummated invitations and gave her my thanks for a lovely evening. My last view of her was her wide-open eyes of amazement and a pretty face of softness and appreciation. I have no idea of whatever happened to her. I don't even remember her name. But I do remember very clearly that it was a beautiful moment in my life, and I hope in hers also. Believe me when I say that I went back to my ship that night more satisfied and more at peace with myself than any of my fellow sailors. I hope that doesn't sound pietistic or proud, because it isn't meant that way. I tell you that story because that's just the way it was, and it's a story that I joyfully and thankfully remember!

Three more experiences characterized that cruise in special ways for me. The first of these experiences is entitled, "I Think I Fooled a Navy Admiral." I had already been in the U.S. Navy for three years in 1948, having enlisted as a 17 year old right out of high school in 1945. That was shortly before the end of WWII, or as I sometimes liked to put it, "The enemy quit as soon as I enlisted!"

In 1947, I served aboard the big aircraft carrier, the USS Midway (over 1,000 feet long), which was finally put into "moth balls" quite a few years ago now, after more than forty years of distinguished service. The next year (1948), I was aboard the cruiser USS Huntington, 750 feet in length with a crew of more than 800 sailors, plus the U.S. Marines unit attached for special purposes. Since I was a Navy medical corpsman with the rate of 3rd class petty officer (same as a sergeant in the Marines or Army), I had been assigned to the U.S. Marines. The Marine Corps does not have its own medical personnel because, technically, the Marines are part of the Navy. I was part of the "Fleet Marines," the amphibious invasion forces especially well-known for their island-to-island operations in the Pacific during WWII.

In the immediate years after WWII, the U.S. Navy's 6th Fleet was our "Big Stick" policy in the Mediterranean Sea to discourage or even combat the spread of Communism in that part of the world, particularly in Italy, Greece, and France. In the spring and summer of 1948, we cruised around the Mediterranean dropping anchor in many places and keeping a wary eye on Israel and the Arab world. In that year of 1948, President Truman, with the support of most of the United Nations, officially recognized Israel as a national state, in spite of dire predictions of violence and bloodshed by the Arab states.

After crossing the Atlantic Ocean to the Mediterranean Sea, we experienced a change of captains on our ship. The new captain, Arleigh A. Burke, was brought aboard in Taranto, Italy. He had recently been promoted to a "four-striper" and this would be the largest ship he would ever command. He had always been a "tin can" (destroyer) man, especially during WWII when he was nicknamed "31-knot Burke" because he was always making his destroyer go faster than it was designed to go and fooling the enemy fleets. From the beginning, we referred to him as "pear shape" because of his physical dimensions. However, it soon became a kind of loving term for him, since he quickly became our well-respected, well-loved captain of unusual skills and ability to command. He was, in the opinion of the crew, a top-notch seaman and captain, as well as a solid Navy man with a great charismatic personality that attracted loyalty to him easily and enthusiastically.

My first encounter with Capt. Burke came on the first Saturday morning, during "Captain's Inspection." I had been put in charge of the Emergency and Treatment Room of the ship. That meant that all cases aboard ship came through us and it was usually up to me to determine who needed what kind of help and treatment, as well as my own direct involvement. I really enjoyed this work and responsibility, and I guess I did it pretty well. When our Marine detachment left shortly before the end of the cruise to go back to the states, our ship's doctor wrote an official letter of commendation for my work on the USS Huntington, signed by Capt. Burke! But, back to the story. Naturally, for this first inspection, I wanted to impress our new captain and have the treatment room in clean, shiny condition and the steel decks and bulkheads perfectly spotless. On that first Captain's Inspection morning, my area was in tip-top condition, including the "knobby" steel decks throughout the area. We knew just about when the captain would be appearing, so I was ready. Then, just before the arrival of Captain Burke, a cook from the ship's galley came running in and was dripping blood all over the place from a cut finger. He had cut his little finger with a knife a few minutes before. Realizing the immediate need to take care of him and aware that the captain was soon to make his appearance, I brought the cook into the treatment room and had someone quickly clean up the blood he had dripped on "my" deck.

Since it was a relatively small but bloody cut, I decided that a good, tight "butterfly" bandage would take care of the problem and I wouldn't have to break open a whole suture kit and administer "sterile technique" in the area. That would have messed up much of my treatment room and made it into a clutter just before the captain arrived for inspection! After taking care of the cook, I asked him if he felt all right, since some men get quite queasy at the sight of their own blood. He responded that he was fine. As I turned to put away the few instruments I had used to treat him, I heard a thud behind me. When I turned around, I saw my "patient" lying down on the deck – out cold! Worse than that, on the way down, he had hit his mouth on the edge of the treatment table and cut open a big gash inside his mouth and was bleeding all over the place and in every direction! After reviving him, I got him up and laid him on the treatment table and began to take care of him. That meant getting out the suture pack and sterilizing it and doing whatever else was connected with treatment. As I was sewing in the five or six stitches to the inside of his mouth, and with the whole treatment room now in a mess and blood all over the place, the captain made his appearance! He immediately came over to the treatment table, watched intently as I put in the stitches (I hardly realized he was there) and then looked at me as he departed and said: "Keep up the good work, doc. You're doing a great job!" (In the Navy, "doc" – as contrasted to doctor – is a colloquial term for a hospital corpsman, similar to a medic in the Army.) As the captain walked out, he seemingly didn't notice the rest of the treatment room and all that I had done to make it look perfect!

Aha! I thought to myself after he left. From that time on, whenever there was a Captain's Inspection, I would survey the Sick Call line and determine who was most in need of "extended" kinds of treatment! Usually, it was someone with lots of bandaging needed, or re-bandaging, or someone with stitches to be removed. Each time the captain came into my treatment room and would see me busy with someone, he would watch for a while, and then comment the same way he had the first time, and depart without really looking over the place. Thus, I never really experienced a thorough Captain's Inspection, and yet I enjoyed his appreciation of my work.

As for Capt. Burke? Well, he turned out to be quite a surprise in another way. During the early 1950s, I was reading a Washington report on President Eisenhower and his Cabinet appointments, and other high-ranking appointments. And right there appeared an article on Arleigh A. Burke, who had been appointed the Chief of Naval Operations for the United States. The amazing thing was that Admiral Burke had been chosen by the wise and perceptive President Eisenhower over 95 senior admirals in the U.S. Navy, to the consternation and criticism of many people. However, Admiral Burke turned out to be the right combination of a bright military mind with political wisdom to handle the delicate and stressful job as Chief of Naval Operations for the United States in the 1950s. But I will never forget the time that I think I fooled an admiral.

But maybe, just maybe, in his graciousness and natural compassion, he allowed me to believe that. Nevertheless, to this day, Admiral Arleigh Burke remains one of my heroes!

The second experience was very special to me personally as I prepared to leave the ship near the end of our cruise. (Our Marine detachment was sent back to the States before the ship completed her cruise a few weeks later.) The day before leaving, Dr. Old and the chief petty officer of the ship's medical department handed me a fairly long letter. It turned out to be a very flattering, written commendation of my work on the USS Huntington for those nearly six months. It would be entered into the official records of my U.S. Navy career.

My only regret is that I didn't ask for a copy, but it didn't occur to me at the time. Besides, we didn't have copy machines then and I don't know if a carbon copy had been made. But that didn't seem to make much difference to me. I felt extremely complimented and it was enough for me to be characterized by one of the senior corpsman in our group who said, "Jim is the best 3rd Class Petty Officer Hospital Corpsman in the whole U.S. Navy!"

I didn't get to relish my honor very long, however, due to my third major experience of that cruise. Almost as soon as I was transferred with my Marine detachment to the carrier, USS Philippine Sea, I came down with an acute case of infectious hepatitis, not too uncommon at the time in the Mediterranean Sea. My first ten days were extremely painful, mainly because I would hide my pain pills under my pillow, rather than take them. Since I was in a somewhat agitated and not too rational state, I was convinced that I didn't want to take any kind of drugs! I had seen what the abuse of them could do to a person, and I wasn't taking any chances. Not too smart on my part. When I got back to the States, I spent two and a half months recovering at the U.S. Naval Hospital in Newport, Rhode Island.

One interesting (and sometimes confusing) thing about being in the Navy but attached to the Marines: I needed a full set of Marine uniforms to go with my full set of Navy uniforms – that is, Navy "Blues" and Marine "Greens." When I was with the Marines, I wore the Marine uniform most of the time, particularly on the base. But the uniform of my choice off the base was almost always Navy, unless I was with my Marine buddies. On a couple of occasions, my Navy status came in quite handy, especially in two different disciplinary situations which I will describe in the next paragraphs. And our Navy status kind of isolated us from some of the Marine things we either didn't like or just found boring. The choice and change of uniforms also proved to be a wonderful asset aboard the USS Midway (and to a lesser degree, a couple other troop ships I was on for maneuvers in the Caribbean). Since the ships (particularly the Midway) had so many men aboard, it was impossible to keep track of everyone, Navy or Marines. Feeding 3,800 men three times a day on the Midway was a gigantic task. So, the Marines who were aboard just for the Mediterranean cruise were given little cards or "chits" which had to be punched for each meal. This procedure wasn't required of the ship's crew! So, whenever I'd have my meal with my Marine outfit and was still not fully satisfied, I'd quickly run down to my bunk and change into my Navy uniform and go through the chow line and eat with the ship's crew! Well, remember, I was still a growing young man of 19, adding an inch in height and 30 pounds since joining the Navy, and I had a voracious appetite in those days!

That pretty well sums up my years in the military, the U.S. Navy. And I have no regrets. I have never looked back with any sense of wanting things to be different or reverses or whatever. The only other parts of my military career that I must mention (I'd rather not, but I must be fair to my own history) have to do with the two times I *could* have been in real trouble for disciplinary reasons. In both cases, my Navy status "saved" me, since both times occurred while I was with the Marines. The first time took place when I was at the firing range with my company. Since I was a corpsman with the U.S. Marine Corps, I was required to be somewhat proficient in the use of firearms. At the firing range that day, we were faced with a gnarled Marine sergeant who didn't realize we were a group of "dumb" Navy corpsmen. Since we also didn't care much for official ranking or rating, we usually didn't have our rates stenciled on our jackets (remember, my rating was equal to a sergeant's). On this particular day, none of us had our ratings showing. Actually, we weren't very interested in all this shooting business, probably because we weren't very good at it. I much preferred to be in the field with my machine gun and mortar platoon, and doing some of their stuff with them. Anyway, there we were on the firing range and I didn't like the poor shooting I was doing. Being competitive, I wanted to do better. All the time we were firing, this sergeant kept at us in a very demeaning and negative way. I had just missed a number of "bull's-eyes" with my "big kick" 45-caliber pistol and was feeling pretty lousy. Along comes this sergeant and starts talking about our poor shooting efforts, especially mine. Then he said in a loud voice, "Hell, my wife can do better than you guys!" That did it! I promptly replied in an equally loud voice, "I don't care what your wife does for a living; I just can't hit that damn target!" He turned to me with this terribly ferocious look on his face and bellowed out that I was on "report." I was in trouble! However, our Navy chief went to him privately and quietly convinced him that putting a Navy man on report would do very little, since our doctor had the final say on such matters, and he wouldn't do a thing. So, I got off! I didn't deserve it, but I accepted it.

The second disciplinary incident was more serious and more threatening. I had been in Company B for a long time and the officers had given me a free hand in my work and medical decisions, such that I was pretty independent in my status and position. Then we got a new company commander – a young, inexperienced man who decided that he needed to "prove" himself and his authority. A week or so after he came, there was a big regimental parade and our company was part of it. That Saturday morning, I had my usual Sick Call for the company. One of the guys was scheduled for dental work and he really needed it. So, I sent him down to the company office with the request that he be sent to the dental office. My new company commander refused permission, indicating that all the men must be in the parade. For whatever reason, maybe my German stubbornness, I took offense at this as an invasion of my sphere of authority. (Heck – I didn't know military protocol very well and have since realized I was in the wrong. I wasn't a very military person anyway, so what did I know?) Therefore, I sent the kid back down to the company commander with the demand that he be given permission. That didn't work either, so I went down myself, and in front of all the officers and sergeants assembled to be ready to start for the parade, I told our dentist on the phone the situation in a voice loud enough for all to hear! The dentist then "ordered" me to send him to Sick Bay immediately. Well, what else should I have expected from the new company commander? He went "ballistic" and put me on three weeks' restriction to the barracks. That's when I found out that military concerns take precedence over medical concerns, although that makes the leader also responsible for his decisions on medical matters. Two days before my three weeks of restriction were to be over, my new company commander found a new reason to restrict me. At that point, I went to my own Navy chief petty officer and told him my problem. He promptly transferred me to Company C, right next door to Company B! When I talked to my new company commander (whom I knew slightly already) and told him my situation, he simply replied: "You are now in my company. I know you, and so just forget the whole thing. His restriction doesn't apply here." And that was the end of that whole thing. I was lucky, even though I was wrong. Sometime later I ran into that new commander and apologized to him, to which he didn't respond.

The rest of my time in the military service was basically uneventful, except for my wonderful times in Wilson and the church there. I did go on one more cruise, but this was to the Caribbean and Puerto Rico and was mostly a bore, although I enjoyed shipboard life. While on one of the islands there, I received late word (mail was slow and we were aboard ship) that my Uncle Harry had died rather suddenly from Hodgkin's disease (curable these days, but not then). This hit me very hard because my Uncle Harry was the major male role model in my early life as a boy growing up (see Chapter 1). He had been the one who had first put into my mind the idea of joining the Navy, if the war was still on after my graduation from high school. I loved him very much and missed him terribly!

My discharge from the Navy would take place about the time that school would begin in the fall of 1949. I had a little problem. If I jumped right into college life, I would hardly have time to "catch my breath" and be ready for the academic life. So, I decided I'd wait until the mid-year start of the second semester, around the first of February, and make up the "lost" semester over the next three and a half years. And so I did, and with excellent grades. (See the chapter, "My Valpo Years.")

Before closing this account of my little more than four years in the Navy, I am going to try to make a kind of summary statement about those four years and what they did to me and what they meant to my life in the years ahead. In the jargon of today, in many ways they were the "defining" years of my life. That is, they served to set me on some course in life that affected the rest of my life in very clear and definite ways. Several things the Navy did *not* do for me or to me: I did not become a cigarette smoker until I got out (which I discontinued some years later); I did not lose my male virginity; I did not come out of the military service with any kind of negative feelings, grudges, regrets, unmet expectations, or emotional or mental scars; I did not have any feelings of being "cheated" out of four good years of a young life! Nor did I come out with any doubts about wanting to get back into civilian life. The U.S. Navy did me one great and tremendous favor for which I will always be truly grateful: Those four years in the Navy gave me that rare opportunity to "find myself" as a person, to look at my life ahead in an unrushed way, to have the time and luxury of planning an agenda for life unhindered by time constraints or economic pressures or needs. I took counsel with no one, other than to ask a few questions, nor did I seek advice from anyone, not even my family. Whatever general goals or directions came to me, it was more through prayer, reflection, and meditation. In other words, I "grew up" in the Navy (as my own Uncle Harry had told me many years before would happen). When I came out, I was really ready to "take on the world," so to speak, and to start making something more of myself, to serve God and His people in whatever way that would happen, and to bring a sense of fulfillment, accomplishment, and satisfaction into my own life. At this time, I don't remember having any high and mighty goals or altruistic plans to "give" myself to church work or any particular spiritual calling.

Spiritually speaking, those four years were also defining years in my life. When I entered the U.S. Navy at the age of 17 (almost 18), I carried with me a great loyalty for my church and for the Lord. However, that loyalty was probably adequate but not very enlightened. I was a "cognitive" Lutheran who loved the church and the people of the church who influenced me and gave me spiritual direction, including the only pastor I really knew all of my life until then. While in the Navy, I experienced a variety of feelings about my religion and my faith, all the way from a form of agnosticism to closeness and commitment to Christ. More important than my pastor in those days before the Navy (except, of course, for my mother and Uncle Harry) was Bill Scheer, my 8th-grade teacher and the youth leader at church during my high school years.

During my Navy years, several things occurred that affected my "journey of faith." First of all, my sense of loyalty to the church, and to those people of the church who were so important to me, was vital to my life. That loyalty saw me through a number of times when I was faced with doubts, uncertainties, temptations, or challenges to my faith. Those important people did not cause me to remain faithful (only the Holy Spirit can do that!), but they were God's instruments in my life up until then to give me guidance, support, and a sense of belonging to Christ and His Church!

The second thing that affected my journey of faith those Navy years were some very positive experiences with my church wherever I went, whether in New York and Long Island, North Carolina, or anywhere else. Good people of God always seemed to be some part of my life those days, even on different military bases or aboard ship with other Christians. And there were the wonderful congregations I was associated with or some of the personal faith-renewing events (usually involving other people).

That leads to another aspect of my journey of faith – the many, many hours of personal, quiet, alone time for reflection, prayer, meditation, and thought aboard my ships. So often I would go up on the main deck late at night after "lights out" and find a quiet, secluded spot along the ship's rail. There, with the beautiful night sky and the galaxy of stars and the special, unique sounds of the water as the ship moved through the sea, I found myself able to think, to pray, to ponder, and even to indulge in some flights of fancy and fantasies of a young man. Those were some of the most meaningful and memorable times of my Navy career, and they set the stage for my major decisions as I prepared to enter my post-Navy life. I am so grateful for those special times and special experiences in my spiritual life!

Finally, one other thing that greatly affected my spiritual life and those years occurred primarily while I was aboard any one of the six different ships I served on – deep, private, uninterrupted study of the Holy Scripture. This, too, was a very special dimension in my life, and these are times which I look back upon with very special joy and gratitude! I had no special goal in mind as I read the Bible, except to enjoy it and know it better. Of course, during such study there were some very wonderful faith-revealing and faith-renewing experiences. In particular, at a very important juncture of my journey of faith, I was filled with a newness of God's grace when I read and re-read and studied 1 Corinthians, chapter 15, the great "Resurrection Chapter" of the Bible! It hit me square "between the eyes of faith" (theologically speaking) and made such a spiritual impression upon me that I still consider and view that chapter with total awe, gratitude, and joy! For me, it was the defining moment of my spiritual experiences in the Navy, and maybe my life! And, of course, it set the stage for my becoming a few years later a Lutheran high school teacher and then an ordained Lutheran minister.

Like many defining moments in my life before and since then, I simply took my life where it was at that moment, accepted whatever was the situation, and just went on from there without looking back, having any regrets, or wishing things had turned out differently. I have never had those feelings in my life and I don't have them now. Given all that's happened to me in my life so far, and with the reality that I'd probably change some things if I could, I consider myself to be an amazingly "lucky" man! Since I don't believe in luck, I will settle for the truth that I am a most blessed person in just about every way imaginable! I believe that God led me into some important and wise decisions along the way, even when I wasn't sure of them, as my story has already shown. For example, when I was getting ready to leave the Navy, they tried very hard to convince me to join the Navy Reserve (an easy way to pick up a few extra bucks with a minimum of effort). Even one of my buddies back home tried it with me, but I told him what I told the Navy: "I really appreciated all that had happened to me in the Navy and I was very satisfied with my four years, but that was over with, and a new period of my life was beginning." A "lucky" decision? How about this for timing, or "luck," or whatever you want to call it: I joined the Navy shortly before the atom bomb brought a sudden and unexpected end to World War II, or I might have been with some of those Fleet Marines invading the Japanese islands as was being planned. End of summer, 1949, I was discharged from the Navy less than nine months before the beginning of the Korean War in June of 1950! Being a medical corpsman with rating, in the Navy Reserve I would have been immediately recalled into service in the Navy and probably sent right to Korea. A buddy of mine (the same one who had been urging me to join the reserves with him), with the same rating, but with a wife and a small child, was recalled and sent immediately to Korea! He returned safely, but with a Purple Heart decoration for being wounded in action. No wonder that I mean it when I say that I wouldn't trade my life for anyone's. I think it was then that I realized, as I would many other times, that God was saving me for something special in His own plans for me. Whatever it would be, I believe that my years in the Navy afforded me the opportunity to take some giant strides in His direction for me. I am proud of my service in the Navy; I am proud of the U.S. Navy; and I am truly thankful for the role of the U.S. Navy in my life!

Chapter 4

My Valpo Years (1950-1953)

Outside of my early years in a parochial school in Muskegon, Michigan, my favorite and most influential school was Valparaiso University. Valparaiso, Indiana is about 60 miles southeast of Chicago and 150 miles directly south of my hometown of Muskegon. During my teaching years in Cleveland, I did some graduate work at Case Western Reserve University, and during my seminary vicarage year in Los Angeles, I took several outstanding graduate courses in the School of Religion at the University of Southern California. Of course, I spent four years (including one year on vicarage) in theological study at Concordia Theological Seminary in Springfield, Illinois (which has since moved to Ft. Wayne, Indiana), where I achieved my Master of Divinity (M.Div.) degree, as did all the sem graduates. However, Valpo was the most important school because of the direction my life took professionally and spiritually while I was a student there. Along with USC, it was the most academically challenging of any place I have ever studied. I attended Valpo for three and a half years, completing my Bachelor of Arts degree during that time, including one summer school session in 1952. I graduated with a 3.50 grade point average. My majors were history and English, with minors in social studies, education, and geography/geology. That last minor was a surprise and a delight to me (I didn't need it to graduate), which happened because I took some extra courses from my favorite prof, Dr. John Strietelmeier. At Valpo, my main focus and interest was, of course, history. I expected that social studies and history would be my main teaching areas, although I was prepared to teach English and American literature.

While I was still in the U.S. Navy, I decided to follow God's direction and my own spiritual growth to pursue a career as a high school teacher. And I would have the financial means to make the possibility a reality through the G.I. Bill. At that time, the "G" in G.I. stood for "general," and the "I" stood for "issue," and it designated everything issued to servicemen upon induction into the U.S. Armed Forces (clothing, shoes, blankets, weapons, etc.) and all continuing physical and military needs of servicemen. Ultimately, the term "G.I." came to refer to all servicemen and women of the U.S. Armed Forces and anything connected with them. Following World War II, the U.S. government, in one of its amazingly wise decisions, passed the G.I. Education Bill, which financially underwrote the cost of college and vocational training to all honorably discharged veterans with the opportunity for post-high school training or education, all the way through a four-year college program for those who so desired. It included full tuition, books, and a small monthly stipend for living expenses. It was one of the most important decisions in our nation's history! Millions of G.I.s took advantage of the opportunity and became part of the great economic and social boom of the post-World War II period. It was based on the principle that if you give young men and women the opportunity, they will respond with a greater effort, and the result will be a more positive contribution to our society and our nation.

So, my G.I. Bill allowed me to enroll at an academically-strong, Lutheran university, despite my rather meager scholastic background in high school. (I had no foreign language and few math credits.) Remember, I had been vocationally-trained to be an "apprentice printer," not an academic person. I took general education and not college prep courses. I think I barely got through high school, and my getting through was mostly because of my grades in history and English! I did do a lot of good reading while in the Navy and was a bit of a bookworm, especially on some of those long sea voyages.

In early 1949, while still in the Navy, I knew I had a chance to go to college! Inspired by the Lord's guidance, much prayer and much thinking, I decided to change my direction and focus in life, and study to become a high school teacher ("In their hearts humans plan their course, but the LORD establishes their steps" – Proverbs 16:9). The decision was simple, but getting into college presented a challenge. Fortunately, the G.I. Bill allowed just about anyone into college or vocational training who wanted it, regardless of their high school background. Even then, I wondered if I could get into Valpo. Well, with a certain amount of youthful self-confidence, I applied to Valpo. And they accepted me! With money that I had saved personally, with regularly-saved U.S. Savings Bonds, and with money I earned with summer jobs, I knew I had enough money (along with the G.I. Bill) to get me through college without depending on my parents. That was important to me! So, with all this going for me, I proceeded into the marvelous era of my life called "Valpo!"

My Valpo Years (1950-1953)

The very idea of my going to college (which I had once said in my teen years that I would never do!) was helped by a very practical reality – the opportunity provided by the G.I. Bill because of my four years in the Navy. However, the main idea was far more important – I wanted to be a high school teacher! That goal motivated me in every way as I proceeded through Valpo. The reason I began at Valpo in February, 1950 (instead of fall, 1949) was due to my desire to have a good time for a couple of months after my discharge from the Navy and before I began my college studies. I did study my mom's college textbooks on English grammar in preparation for the "Grammar O" test that every incoming student was required to take at Valpo. It worked! Whatever gave me the feeling or the idea that I could handle college curriculum demands after my years in the Navy, I don't know. Somehow, I believed that I could. Valpo accepted me and I accepted Valpo, and that was it.

When I began at Valpo in February, 1950, I discovered that the on-campus dormitories were full and I would have to live off campus. That was all right with me, and I found myself in an apartment-room on the second floor of a house. Actually, that turned out to be a real blessing. Our landlords, Frank and Marge Doyle, were wonderful people. They owned and operated a successful restaurant and drive-in right behind their large house on the main street of the city of Valparaiso. There were three other Valpo students living upstairs – all 18 years old and freshmen. Of course, I was the "elder" and that turned out to be a blessing for the Doyles and for me. I became the moderating/counselor influence and the Doyles were extremely happy with my more mature presence upstairs, especially when a couple of cute teenage girls from across the street would wander over from time to time with some "ideas" about us! The four of us took turns cooking the main evening meal (sometimes with disastrous results – e.g., when I cooked tongue until it was totally impossible to eat). We established definite study hours and quiet time, and generally did very well together. I was able to establish a deep and warm friendship with the Doyles during that one and a half years I was in their upstairs apartment-room. My last two years at Valpo, I was Freshman Dorm Counselor on campus and enjoyed that very much, especially since my room was the best "viewing room" of the girls walking past our dorm on their way to the old campus several blocks away! However, I never forgot the Doyles and often spent some good times with them at their restaurant or in their home. During the one and a half years in the Doyles' house, I met and became a lifelong friend of Dave Brueggemann, from Rocky River, Ohio (immediately west of Cleveland). To this day, it continues to be one of my very special friendships, which both Betty and Nancy have also enjoyed, together with Dave and his wife, Lil.

After describing some of my life when I lived off campus, I now must add a couple of paragraphs about dormitory life on campus. Near the end of my time at the Doyles', I applied for on-campus housing. When I did, they asked or suggested that I might want to be a Freshman Dorm Counselor. It would help them and also give me a few extra dollars. It seemed like a good idea and I accepted. Later on, I found out that after I'd told Frank Doyle that I would be on campus the next fall, he called the university housing people and suggested that I would make a good dorm counselor, based on his experience with me when I boarded at his place.

Life in a dorm at Valpo was no problem – not after my years in the Navy and Marines with bunk beds, large barracks, and cramped shipboard sleeping arrangements! My dormitory was simply labeled "Lower Dorm B," as compared to "Upper Dorm B" and "Upper and Lower Dorm A." It sounds almost like something taken right out of Al Capp's *Li'l Abner* comic strip ("Lower Slobovia"). The four dorms, with Lower Dorm B being the only one for freshmen, were former U.S. Navy WAVES (Women Accepted for Volunteer Emergency Service) barracks. First of all, the rooms (with two students to each room, except for the counselor), were small by any standards we'd use today (little closet space, little study space, and very crowded together to the adjoining rooms). The two long dorm facilities were joined in the middle by a central area of washroom sinks and mirrors, and with many individual shower stalls (where the guys loved to pour ice-cold water on unsuspecting guys who were showering and responded with appropriate screams of agony). Toilet-wise, there were, of course, no urinals! Just a long row of enclosed toilets! The walls in the dorm were so thin that you always knew what was going on in the rooms on either side of you. This sometimes led to arguments and acrimony, but was generally accepted as the way of life at Valpo. Since there was no refrigeration, many guys, including me, built little wooden boxes that fit the size of the sliding outside windows of the room, and used them in the winter to store meat, cheese, and other perishable foods. Quite primitive, but very useful. In the warmer weather months, we used outlawed "hot plates" for grilled cheese sandwiches at night, and whatever other uses for our late-night appetites!

With such thin walls and low ceilings, a number of "break throughs" occurred, so that the university was constantly repairing holes made by the students, some of them quite accidentally. However, one guy, a good friend of mine, challenged the low ceiling one day by jumping up as high and fast as he could to put a head-sized hole in the ceiling. Unfortunately, he chose a section with an unseen crossbeam and knocked himself semiconscious for a while! I had a number of freshman students whom I came to love and care for very much – all the way from the kids who weren't interested in education and didn't last very long at the university, to those who had wonderful academic or athletic skills (e.g., Art Muchow, a brilliant scholar and good friend, and Fred "Fuzzy" Thurston, of later Green Bay Packer fame in professional football). Several of my boys went on to become academic scholars in various fields; some went on into the Lutheran ministry; some went on to great teaching careers; and some went on to become experts in their particular disciplines. I do remember helping any number of them in various academic ways, especially some of the engineering students who needed help with writing English compositions. Also, I remember helping some of the students researching American literature, finding historical references, or dealing with professors who "didn't understand them." And, of course, I had to help some of them with their "girl problems." I was good at that!

With this great group of freshmen in Lower Dorm B in my senior year as counselor, one of my proudest moments came in late spring, not too long before graduation. In the spring of each year at Valpo, they conducted an athletic "Field Day" in which every group or organization on campus was invited to compete, including the dormitories. In reality, it was mainly a fraternity Field Day and few other organizations were well-enough organized or had the time to put together what one might simply call a "track team" that could be competitive – not even the dormitories. Even though the fraternities would dominate Field Day, we were expected to have a team. Most of the school's athletic stars were, as you might expect, in the fraternities, including many of the guys in the dormitories, except for the Freshman Dorm. So, I began putting together a "track team" and discovered that we had some very good track athletes, and they were anxious to prove we could be competitive. I spent a lot of time teaching some of the guys how to do some of the trickier things in track, such as successfully handing off the baton while running at full speed in relay races. We actually took time to practice some of the events at the school's track. As a former athletic coach, I quickly recognized many talents among my freshman group. On Field Day, I didn't really know what to expect, except that we would make a good impression and do as well as we could against a "stacked deck" of many outstanding athletes in the fraternities. Well, my kids did exceedingly well, to everyone's amazement, coming in third place – ahead of almost all of the many fraternities. Except for our 440-yard runner collapsing just before the finish line, we might have been in second, or even first place. The awards assembly was mostly a farce – simply a fraternity function in which we were treated as interlopers on their fun. I also let a few people in the university Athletic Department know my feelings about the fraternities and their attitudes. Nonetheless, I was never more proud of a group of kids than my freshmen in the spring of 1953! That dormitory counseling time was a wonderful, growing, enlightening time in my preparation to be a Lutheran high school teacher, and those freshman kids of mine will always be very special in my memories of Valpo. And my work with them in my senior year was recognized by the university at the end of the school year with a special award for me.

~

The next section of this part of my story will simply include a number of vignettes of those three and a half years at Valpo. Academically, it was a bonanza for me! I thoroughly enjoyed nearly every class I took, including science (not my strong suit) and education classes (which were a bit boring at times, but they included some good profs and student friends). I did not enjoy or particularly appreciate a couple of the psychology courses and their multitude of True/False or multiple-choice test questions. The only "C" I received at Valpo was in one of those psychology courses. I simply couldn't get on the same wavelength with that particular prof, and it didn't seem to make much difference to him. Maybe not a fair evaluation, but that's the way I felt. Otherwise, there were so many great professors and university people with whom I was involved and/or took courses from, that in all fairness I will simply list them by name. I am grateful to Dean Bauer (history, and my majors advisor), and Professors Gahl, Schaeffer, Rickels, Hoffman (history and government), Friedrich, Umbach, Essig, Tuttle (English), the Ruprechts (V.P. and his wife, and good friends all the way out to California Lutheran University in Thousand Oaks), Doering (Public Relations), Krekeler, Kuster, Bloom (biology), Meyer, Buls, Kowitz (geography/geology), Vikner, Waldschmidt (education), Schoenbohm (choir... I didn't sing – I just fully appreciated!), Koenker, Koepke, Bertram (religion and philosophy), and, of course, John Strietelmeier (geography/geology... with whom I became good friends in later years after Valpo). And leading this cast of inspiring, Christ-centered people was the president, Dr. O.P. Kretzmann, affectionately known as "O.P." He was a marvelous orator, preacher, and spokesman for Lutheranism. One could spend much time and many lines describing O.P. That has been very well done already in *Flame of Faith, Lamp of Learning: A History of Valparaiso University* (St. Louis: Concordia Publishing House, 2002) by the Rev. Dr. Richard Baepler, the son of my seminary president at Concordia, Springfield in 1957-58.

- Special note – In addition to these profs whom I appreciated, were the two pastors at Immanual Lutheran Church in town who served the university those years. They were:
  o Dr. Armin Oldsen, former Lutheran Hour speaker, sociology prof, later my pastor at Lakewood in Cleveland, and whose sons I had as students at Cleveland Lutheran High from 1953-1957
  o Rev. Otto Toelke, my friend Dave's pastor in Cleveland before coming to Valpo, and a good friend in Ohio District when I was pastor in Solon, Ohio, and he was district president

~

While I was a student at Valpo, O.P. was always around on campus – meeting students, talking with colleagues, or just walking about and enjoying his university and its people. From time to time, just about every student somehow "ran into" him, and it was a wonderful and exhilarating experience! He was beloved by many! From a human point of view, O.P. made Valpo into a better school than it had been before – in the early years after Lutherans bought it in 1925. He set it on the good course it is now on! My best memory of O.P. was the special class in his office, once a week for senior students only. Only 25 members of the senior class were invited, including me (which surprised and delighted me, of course!). We met every Tuesday evening in his spacious office, which held 25 students quite adequately, if not always comfortably. Who cared? From behind his large desk (with piles of papers on top of it) he would begin each session with prayer, then go right into a reading or a long quote on a current religious subject, or something from a Christian apologetic writer. Sometimes we'd discuss the contents, and other times we'd just proceed to the next reading, which occasionally was a letter he had received that week concerning a theological or moral topic or issue. It was so stimulating and challenging! Often, he would just expound on anything that was on his mind (and he had an uncanny sense of what was on the minds and hearts of his students) and share with us in many edifying ways. We had chapel every morning, and after our freshman year we were free to attend or not. Well, when O.P. was scheduled to preach in chapel, the place was filled. He had that special charisma and special way of putting words together that attracted and sometimes mesmerized those who heard him. Many of his writings are a beautiful legacy he has left to us, especially his many back pages, a series entitled "The Pilgrim," of the university magazine *The Cresset* (edited at that time by John Strietelmeier), which came out monthly for many years, and continues with five issues a year to this day.

In that Tuesday evening class, O.P. first introduced me to the mind and writings of C.S. Lewis, for which I will be forever grateful! The only difference between an "A" and a "B" in his class was whether you did a thorough report on any one of a number of theological or religious writers. Almost needless to say, I chose C.S. Lewis and received my "A." But more than that, I grew spiritually from that experience and enjoyed it immensely! O.P. was a teacher in the best sense of the word! His insights, humorous stories, and commentaries (e.g., "Campus Commentary" publications for pastors for a number of years, which were priceless!), his solid biblical theology and remarkable sharing of wisdom are a continuing legacy which I treasure personally to this day. Years later, in 1970, he and I would establish a close and unique relationship when he spent six months in Thousand Oaks, California, where I was pastor at Redeemer Lutheran Church. He was a six-month visiting professor and lecturer at California Lutheran University. That time with O.P. is a story in itself, which I have added as a subsection at the end of this chapter.

My Valpo Years (1950-1953)

~

Now, back to my main reason for going to Valpo – I wanted to be a high school teacher! Looking at my mother's teaching career (and I knew she was an excellent teacher), I had early in my life decided that I would never become a teacher. I knew what it took to be a good one, and I realized what a tremendous amount of sacrifice it required and how little recognition one would receive, both financially and in society. Nevertheless, from my own limited teaching experience in the Navy and in my own maturing, I discovered that God was calling me to be a teacher. And so I followed! For the first couple of years at Valpo, I envisioned myself as a public high school teacher somewhere in the Midwest. However, toward the end of my junior year, one of my history profs, Dr. Rickels, asked me about teaching in a Lutheran high school. She had just come out of that experience in Chicago and suggested that I might give the idea some thought, even to the point of directing me to visit the Luther Institute in Chicago and meet Dr. Meyer, the principal. When I finally visited there in late spring of 1952, I was totally unimpressed by the gray, foreboding-looking, old-fashioned buildings, but I was completely sold on Lutheran high school teaching! Going to Chicago was also convenient for me because I was already "going with" a girl there who, along with her wonderful family, made many weekends away from Valpo very enjoyable!

One year later, in the spring of 1953, I did my student practice teaching at Hobart High School in Hobart, Indiana, about 12 miles from Valpo. Probably one reason I was chosen to practice teach there was I had a car (a wonderful but not always reliable 1928 Model A Ford coupe with a rumble seat!) and I could therefore drive to Hobart each day for a full morning of teaching. It was a terrific experience! My classroom was right next to the school office, so the principal was always nearby. The social studies and history teacher, who was supposed to be my "teaching mentor" and supervisor (whose classes I was to work with in the mornings), turned out to be a bit lazy, not very motivated, and very content to let me "take over" his two main classes in U.S. history. While I did this, he spent his time in the teacher's lounge, snoozing and smoking. However, I loved such an arrangement! I got so close to the students, and they to me, that those classes were a constant and rewarding joy to me! They used to tell me that they would wait with "bated breath" each morning (especially in wintertime) to make sure I arrived in my little Model A Ford! For my last time in each class at the end of the semester, each class threw a party with cake, ice cream, cookies, lots of cards, and many best wishes. The principal peeked in once to see what was going on and decided it wasn't really worth finding out (he was very strict and always very serious). Those kids at Hobart High School will always hold a special place in my heart in terms of my overall teaching experiences and my wonderful relationships with them! Public school teaching would have been just fine with me.

While my spring semester of 1953 was filled with classes and student teaching, I needed to consider where I might eventually teach after graduation. While I made up my mind before the end of the semester that I wanted to teach in a Lutheran high school, it remained to be seen if such a position was possible or available. Here my friendship with Dave Brueggemann in Cleveland became an even greater blessing. Dave had become a good friend and buddy of mine at Valpo, and during that time I even spent a couple of weekends with Dave and his family at his home in Rocky River. This continued even after he went into the U.S. Army (and Korea). I was invited to spend a few days in Cleveland with his parents during my senior year. In the spring of 1953, while concerning myself with classes and student teaching, I received a formal letter from Dr. E.F. Sagehorn, principal of Cleveland Lutheran High School, asking if I would be interested in a teaching position there. The teaching position was in history and social studies, ranging all the way from freshmen to seniors. Since I had already met Dr. Sagehorn a couple of times at Dave's house (his father, R.F. Brueggemann, was Chairman of the Board of Directors of Lutheran High), I suspect that my "in" to the teaching opportunity came from that association. At almost the same time, I was offered a similar teaching position at Hobart High School. In fact, the principal interviewed me for the position personally before he made the offer. Such an offer from him was unusual, since he had Valpo student teachers every year and had never offered any of them a position at Hobart High. This was possibly because no position was available at the time. Still, what a compliment to me and my teaching experience at Hobart High! However, I was ecstatic about the Cleveland Lutheran High offer and immediately accepted it! My goal for attending Valpo had been reached far beyond what I could have anticipated, and I truly felt led by God in the direction I was headed, even though I hadn't expected or considered Lutheran high school teaching when I began my studies at Valpo.

My Valpo Years (1950-1953)

~

Having said all this about Valpo, I also want to describe a bit about other facets of my life at Valpo in those years, besides the academics and my dormitory experiences. I didn't make a big "splash" on campus with involvement in a lot of activities and social doings, but I did make a number of wonderful friendships, some of which I treasure to this day through correspondence and personal contact in various parts of the country. Since I began school at Valpo half way through the 1949-1950 academic year, I didn't have to put up with a lot of the rather inane freshmen antics – hazing and high jinks which characterized college life in those years for freshman students. I wasn't interested in fraternities (although I was invited to several of them) because I considered them a bit unnecessary and mostly a way for freshmen and sophomores to get into the social scene more comfortably, as well as for other students to achieve some special status in the campus community. It was fine for them, and many of them were my friends and buddies while I was at Valpo. I focused on my studies as my first and most important priority, and participated in life on campus as best I could (intramural sports, music programs, campus functions, and special academic and social events and opportunities). I was active on campus as president of FTA (Future Teachers of America) and with Pi Gamma Mu (National Social Science Honor Society). I almost decided to play varsity baseball, but a couple baseball-playing buddies of mine discouraged me because of the time demanded in the spring, the away games, and the many rainout games that had to be made up near the end of the semester with finals and term papers coming due. It certainly would not have worked when I was doing my student teaching at Hobart High in the spring of 1953. Besides, I had summer semipro, Industrial League baseball back home with a lot of ex-high school and ex-college players whom I knew and with whom I had played before. I had a great time playing baseball those summers, in particular the two summers when I was also working during the day at a local brewery!

While at Valpo I did a certain amount of dating, but not very seriously since I usually had "something going" back home in Muskegon and then for a couple of years with a wonderful girl in Chicago (now a Lutheran pastor's wife). When I attended summer school in 1952, there was a lot of casual dating and many informal social opportunities. That summer was also a great experience for me in another way. Ten last-year sem students from our seminary in St. Louis were enrolled for the summer session at Valpo. They had tremendous credentials as students and as future pastors in our Church. They turned out to be some of the greatest guys I could have wanted for friends and fellow students. All of them were single (the sem didn't allow married students in those days) and they discovered that a coed school like Valpo was just about the best thing in all of Lutheranism! They were constantly organizing social events, outings, Sunday afternoon picnics, coed softball games, and anything else to get them together with the girls. Since they had spent most of their academic years in one of our pre-seminary schools, they had never been to a school that included girls, especially ones in halter tops and shorts on hot days! They couldn't believe their good luck! One of the guys (John Saleska) met his future wife that summer, and he continued on in the ministry and ended up teaching at one of our seminaries years later.

As great as that social and community aspect was in my years at Valpo, there was something else that stands out as being far more important – the top-flight, Christian professors in my various academic disciplines. Almost without exception, they were academically and intellectually strong; they were up-to-date in their fields of discipline; they imparted their knowledge and wisdom in many theoretical and practical ways; they exhibited powerful moral, spiritual, and Christian attitudes and bearing in their presentations as teachers, counselors, and personalities; and they were, in almost all instances, wonderful examples of Christian virtues and ideals. I must put it this way: I was more influenced, more impacted, and more Christ-directed in my walk of faith by the staff and professors of Valpo than by any other element. It was not, per se, the religion faculty, or the various religious colonies on campus, or the worshiping community which affected and influenced and directed me spiritually the most those years. It was the day-to-day, class-to-class, professor-to-student Christian example and dependence on Christ that inspired and motivated and serviced me the most in my growing belief and commitment to serve Christ as a Christian teacher. For *that* I am eternally and joyfully grateful to Valpo and to our gracious God, Who gives us life, breath, and eternal life through His Son, our Lord Jesus Christ!

~

My Six Months with O.P. Kretzmann

Earlier in this chapter, I devoted quite a bit of space to the president of Valparaiso University when I was a student there, Dr. O.P. Kretzmann. When using the name "Kretzmann," one must remember to use their first two initials, since a number of Kretzmann boys from New York became well-known in Lutheran circles, i.e., A.R., J.P., and some others. In the early 1930s, O.P. became president of Valpo. During his long presidency, he really put Valpo "on the map" academically, theologically, and Lutheran-wise. He was probably at the height of his presidency through the years that I was a student (1950-53) and for many more years after that – a slightly biased comment. As near as I can recall, by the mid to late 60s, his health was becoming a serious problem with deteriorating eyesight and being quite overweight (he was a big man to begin with). Very early in 1970, he took a six-month leave from Valpo to be visiting professor and guest lecturer at California Lutheran University ("College" at the time) in Thousand Oaks, California. I think he was no longer active as president of Valpo, but he was very much a presence there, as well as being in high demand as a writer, speaker, and preacher. Thus began what I will call "My Six Months with O.P. Kretzmann."

In January, 1970, I had been pastor of Redeemer Lutheran Church in Thousand Oaks for almost two years. "T.O." (as Thousand Oaks is often called) was a growing community, as was the congregation. Located about 45 miles north of Los Angeles and 30 miles south of Santa Barbara, it was well known as the "Valley of the Pilots," since so many commercial airline pilots had spotted Conejo Valley, including T.O., and decided it was an ideal place to live. T.O. was also known for its 12-year-old Lutheran college, located on more than 500 acres of land. It was also the home of the six-week summer training camp of the Dallas Cowboys professional football team and its famous Christian coach, Tom Landry. (I can attest to his humble, active faith.) O.P. came to Cal Lutheran in January and stayed through to the end of the academic year in June, 1970. While I looked forward to seeing him again (since I knew him fairly well from contact on campus and being in his special course for seniors), I wasn't sure how his presence would impact my busy ministry in T.O. and increasing involvement at Cal Lutheran. However, I also realized that I would, in a sense, be his pastor while he was in the area and part of my "diocese." Since I didn't know exactly when he would arrive in town, I waited to hear about his arrival. My first contact with him was a difficult, but important one. One afternoon in the middle of January, I was called to the local hospital (where my wife worked as a pediatric nurse), Los Robles Regional Medical Center. The hospital chaplain was a good friend of mine and whenever a call came for a Lutheran pastor, he would usually call me first because he knew I'd come as quickly as possible (our training at the sem in pastoral care had been good). I was told there was a Mrs. Kretzmann in the hospital. When I arrived and found her room and walked in, I was met with an all-too-familiar scene for a pastor: a spouse sitting at the bedside of their loved one, looking somewhat forlorn, concerned, and lonely. In this case, the reason was simple, for O.P.'s wife, Florence, or Flo, had been hospitalized because of an ongoing health condition, a recurring issue that she was again getting treatment for. O.P. was just sitting there like any loving, caring husband – no different from any other mortal human being facing a crisis. His recognition of me, the warmth of his greeting, and his simple delight in my presence made me feel right at home in that situation. We talked, shared, and prayed together that afternoon in humble submission to our Lord and in total dependence on His grace and love! What amazed me at the time was that neither of us seemed to feel uncomfortable or ill at ease in the kind of "reversal of roles." That is part of the glory and joy of the Lutheran ministry and pastorate: we are all saints and servants in the Lord!

At this point, let me say a few things about Flo. I met and was acquainted with her only through our special senior class with O.P. and our special time at their home before we left for Christmas vacation. That was a most unique and beautiful experience that both she and O.P. gave 25 students on a marvelous evening in December, 1952. Because of their coming to Cal Lutheran and Thousand Oaks, I got to know and appreciate Flo in some ways that many people in Valparaiso never experienced. Her six months in T.O. was one of the best periods of her life with O.P., as she told me some months later before leaving. And I think there were a couple good reasons for her feeling that way. First of all, she was "free" of Valpo. For one so sensitive and so caught up in O.P.'s role as president, this "freedom" was important to her. It's not that she wasn't a wonderful university president's wife and hostess, but it was that she didn't have to be that for six months in California! Secondly, when she came to T.O., she renewed a very good friendship with someone from her own past in

Valparaiso – Olga Barth. Olga was the choir director for my congregation at Redeemer and was an excellent public school teacher. (I can fully attest to that through one of our son's time as her student in the 2nd grade in a nearby school.) When living in Valparaiso, Olga had been a teacher at Immanuel Lutheran School. There were times, Flo told me, when she and Olga would go shopping, or go into town to the local mall, or just walk around in T.O. and no one would recognize her! She really enjoyed that anonymity! Other than that, it must have been a difficult and lonely year for Flo, and I really found myself being as much a pastor to her as I could under the circumstances. I really liked her very much! I would often go their home in T.O. and she always seemed happy to see me and spend a little time together, even when O.P. was anxious to "get going." One morning I went over to their home to pick up O.P. for some kind of meeting or conference, and Flo ushered me into his "study," which was the front dining room! There O.P. sat at a typewriter, working furiously. "Just a minute, Jim, and I'll be ready as soon as I finish this article which is due tomorrow back at Valpo!" But that wasn't what fascinated me. On top of the small table he was typing on were overwhelming piles of papers, documents, letters, and writings. I could hardly see his typewriter! On the floor around him was an even larger collection of such piles of papers! As I looked at the seeming chaos, he pulled a sheet of paper from one of the piles and announced proudly, "I've found it!" And then he continued typing. When he was through a few minutes later, he handed it to me and said, "Read it and tell me what you think of it." Of course, it was very, very good, and I told him so. He replied with a bit of nostalgia, "I miss my secretary!" Flo just stood there smiling.

    Now, back to O.P. That six months with him was one of the most enjoyable, inspiring, and celebrated times of my ministry. Since he couldn't drive himself anymore because of his deteriorating eyesight, I had the privilege of being his "driver" on many occasions. Not only that, but I also became what I referred to as his "seeing eye dog" for all the places where we went. We went to speaking engagements, pastoral conferences, lectures on various campuses, presentations to churches, and to whatever other places he was asked to be present. Of course, I didn't do all the driving, since Flo did a lot of it. However, I would usually drive when it involved LCMS circuit conferences or Southern California District conferences, e.g., at Arrowhead Lutheran Camp in the San Bernardino Mountains. He loved being "with the guys" of the LCMS, and probably was at his best on those occasions. When I would drive him along the coast between Ventura and Santa Barbara, he would often rhapsodize, "Oh, look at those beautiful mountains! Look at that gorgeous ocean! I can't get over the beauty out here along the Pacific coast!" Such times as those, along with many great conversations, caused me to dub myself his "happy chauffeur!" Because of his growing infirmities, he sometimes needed a little extra help. I accepted it as part of my personal role for a man whom I loved and admired and felt for in his physically uncomfortable state. I was happy and privileged to serve him, Flo, Valpo, and our Church in any way I could. I loved the man! Next to my favorite prof at Valpo, John Strietelmeier, O.P. was the one I admired and appreciated the most.

Concerning his time in Thousand Oaks and Cal Lutheran, I suspect that he didn't say much about it when he got back to Valpo. I'm sure those months were not always pleasant, memorable, or comfortable for him, especially in light of his health and so much discomfort. Because of his increasing weight, he could not stand for any real length of time. So when I had him at Redeemer to preach for me several times, he sat in a large, comfortable chair in the middle of the chancel with a microphone and held forth! My congregation loved him!

Cal Lutheran also loved him and made much use of him. They were only disappointed when he sometimes showed up late for a presentation (but not when I was driving!), or when they felt he was pushing too much for Cal Lutheran to be a "Valpo on the West Coast." He really believed, as I did at the time, that there could be an accommodation to bring Cal Lutheran and the LCMS into a workable relationship. Such an arrangement would do two things: express in theological and practical ways that we Lutherans could operate together at such a level; and, it would be much better financial stewardship than for the LCMS to build a whole new system and campus in Irvine, California (where Concordia University, Irvine now exists). However, almost needless to say, this never went anywhere because of LCMS authorities in St. Louis. In spite of that, O.P. was very popular on campus and was always a "hit" wherever he went and whenever he spoke. His presence also gave more authenticity and creditability to my role at Cal Lutheran as a representative of the LCMS in an open and evangelical way. This was best expressed in 1985 when I was given the California Lutheran University Distinguished Service Award.

~

All in all, the personal experience of being with O.P. for that six months in 1970 is part of my special memories of 40 wonderful years of ministry: a Lutheran high school teacher in Cleveland for four years and a pastor in our Church for 35 years. So I say, "Thank you, God! Thank you, O.P.! Thank you, Valpo!"

Chapter 5

My Life as a High School Teacher and Coach

From 1953-1957, I taught all four grades at Cleveland Lutheran High School on Prospect Avenue, near downtown Cleveland. At that time, there was only one Lutheran high school with more than 500 students. Today, there are two such high schools in Cleveland: Lutheran High East and Lutheran High West. Interestingly, or maybe prophetically, Cleveland Lutheran High School began its first classes on my birthday, September 7th. The year was 1948, and at that time I was on duty in the Mediterranean Sea aboard the USS Huntington, and totally unaware of how that momentous occasion in Cleveland Lutheran history would intersect my life some years later.

During my first year of teaching, in early 1954, I experienced God's protection in a very traumatic way.

~

Train Story

My first year of teaching included an event outside of my teaching experience. It was an event which almost cost the lives of three young men, including me. It happened back in Michigan when I came home during the school semester break in February 1954. The reason for returning was to be best man at the wedding of one of my best friends, Harland Reister. He was a very successful farmer in the Sparta/Conklin area east of Muskegon, near Grand Rapids. We met years before through our church youth program called Walther League, named after the first president of the Missouri Synod. I became very good friends with Harland and his wonderful farming family, making many visits to their farm. One day, I even tried to drive a tractor. When I pressed the wrong pedal to turn, I ran straight into an apple tree. So much for my becoming a farmer!

On the Saturday evening of the wedding, Harland, his 12-year-old brother Herbert, and I started the drive to Jan's church in Nunica, several miles away. Perhaps Snoopy would begin this story, "'Twas a dark and stormy night." It wasn't really stormy, but it was dark, wintertime, with some snow, and icy, slushy roads. The three of us sat in the front seat of my 1950 Mercury which I was driving, with Harland's brother in the middle holding the wedding cake. As we drove in the light snow down that country road, we approached a crossroad with a railroad crossing coming right after that. The railroad track with trees at both sides came at a slight angle behind me and to my left. When I got to the intersection, I looked to my left and saw a light some distance away which I assumed was another car. So I continued on, preparing to cross the tracks. As I crossed the intersection and approached the railroad crossing, I saw the old-fashioned railroad crossing sign on the right-hand side of the road. They had no crossing lights in those days. Getting close to the tracks and trying to see the road more clearly, I suddenly heard Harland's voice cry out, "Jim, the train!" A bit to my left, I saw the huge engine of the train bearing down at high speed. I had a split second to decide whether to beat it across the tracks, or try to stop on the slippery road. I put on the brakes as Harland yelled, "Head for the signpost." I quickly turned toward the sign which had a ditch behind it. The car began sliding toward the speeding train. I waited ever so briefly for the terrible impact. My front wheels caught the gravel on the side of the road and turned the car sideways. With no time to think, I waited for the inevitable, horrible impact. As the train roared on with its whistle screaming in the night air, the car, so close to the train, suddenly came to a stop with a slight jolt. Sitting there as the train thundered by for those few seconds, I remember praying that there wouldn't be something protruding outside the train that would hit the car. After the train had gone by, I rested my head on the steering wheel and simply said, "Jesus, oh Jesus!" We each got out of the car to examine how it might have stopped sliding so suddenly. We figured that the front wheels catching the gravel on the side of the road caused the car to turn sideways. As the car slid sideways toward the train, the weight of the car shifted to the left rear tire, which made a path through the icy slush on the pavement. Sliding sideways the right rear tire followed straight behind the sideways path to get a grip on the road and bring the car to a stop. There we were – hearts beating wildly – and the only damage was a dent in the side of the wedding cake. That's the way we figured it happened. I believe there was another dimension involved. Fifty years later, Nancy and I attended the wedding anniversary for Harland and Janice. Each of us spoke a few words, and then Harland's brother said something about that night and the train. After he told the story, his sister spoke up and said, "You must have had a lot of angels around you that night!" to which I quickly quipped, "Yes, there were feathers all over the place!" All three of us realized that God had something more in mind for us in this world when He saved our lives that dark, snowy night.

~

During my first two years of teaching, I taught Freshman Social Studies, along with World History (sophomore year) and American Problems (senior year). During my third and fourth years of teaching, I taught only U.S. History (junior year) and Senior American Problems. Those were the two levels of teaching that I enjoyed the most, and received the most response from students, especially the Senior American Problems classes, which were always full! During those four years, I had just about every one of the students in at least one of my classes, and even the ones I didn't have in class (like Nancy Precker!) I knew. As in most Lutheran schools at any level, the faculty was involved in many of the extracurricular activities of the school. Late in my second year of teaching, I expressed an interest in the athletic program, so my third and fourth years also found me as Assistant Coach in football and Head Coach of the baseball team. Another area of extracurricular activity was the informal, impromptu, and personal counseling time with students, which ultimately became a part of my larger decision toward the pastoral ministry of our church. More about that later. Suffice it to say, those four years of teaching were monumental and defining years for me, and they forever characterized the rest of my life of service to the Lord and His people. When I was honored to be the preacher at the 50th Anniversary Worship Service of the Cleveland Lutheran High School Association at "Old" Trinity Lutheran in Cleveland, in August of 1998, I opened my sermon with the indication that I had recently retired from the active pastoral ministry after serving four congregations in New York, Ohio, and California during the previous 35 years. Then I paused, and with all the sincerity of my being, I said:

> But four congregations is not correct. My first "congregation" was a group of 400-500 students at Cleveland Lutheran High School from 1953 to 1957 who meant as much to me as any congregation that I served as pastor! That's why I am here today: to meet, to share, and to speak to my first "congregation," so many of whom are present today. A unique and rare privilege! Believe me, every trip through one of the yearbooks of those years is a journey of remembrance, joy, nostalgia, and many smiles, plus a few tears.

That particular occasion also gave me the opportunity to pay honor to Mr. R.F. Brueggemann (who was not mentioned in any of the 50th Anniversary materials and remembrances), who almost single-handedly kept Lutheran High financially and emotionally afloat during those critical early years. I really enjoyed honoring him!

So what started me on this marvelous and defining time of my life as a Lutheran high school teacher? Here I cannot claim any particular "revelation" or sudden "inspiration." Actually, God really does act "in a mysterious way His wonders to perform" (Cowper, "God Moves in a Mysterious Way," *Lutheran Service Book* (St. Louis: Concordia Publishing House, 2006), 765, 1), and I am evidence of that. While I was still in the U.S. Navy in the late 1940s, I needed to make some very important decisions about my life in the years to come. I had joined the Navy in the summer of 1945, shortly before the atom bombs on Hiroshima and Nagasaki, and the cessation of war on August 14th, 1945. Before I joined the Navy, I had been educated and trained as an Apprenticed Printer through the Vocational Training School at Muskegon High School, a full two-year program. As I indicated in my pages on my Navy career, I was good at my job and was promised that job when I returned from my Navy service. Once I was in the Navy and discovered that I could not pursue my printing career there, I decided to serve as a Hospital Corpsman, in the medical branch of the Navy and Marines. It was in this capacity that I flourished and did so well that I received a peacetime commendation for my work and service as a medical Hospital Corpsman aboard ship. As I approached my fourth year in the Navy, and realized that I did not want to continue in the military service (as worthwhile as it had been), I had to start making some decisions about my life ahead. I realized that I did not want to go back home and resume my job in the professional printing business. To me, that whole scenario seemed boring and no longer interesting to me. But mostly, I was restless to do something else and go somewhere else.

As I prayed and considered various ideas, thoughts, and directions for my life ahead, I was suddenly cast into a "teaching" situation. I was told that I was to teach a class of Marines about potential battlefield procedures and medical attention. I was scared! Here I was, a Navy guy who was responsible for teaching Marines how to administer not only first aid but also basic medical help on the field of battle. That teaching experience, which lasted for almost the whole last year of my military service in the Navy and Marines, gave me such a "rush" and such a feeling of giving someone something worthwhile, that I was "hooked!" I wanted to teach! When I mentioned this to my mom the next time I was home on leave, she just about fainted! I knew from her experiences as a teacher the time and effort and long hours involved in being a good teacher (which she certainly was!). And I remembered how I had felt – and said a number of times in previous years – that the one thing I would *never* be is a teacher! After her initial surprise, she was very happy and supportive, and I was on my way.

The first problem I had to deal with was my grades and records in high school. I had taken general prep courses, not college prep courses. Therefore, it could have been a question about my even getting into college after my time in the Navy, without a lot of extra pre-college courses. Fortunately, the G.I. Bill allowed me (as well as millions of other GIs) to enter colleges and universities without all the proper prerequisites. During the last few months of my Navy career, I applied to a number of colleges and universities for entrance (e.g., Central Michigan, where my mom attended, Michigan State, and others in Michigan). However, the place I really wanted to attend was our own church's independent, forward-looking, and academically strong university, Valparaiso University in Valparaiso, Indiana, 150 miles south of my home in Muskegon, Michigan. When I received word that I had been accepted at Valpo, I was ecstatic and anxious to get out of the Navy and begin school. Of course, it wasn't quite that simple. I had extended my time in the Navy to a full four years after my initial enlistment in the summer of 1945, meaning that I would not be released until the middle of September, 1949. Beginning at Valpo at that time would have been a bit difficult, both because I would be a couple of weeks behind my class at the beginning, and because I needed to "bone up" a bit before starting school, since I had been away from academics for more than four years. Thus, I began my college career at Valpo on February 1st, 1950, with the intent to graduate with my class in three and a half years, which I did! (Please see my chapter entitled, "My Valpo Years.")

During my last two years at Valpo, my desire to teach high school was intensified, and I hoped to teach in a public school system somewhere in the midwest. To this end, I did my practice teaching in a large high school in Hobart, Indiana, about ten miles from Valpo, during the Spring Semester of

1953 (February to June). That experience alone convinced me that I really did want to teach high school! Actually, the experience in Hobart turned out to be even more extensive and thorough than expected, which worked to my benefit. The U.S. History teacher, whose class I was to be involved with, was a former basketball player at Valpo, but not a particularly good teacher, and just a bit lazy. When he discovered very quickly how "gung ho" I was to teach, he basically "gave up" his two morning classes in U.S. History and gave them over to me. He spent that time in the teacher's lounge, smoking and taking it easy. He was supposed to supervise me, but really paid little attention to me or the classes and was very happy that I "took over" his classes. As it turned out, so were the students! The kids were just great with me, and it was one of the truly wonderful experiences of my life in teaching! In fact, it went so well that the principal, at the end of the semester, offered me a position to teach at Hobart High School the following year. I was told later that this was very unusual. On my last day of teaching my two classes in Hobart, the kids "threw a party" in each class on my behalf, which was a great compliment to me, but a surprise to the staff and administration. It apparently had never happened before. The kids and I enjoyed those special moments, even when the principal peered in once or twice to see what was going on! I would have really enjoyed teaching at Hobart (I loved the kids there!), but something else happened in my preparations to teach high school. During that junior year at Valpo, as I contemplated my teaching future, one of my history professors, Dr. Rickles, a very bright woman teacher, had rather casually asked me one day if I had ever given any thought to teaching in a Lutheran high school. Since I didn't even know there were such "things," I answered her in that way. Well, she suggested that I ought to look into it, because she thought it might be something I would appreciate and enjoy in a special way. She even gave me the name and place of the Lutheran high school in Chicago, where she had previously taught, and suggested that I visit there. Since I rather regularly went to Chicago for some "romantic reasons," I did visit Luther Institute (as it was called then), met the principal, and toured the campus. While I was not impressed with the rather dreary, gray-looking campus, I was very impressed with the idea of teaching in a Lutheran high school somewhere. That pretty much ruled out teaching in Hobart, even though the offer there was financially more than anything I would receive from a Lutheran high school. I owe a great debt of gratitude to Dr.

Rickles and her advice. It helped me make the decision to teach in a Lutheran high school!

During this time, something else was happening to influence my decision to teach in a Lutheran high school. While at Valpo, I had become a very good friend of Dave Brueggemann, from Rocky River, Ohio, just west of Cleveland. We had become such good friends that I spent some of my college vacation days with Dave and his family in Rocky River. It was during one of these times that I not only met and stayed with his parents, but also came to realize that his father was Chairman of the Board of Directors of Cleveland Lutheran High School, and a very close friend of the principal, Dr. E.F. Sagehorn, a pioneer in Lutheran education in this country. While I was doing my practice teaching in the spring of 1953, I received a letter and an offer to teach at Cleveland Lutheran High School for the coming academic year of 1953-54. This astounded and amazed me, but I was ecstatic and totally committed. I quickly signed an agreement contract, in spite of the better financial offer from Hobart High School. I began preparing myself for teaching in Cleveland.

Thanks to my connection with Dave and his family, I found myself quickly accepted into the Lutheran High community and all that it encompassed, including the supporting congregations of the Cleveland area. To this day, Dave and his wife, Lil, remain as two of my most favorite people and friends. Actually, I was with Dave in that first year at Lutheran High when he met Lil at a Walther League get-together. Later, I was one of his groomsmen at his wedding in historic Zion Lutheran Church on East 30th in Cleveland, just two blocks from the high school's location. Before that time, Dave had spent a couple of years in the Army, mostly in Japan, but his family always made me feel like one of them. When he came back from the Army, I was in my first teaching year at Cleveland Lutheran High School. What a magnificent "coincidence!"

The first and maybe most important thing I want to say about teaching, before I detail some of my experience, is this: It takes at least three or four years of teaching to become a good teacher, even when you are trying hard! At least that was true for me, and I've found agreement among many of my teaching colleagues over the years on that realization. By that, I don't mean that I don't think I was a pretty good teacher the first couple of years at Cleveland Lutheran High, but it does mean that I learned a lot and matured so much as a person and as a teacher, that I will forever be grateful to Cleveland Lutheran High for those four years of teaching, coaching, maturing, and growing spiritually. Those four years at Cleveland Lutheran High were as much defining years for me as had been my four years in the Navy previously. I value those years as some of the most beautiful years of my life. Some of the greatest and most wonderful people in my life I met and associated with during those four years in Cleveland!

Without going into too many details, let me sketch briefly those years in Cleveland. During those four years, I lived in four different places. The first year I rented a room on the West Side in Lakewood from a widow, Mrs. Reinker. She was glad to have me around, most especially during the week that Cleveland was snowed-in, and the city and suburbs were almost totally paralyzed. I loved being home those days in early 1954, in order to watch the Army-McCarthy Hearings from Washington, and witness the self-destruction of Sen. Joe McCarthy, whose type was as dangerous to democracy as many of the forms of Communism he sought to fight with his undemocratic ways. At times, I was amused and bemused with Mrs. Reinker and her two widowed friends, as they came over often and did much together. Their chatter and good fun together, along with some of their eccentricities, made for some interesting moments for me as an observer. I liked them, but I thought them a bit strange at times, and quite amusing! My second-year landlady, Mrs. Pine, also a widow, was much quieter and communicated very little, but she was a nice woman. She had an interesting habit or routine once a week when Liberace was on TV for his program. She would completely darken the room and sit there watching him, talking to him as if he were right there personally in the room with her. And she always called him, "Lee," not Liberace!

My third year I spent renting a room on the East Side in Euclid, from one of my favorite teaching colleagues, Bud DeWitt, his wife Doris, and their three small boys. That was a good year because I ate regular, balanced meals, and I was part of a most delightful Christian family. My favorite of the boys was the youngest one, four-year-old Billy. He loved to sit on my bed in my little bedroom and listen to my classical music records and chatter away about anything, just to be with me. My fourth place in Cleveland, in my fourth year, was an upstairs apartment in East Cleveland with my new bride, Betty. It was a bit rickety, with a long stairway outside leading up to our apartment that was downright dangerous on rainy days or in the icy winter. The whole apartment sloped decidedly westward. I would place a marble on the floor in the bedroom at one end of the apartment and it would roll with increasing velocity down the hallway, across the kitchen floor, and go banging into the large closet/attic area on the other end of the apartment! Such was our entertainment at times.

While living on the West Side the first two years, I attended St. Paul's Lutheran Church in Lakewood, where the pastor was Dr. Armin Oldsen, my pastor in Valpo during my first two years of college. He had just finished a brief stint as *The Lutheran Hour* speaker in St. Louis. He felt harried and intimidated by our synod's special kind of "censorship" and it finally "got to him," so he decided to return to the parish ministry. During my four years at Lutheran High, I had two of his sons as my students, so I got to know him even better and liked him very much. He was a terrific pulpit preacher and the best after-dinner banquet speaker I have ever heard.

During my third and fourth years, in Euclid on the East Side, I went to Shorehaven Lutheran and my pastor was Rev. E.C. Abendroth, one of the sweetest, kindest, and most Christ-like men I have ever met, with a wife to match! One of my favorite students (yes, like every teacher, I had some "favorites") those years at Lutheran High was his daughter, Dorcas. She was one of those who first suggested that I go to Camp Pioneer the summer of 1955 as a Camp Counselor. And it was at Camp Pioneer that I met Betty! And it was at Camp Pioneer that the first small, almost unnoticed feelings about the pastoral ministry occurred, somewhat due to my opportunities to lead worship and "preach" in the camp's "Chapel in the Woods." Because I had students from all over the Cleveland area, I made it a point to visit often many of the churches they came from, and also to get to know their pastors better, many of whom preached at our school's chapel services during the school year. I wound up teaching a Sunday morning Bible class at one of these churches during my third year in Cleveland. During my fourth year of teaching, when I began giving serious thought to the pastoral ministry, I taught the 8th-grade Confirmation class of 35 kids for Pastor Abendroth on Saturday mornings, as well as the Sunday morning Sunday School class of mostly the same kids. It was good training and preparation for me, but I would have done just about anything for Pastor Abendroth!

One of the most amazing and impacting educators in our church in those years was my principal, Dr. E.F. Sagehorn, whom we lovingly called, "Sage," but seldom to his face! But sage he was. He almost literally "made" Lutheran High happen in Cleveland, and I honored and respected him immensely, both as an educator and as a person of Christ. However, as one of his young teachers, we had our "moments." One of the first of these "moments" came early in my first year of teaching. Because I was already well-acquainted with Dave Brueggemann's parents, it was quite natural for me to be invited over to their home for supper from time to time, even though Dave was off in the Army. About two months into my teaching career, I was invited over. And of course I showed up very hungry, as usual. Also invited were Dr. E.F. Sagehorn, and his lovely wife. No problem – good food and good company. Dave's mother is one of those "sweethearts" of the world whom everyone loves, and I loved her too (she turned 100 in 1999!). I totally admired, respected, and liked Dave's father, but didn't always agree with him in certain areas. About halfway through this marvelous meal, with a wonderful conversation going on, Dave's father began making a number of political and philosophical comments which I didn't entirely accept or agree with. This was the "I like Ike" era, and ex-President Truman was probably at the lowest point of his popularity, following the Korean War. Time and retrospect would change a lot of that feeling about Truman, one of my favorite people in our history. Anyway, I found myself disagreeing with some of the things Dave's dad was saying, and I finally could keep my silence no longer. I spoke up very clearly in disagreement. Then ensued a wonderful, lively, and stimulating conversation, mostly between Dave's dad and me. During this time, I looked over at my principal a couple of times (he wasn't saying anything). The first time I looked at him, he just blanched when I began to disagree. From then on, he just looked apprehensive as I continued vigorously with Dave's dad. The look on my principal's face said: *This is the Chairman of the Board of Directors of the high school with enough authority to make or break the school and you are disagreeing with him on politics? Are you crazy?* But I knew something about Dave's dad that maybe my principal didn't know: R.F. Brueggemann was one of those kind of men with whom you could disagree, and he would listen carefully. As long as you had good arguments and an honest approach and feeling, he accepted you and lovingly respected you. I admired the man greatly and deeply honor his memory to this day!

One of the other incidents I had with my principal involved a very professional situation. I had a totally marvelous group of senior students in my first period American Problems class. From the very beginning, we had a special relationship, and it really encouraged my "first-year" teaching spirits. However, one morning, completely unannounced, Dr. Sagehorn "slipped" into the last row of my class from a side door entrance, and stayed there the whole period. This upset me a bit, since I was operating under the unwritten rule or maxim that a classroom is a teacher's "ship," and that he/she is the "captain" of it. In light of this, I was surprised that anyone, even the principal, would "come aboard" without the captain's permission. Of course, I became a little tense, although I did have a good lesson plan ready and it went well. Along with me, the students tensed up, too. But then they rallied to my cause and became the most ideal class, and were perfectly great! I could have kissed every one of them! The next day, I made an appointment with Dr. Sagehorn and had a brief meeting with him. I simply said to him, "Please, I prefer that you not visit my class unannounced and unexpectedly. I'm sure you can appreciate that this is a disruption to me and especially the students. You are always welcome into any one of my classrooms at any time, and we would all be honored. But you do owe me the privilege of advance notice." He listened and accepted my statement, and even apologized to me. He indicated that probably wasn't the best way to handle the situation. But he also indicated to me how very much he wanted me to be a good and successful teacher, and that he had been very impressed with my class and the way the students were learning. That was good enough for me! And I told the students that the next morning! However, from that time on, he never came into one of my classes unannounced, nor did he ever challenge any of my teaching methods or abilities, even if some of them were a bit questionable! I loved him and deeply appreciated his professionalism. Later, in those first two years of teaching, I would have occasion to "sit down" with him again in his office, but these were less serious and even a bit humorous, since they had to do with my "romantic escapades" (as he viewed them) before I met Betty in the summer of 1955, between my 2nd and 3rd years of teaching. All in all, however, we got along very well, even though I did challenge him later on about another more important issue than the women in my life.

That challenge occurred in my fourth year of teaching, the 1956-57 school year. Every morning we had chapel at Cleveland Lutheran, with more than 500 students gathered for worship in the auditorium. Along with my fellow faculty members, I listened to some very good and some not-so-good chapel sermons and devotions by faculty members and Cleveland area preachers. The faculty members had been trained in one of our Concordia teaching colleges, and were thus "qualified" to conduct a Lutheran school worship service. Some of us who had not been "Concordia trained" and were not allowed to lead worship began to question this exclusiveness. We made known our feelings and thoughts on this matter to Dr. Sagehorn. Primary as my ally in this "battle" was my good friend and the finest teaching colleague I ever had, Julius "Ju-Ju" Lorko, also a Valpo graduate. After a number of entreaties to let some of the non-Concordia faculty members conduct worship services if they so desired and felt competent enough to do so, our principal gave us permission with some reluctance. Well, it worked out very well and we all seemed to benefit from this added dimension to our chapel services.

For me, this experience had a special and extra benefit. When I prepared to give my first chapel devotion, I worked on it thoroughly and came up with what I thought was a good "sermon-devotion." I typed it up perfectly and *read* it expertly at chapel. Since I had a Senior American Problems class right after chapel, I had indicated to them that I was "preaching," and that I wanted an evaluation from them after my first attempt. They were all very positive about the *content* of my "sermon," but they were very clear about the fact that they didn't like my delivery. I had *read* the "sermon," word for word, with very little eye contact with my audience. I didn't engage my audience with my thoughts, feelings, and words very well, and they let me know this! Wow! What a lesson! The next time I "preached," I used no notes and no manuscript, kept eye contact, and expressed myself with more feeling. When I came back to my class after that chapel service, my class greeted me with applause! And they let me know why they were applauding: my delivery with no manuscript and no word-by-word reading. From that time on, I would never go into a sermon without completely knowing it and nearly memorizing it word for word. And what a freedom that gives to the preacher, when he comes before his people on

Sunday or other worship occasions! Right now, well into my retirement from the formal and active pastoral ministry, I believe that I am a better preacher than I have ever been, and the lessons I have learned and am still learning are the reasons for that!

Before getting to the favorite aspect of teaching, my students, I must mention a couple more names. At school, the custodians were Rudy and "Ma" Mix. He was quiet and much smaller than Ma. Ma Mix was built like a combination of a football linebacker and a beer stein-carrying waitress at the Hofbräuhaus in Munich! And she used her size and voice to intimidate everyone! But something else even more important about her: She loved everyone, especially the kids, and we all loved her in a crazy, wonderful way. She also had a very soft heart for kids in need – even supplying one boy in her church with a new suit (which his family couldn't afford) for his Confirmation. That boy went to Lutheran High and into the pastoral ministry of our Church. Ma Mix was something else, but most of all a true practitioner of her Christian faith.

The other name I'm going to mention is the name Puls. "Ma" and "Pa" Puls, as they were known to all of us, teachers and students alike, were into the Lutheran High movement from the very beginning, even though their two oldest sons were beyond high school age. They had three more younger sons, all of whom would attend Lutheran High, all of whom I had as students, and all bright, good kids. The Puls' opened up their home to all of their children's friends for parties, singing, and other fun stuff, with Ma Puls banging away on the piano in what I would simply call their "high school romper room!" Some of the graduation parties were "controlled wild" and great! I became quite close to them, and then became even closer after I met their oldest son, Art, and his wife, Gloria, just after he had been released from the Army in 1957. Art and I took an immediate liking to each other, especially when he said he was going to attend the seminary. Over the year we kept in touch (mostly through his folks), and when I made my decision to attend the seminary (I now had a wife, Betty, who like Gloria, was a nurse), we all four became very close friends. We shared much at the seminary, including each other's apartment when the other of us was out on vicarage. To this very day, I count Art as my closest friend in the pastoral ministry, and we have enjoyed our close relationship for many years out here in California, where we are now both retired. The best way I can describe my relationship with the Puls family over the years was summed up by Ma Puls one time: "Jim is one of my boys!"

Now, back to Lutheran High and my students. All during those four years, I had a very close rapport with the students, and they with me. Over several years together, there developed a special bond between teacher and student. It is a bond that cannot be easily explained, but it's there and it is what keeps good teachers teaching, even under difficult circumstances. In four years, I established many such bonds with many students, whether in my regular course classes, my very special homeroom kids, or with the football and baseball players. Over the years since then, I have encountered many of my former students, and every contact is very special and very meaningful to me. Being back in Cleveland in August of 1998 for the 50th anniversary of the high school was one of the real high points of my life in recent years, as I've indicated earlier. Those many students of mine, without any of us realizing it, were the making of me for my later pastoral ministry direction. I owe them a lot!

In my academic classes, I tended to enjoy the two higher levels the most – juniors and seniors – partly because I had almost all of them in U.S. History and then in American Problems, and partly because I seemed to relate a little better to the older teens. That may also have been God's way of preparing me for my future ministry with college students at Cornell University and Ithaca College in Ithaca, New York, and California Lutheran University in Thousand Oaks, California. My Senior American Problems classes were the most enjoyable and appreciated, probably because they were the most flexible and allowed the most creativity. Let me give some examples. Each school year I would hold a week-long court trial in my room in order to teach graphically about the judicial system in our form of government. I allowed the students to be creative in writing up a "trial story," in choosing the roles for the students, and taking students out of their boring study halls to be our juries. Of course, I was the judge (even using a black choir gown and raised platform and desk from which to run the trial – "Judge Judy" has nothing on me – I was "Judge Jim" in those days!). Another example: I had my students involved in community projects and volunteer work in Cleveland as part of the course requirements. One boy, considered almost a "lost cause" by some of the faculty and administration, turned out to be the Cleveland Lutheran High School "Volunteer of the Year" for his work with inner-city kids. Also, I conducted very popular "seminars" (using pastors and other experts) on love, engagement, marriage, and sex. And we got into some in-depth study and discussion of current events, politics of the day, and many other areas of concern. All in all, those were terrific classes, and the response of the kids many years later seems to verify that. We had a great time together!

Over the years, I've been asked once in a while if I ever "fell" for any of my female students or felt romantic about any of them. Of course, there were some terrific girls in my classes, but I never really desired to get romantic with any of them. Besides, I didn't believe teachers should get that way with students (especially high school students!), at least not while we were in school together. My usual answer to the question was, "I'm having too much fun with girls my own age to want to be involved with teenyboppers!"

Another great dimension of my teaching career was coaching. After my first two years of teaching and maturation, I was asked to be the assistant football coach and the head baseball coach. I was delighted and excited, and plunged into that aspect of my teaching career with enthusiasm and enjoyment. In football, I helped in whatever ways the head coach wanted, mostly helping with defense (where he and I didn't always agree, until I would literally show him by taking part with the team on the practice field). I usually wound up coaching the junior varsity team, which I preferred. That included driving the big bus to our games (which I wasn't licensed to do, but which I also did when we played varsity games out of town in Detroit and Fort Wayne). My junior varsity kids were super, and played their hearts out against bigger and better teams. And we often won, too! However, baseball was my primary coaching area and I loved it! For two years I coached a group of the most wonderful kids around. Our baseball program had not been going well for several years, so whatever I did would be an improvement. It wasn't easy. We had no field of our own, so all our games were "away." Every day for practice we had to carpool to the ball fields on the lakefront of Cleveland. But we did have fun, and we did learn, and we did become close! It went so well that after my fourth year a number of the boys from current and previous years asked me to be their coach in the very competitive Summer League in Cleveland in 1957. I started with them, but had to decline further coaching when I found out that I could do my Greek language requirement for the seminary that very summer in

Milwaukee. But it does say something about their regard for me as a coach and as a teacher and as a friend. That meant a lot to me!

So after all this, the question becomes: *Why did I stop my teaching career, which had been so rewarding up until that time?* And similarly: *Why did I decide to go into the parish pastoral ministry of our synod?* The only way I can adequately answer these questions is to go back to something I inferred earlier – counseling. During the last two years at Cleveland Lutheran, and particularly the last year, I found myself in the classroom and at the after-school "Snack Bar" with kids and all their questions, comments, thoughts, and wonderings about their faith and their spiritual, moral lives. For some reason, I had kind of made myself "available" almost every day at the Snack Bar at school, as well as in my room after school hours. I often spent hours with them in serious and sometimes almost critical conversation about what was happening to them spiritually, that had very little to do with my formal academic classes. My closest friend on the faculty, "Ju-Ju" Lorko, had the same experience and ultimately began his preparation for the pastoral ministry some years later. At some point during that fourth year at Cleveland Lutheran, this conclusion came to me: Since it now meant more to me to deal with these kids on these moral, spiritual, and theological levels than on just academic levels, maybe I needed to go in the direction of the pastoral ministry. During this time, I was also having some great experiences in the church ministry through teaching Bible classes, Confirmation classes, and Sunday School, and sort of "helping out" Pastor Abendroth at times. Somewhere along the line of that school year of 1956-57, God's Spirit moved me to make a decision to go into the parish ministry of our synod. When I first mentioned this to my wife, Betty, in our first year of marriage, she wasn't exactly ecstatic. After all, she had been raised in a parsonage all her life until she went into nurse's training. She had seen firsthand what parish life for a pastor and his family was like, and she wasn't convinced about the greatness of it! Or, as she commented to me one day,

> When I agreed to marry you at the time of our engagement, I thought I was marrying a Lutheran teacher. I was already planning and thinking about where we would ultimately buy a house in the Cleveland area and settle down. Now I find out that my teacher husband wants to be a pastor. Since I had often felt and said to others that I would never marry a preacher, this news of yours amazes me, even though you had

intimated it several times recently! However, Jim, I am with you all the way, and will do all I can to help you realize such a goal. I think I know how to be a good pastor's wife!

Betty's support and strength at this time in my life was one of the most important moments of my life. I can never thank her enough for just that kind of love and support. And, yes, she did make a great pastor's wife and mother of a bunch of "preacher's kids." In early spring of 1957, Lutheran High was forced to decide not to start Lutheran High West that next fall (as had been anticipated). The state of Ohio wanted to do something with our school property – build an interstate highway right through the middle of it – and the negotiations on it would take more than a year. I then decided at the last minute to start the seminary classes that very summer of 1957.

Thus my formal high school teaching career ended at the conclusion of the school year in the spring of 1957. My seminary time of four years I will write about in another chapter. I will conclude this section of my story by answering the most-asked question I have encountered from time to time over the years in the pastoral ministry: "Do you ever miss teaching, and do you ever wish to go back into it?" Answer: "Yes, I will always miss my formal teaching years. The students alone make that part of the answer obvious. But, no, I have never found myself wishing to go back into formal teaching." The reason I have always answered that way is very basic: So much of my ministry over the years has involved and included a lot of teaching anyway. So, in a very real sense, I had the best of two worlds: teaching in its many aspects, and pastoral ministry in its many aspects and dimensions. I credit my years of teaching at Cleveland Lutheran and the hundreds of students I was associated with as some of the most important and vital training I ever had in preparation for my 35 years of pastoral ministry. I am indebted to Lutheran High, its marvelous and challenging students, its Christ-focused administration and leadership, its many, many supportive congregations, and its wonderful and amazing faculty! I remember and delight in thinking of each of them, even after all these years. How very blessed I was by all of those people in my life who contributed so much toward helping me be a servant of Christ in His Kingdom here on earth.

Chapter 6

My Life in Sports (Mostly Baseball)

While most of the following pages will dwell on my favorite and best sport, baseball, it's important to know that I played every major sport there was: football, basketball, hockey, skiing, and some track events. We played a lot of sandlot football during the fall and into early winter, usually in the park across from my house (Harmon Park, but now known as Sheldon Park) in East Muskegon, Michigan. It had a large, grassy area, almost the size of a football field. For baseball there was also a clay diamond and a high mesh-wire fence for a backstop, with benches on both sides of the diamond. We didn't learn basketball very well, because the winters tended to force the game indoors, and there were only the local schools and the YMCA gymnasiums to play in. We did have a backboard on our garage in the alley, but leather basketballs in snowy, wet weather weren't too much fun. But we played anyway! However, because of the weather we played a lot more hockey than basketball in the winter. There was a bowl-shaped depression in the park across the street which allowed water to collect and freeze over, forming an ice pond. We also made our own ice pond in the vacant lot next door during the cold months of January and February. We enjoyed there more, because it was "ours" and we built big snow banks all around the pond to "dive" into as we were playing hockey.

But more than hockey, I loved skiing almost from the time I could stand up. Very early on, at various places where we lived, I would find hills to ski on. When we moved to East Muskegon when I was ten years old, I was in "ski heaven." The best hills were next to the nearby celery farms. Celery farms are built on very low-lying, flat land with a series of irrigation ditches connecting them to get lots of water to the celery plants. That meant there were lots of hills surrounding the celery farms, ideal for skiing because many of the trees had been cleared. Sledding and tobogganing were part of the picture, too, but skiing was the greatest enjoyment. I became a very good skier and spent many, many hours during the weekends of each winter on the slopes. Now remember, the kind of skis we used were simply two good, narrow pieces of wood made into skis with grooves on the bottom and very carefully waxed and taken care of. We did not use (nor did we have) ski poles, clamps, or ski boots. There was a thick leather strap that went through the middle of the ski, and we simply jammed our boots or shoes into them as hard as we could and went downhill. Gravity took us down and gravity kept our feet in the ski straps. If you fell on the way down, you might lose one or both skis to the bottom of the hill, which you retrieved on your own. There were no ski lifts or ropes by which to get back to the top of the hill. We even made our own ski jumps and enjoyed our frequent use of them.

I clearly remember a big jump that continually challenged me. It was for older guys (I was only 12 or 13), but I kept trying and I kept falling. One Sunday in the late afternoon and early evening, I tried at least 50 or 60 times without success, even drawing a crowd to cheer me on. When it finally got too dark, I went home, quite discouraged but very determined to make it the next weekend. The first time out the following Saturday, I took to the ski jump and landed perfectly. From then on, it was a breeze, but always a thrill! And I learned a great lesson: learned skills, persistence, patience, hard work, and determination pay off. I also learned something about my own personality and character that I would apply to my life in the years ahead. All in all, with all the places and space around us, we boys had a great environment in which to live and play, and be close to home for my years of 10 to almost 18.

Other than the winter sports (including basketball), my main interest was in baseball and football. And I lived in the right part of the state in which to play these sports. It seemed that every boy played sandlot baseball and football until high school age (in those days there were no organized sports before high school). Western Michigan routinely turned out the highest-ranking high school teams in the state. This is attested to by the fact that my Muskegon High School football team won the Class A (highest level) state championship two of the three years I was there. In baseball, we won 55 straight games over a two and a half year period. In high school, I was quite small and light (5' 6" and 120 pounds) until my senior year. Even though I was a good passer and a swift runner, I just didn't have the size to do much in football until that last year.

However, whatever hopes I had for football in my senior year came to an end the spring before. I tore up my ankle in one of our "sliding pits" at baseball practice early in the spring of 1944 – my junior year. Not only did it mess up my high school baseball season (I was "looking good," as the saying goes) but it wiped me out for that summer in baseball, as well as football in the fall. In those days, there wasn't a lot of attention paid to "little injuries." It needed to be a broken bone or something "serious" to warrant much consideration. Well, we didn't have a very sensitive coach (good baseball man, but not too good with kids otherwise). When I injured my ankle so severely, the only thing he said to me was, "Get an X-ray tomorrow." I even walked all the way home the day I hurt my ankle – the most painful two miles I've ever walked! Since many ligaments and tendons were badly torn, I should have had a cast put on it for a while (as they would do now) and given it some time to heal. Instead, I went to practice every day, limped around a bit uselessly, and went with the team to our games. I was always considered a part of the team, although I did nothing after the injury. It was so bad, I still couldn't run on it that summer of 1944. So, I took on the American Legion managing job for one of our teams in East Muskegon, with my friend Fred (one year younger than me) as my star player and pitcher. That made it a wonderful summer, even though we got "snookered" out of first place on a very biased decision by the director of the American Legion baseball program. I discovered at that time, even though I didn't realize it then, that I had a gift for teaching and coaching younger people.

Nonetheless, I coached that team while I limped around most of the summer in a bit of pain, but mostly inconvenience. Somehow, my mom and stepfather never got too concerned about me. That was because I was able to hide the worst of it most of the time, and just kind of dismissed it whenever they asked me about it. I was used to that with some other injuries I'd suffered previously that had nothing to do with baseball, but which would have probably made trouble for me with my parents if they'd known how the injuries happened. For instance, in the late summer of 1940, just before the beginning of 8th grade, I tried to do a "bicycle hill climb" up a rather steep and high mound of beach sand that had been dug out for the basement of a new house (very common in the Western Michigan coastal areas along Lake Michigan). In my "daringness," I forgot that if I made the hill climb successfully, and went over the top, there was only the downside of the hill on the other side. And there was a 10-foot deep hole of a basement awaiting me! As it turned out, I succeeded in making the hill climb! In the fall down the other side into the basement hole, I sprained my right wrist very badly. But I would never "let on" to anyone, particularly my parents. It took a long time to heal. There are several other of those kinds of incidents and accidents, probably like most kids growing up who don't tell their parents everything.

Anyway, my active "baseball career" was put on hold the summer of 1944, but would be revived wonderfully after that: in high school, in the military service, and back home in Industrial League baseball after my years in the U.S. Navy.

My baseball life began with almost total disinterest in the sport. My dad took me to a doubleheader between several local Industrial League teams when I was about six or seven. He loved it, but I was completely bored with sitting for so long watching something I didn't really understand and didn't care about. I'm sure that my dad, an avid baseball fan, as was my mother, was probably disappointed in his eldest son. Well, sometimes those kinds of things take time, and I just wasn't ready yet. I'm also sure that's the reason I'm rather concerned when we adults "push" sports and other activities on our kids too soon and project upon them too much of ourselves and our own "ambitions" for them. Our job as parents is to introduce them to these things, let them find their way in terms of interest, skills, and abilities, and then be there to encourage, stimulate, and help out. Neither of my parents pushed me at that time, but somewhere along the line, at about age eight or nine, I suddenly caught "baseball fever." I was hooked! There is no specific event or occasion that triggered this interest so suddenly. It was probably just a boy growing up at a time when baseball was truly the "national pastime," and every kid played ball to some degree or another, especially in school. At my little parochial school at Trinity Lutheran Church in Muskegon (where I attended through the 8th grade), the boys played ball at every recess and noon hour time. The younger, smaller boys were gradually worked up into the more "serious" game as they approached 5th and 6th grades, depending on their abilities at that point in life and growth. At any rate, I loved baseball from that time on, and it became my special interest in sports, even though I would continue to play all the other major sports over the years (as we all did in those days).

One very major event in my life took place around this time – the divorce of my parents in late 1936 or early 1937. Several things stand out about this particular time in my life. I do not recall any negative things between my parents those years before the divorce (they were wise and good to somehow keep it to themselves and not involve my brother and me in the ongoing stresses and friction). Also, my focus on school and sports (school because I had to, and sports because I wanted to!) must have somehow shielded me from whatever negatives were going on so that I didn't feel any great or cataclysmic disruption in my life. It was during this time of moving from house to house that I discovered that baseball was my introduction to any new neighborhood we moved into. I'd just take my bat, ball, and glove and start checking things out until I found other kids for whom baseball was a wonderful pastime, and our friendships began. This worked very well for the three moves we made in 1937-38: first with my mother and brother, then a year or so later with my new stepfather, and then the summer of 1938. I had become a die-hard Detroit Tigers baseball fan; much of this was due to my own interest, but it was also due to the fabulous Tigers baseball radio announcer, Harry Heilmann (a Hall of Fame player himself). The Tigers' first baseman, Hank Greenberg, had already become somewhat my "hero," but before long he would become my all-time and continuing favorite. The summer of 1938 cinched it for me. Unbelievable! I simply call it, "1938: A summer to remember!"

~

It was a clear, starry, beautiful late evening hour as we gazed out of our car at the brightly-lit Michigan State Capitol Building in East Lansing in the summer of 1938. My stepfather drove into the driveway of the house we would live in for the next two and a half months. My mom and dad had divorced almost two years previously, and my mom had remarried early that spring of 1938. My stepfather was a good man, so I seemed to have little difficulty handling all that had happened. His real name was Milton Sevrey, but everyone called him "John," and that's the way I'll refer to him. Maybe part of the reason that I had little difficulty dealing with everything that was happening in our family was due to the fact that I had fallen in love with baseball. I had my bat, glove, and a baseball with me in the car as we traveled the 95 miles to East Lansing from Muskegon. Here John would attend some special classes in electrical engineering at Michigan State University for the summer. My eight-year-old brother, Aubrey (later changed to "David") was with us and would be my "tagalong" for the summer! Years later, I would be asked how I was able to handle my parents' divorce and the many moves we made during the Depression of the 1930s. I could not and cannot recall anything very negative (thanks to both of my parents), but whenever we moved to a new neighborhood, I just took my bat, glove, and ball and looked for other kids with whom to play baseball. It always worked and I made friends easily that way. In East Lansing that summer, we lived in an upstairs apartment and I very quickly adapted myself to the situation with some other boys in the neighborhood, especially when they found out that I could play baseball very well.

However, the high point of that summer came in the third week of July. My stepfather had bought tickets to a Detroit Tigers baseball game in what was then called Briggs Stadium, on Trumbull Avenue in downtown Detroit. I was ecstatic! Growing up in Western Michigan, an equal distance from Chicago and Detroit, we had a choice of teams to support. Early on, I became a Tigers fan, mostly because Detroit's broadcaster, Harry Heilmann, was a wonderfully descriptive radio announcer and very fair in his broadcasting. But more than that, I was a fan because Detroit was in the state of Michigan and because one of baseball's truly great players, Hank Greenberg, was the Detroit first baseman. He was the first Jewish player of any renown in baseball, which I didn't know at the time, nor would I have cared. He was my idol!

Our seats in Briggs Stadium that day were box seats right behind home plate. What a place to watch my first Major League Baseball game and to watch Hank Greenberg up close! On top of that, it was a doubleheader against the Philadelphia Athletics (now known as the Oakland A's). Their manager was one of the most famous and most revered of all time in baseball, Connie Mack. He would dress in a dark business suit, starched collar and black tie, and would stand in the dugout and signal his players with an ever-present scorecard. What a treat! And the Detroit manager was another Hall of Famer, Mickey "Black Mike" Cochrane. I was in baseball heaven! But it wasn't only the ecstasy of being there and it being my first exposure to the major leagues. It was also what happened in those two games that was really amazing and memorable for me all these years.

To begin with, to this day I remember the starting lineup for the Tigers, as well as the names of the starting pitchers in each game. The catcher for both games for Detroit was a rookie by the name of George "Birdie" Tebbetts, who later became a well-known manager of the Cincinnati Reds. He was catching both those games because Rudy York, the regular catcher, had been hit in the head with a pitched ball the previous week, and was still recovering. However, he was in uniform that day and I got to see him. York was a full-blooded Native

American who had set the existing record for most home runs in a single month (18) the year before, in his rookie season (broken in 1998 by Sammy Sosa of the Chicago Cubs). Although he played many good years in baseball, he never again approached that zenith in his career. At first base was Hank Greenberg (Hall of Fame); at second base was Charlie Gehringer (Hall of Fame); at shortstop was Billy Rogell; at third base was Marvin Owen. If my memory serves me, in left field for the first game was the aging Al "Foot in the Bucket" Simmons (Hall of Fame) – then on his last legs as a major leaguer – and for the second game was the good humor man, Leon "Goose" Goslin (Hall of Fame). In centerfield was Pete Fox, and in right field was Joyner "Jo-Jo" White, an extremely fast runner. The starting pitcher for the first game was a rather small player with a tremendous curveball, Tommy Bridges. The starting pitcher for the second game was a real character, Cletus "Boots" Poffenberger, who lived up to his unusual nickname. But it was the relief pitcher in both games, Harry Eisenstat, a 22-year-old left-hander, the only other Jewish player in baseball at the time, who came out of that doubleheader with a very special distinction, along with Hank Greenberg!

Now, for the strange uniqueness of that baseball doubleheader. In one of the games, Jo-Jo White beat out a bunt down the third base line and then continued on to second base as the other team watched and hoped that the ball would roll foul. When they belatedly threw toward second base, White continued on to third base. How often will you see a bunt of 60-70 feet wind up with the bunter going all the way around to third? However, the most unusual thing about those two games was the way the Tigers won both games. In 1938, Greenberg was in the midst of his greatest home run season in which he would hit 58 homers, the closest at the time to Babe Ruth's record of 60. That July, Greenberg was on track to break the record. On that particular day, he hit his 36th, 37th, and 38th home runs of the season! And I saw and thrilled to each one of them! More than that, it was how those homers, especially two of them, affected the outcomes of the games. Detroit won both games by the identical score of 8-7. In the 8th inning of each game, with the score 7-6 in favor of the Athletics, Charlie Gehringer came up and singled. And both times, Hank Greenberg was the next batter and hit a home run to put the Tigers ahead, 8-7. On top of that, in both games, Harry Eisenstat came in as the relief pitcher and became the winning pitcher, throwing five shutout innings in the first game and four shutout innings in the second game. After the doubleheader, Greenberg said to Eisenstat, "Hey, Harry, let's us Jews go out and celebrate!" Mickey Cochrane, the manager, added these words to his team, "Hey fellas, lock yourselves in your rooms tonight, because the Jews in Detroit are going crazy!" (Hank Greenberg with Ira Berkow, *The Story of My Life* (New York: Times Books, 1989), 104-105) Is it any wonder that my first baseball mitt was a first baseman's mitt?

Some years later, in the 1950s when Greenberg was general manager of the Cleveland Indians and I was teaching at Cleveland Lutheran High School, I made an appointment to see him for a few moments at his office at Municipal Stadium. I didn't stay long and I didn't ask for his autograph or anything like that (besides, I never really cared for that kind of stuff anyway). But I did remind him of that summer of 1938 and he, of course, remembered it very well and enjoyed my sharing the experience with him. Many years later, when I lived in Thousand Oaks, California, I got to know Sparky Anderson in connection with our joint golf tournament sponsorship with Sparky and the Thousand Oaks Kiwanis Club, of which I was president. Sparky had been the manager of the "Big Red Machine" – the Cincinnati Reds during the 1970s – and at the time I got to know him, he was manager of the Detroit Tigers. In talking with him one time (he lived in Thousand Oaks), I mentioned those games I saw in 1938, the uniqueness of them, and the strange coincidences of how they were won and by whom they were won. He looked at me a bit incredulously and then told me he'd check it out the next time he was in Detroit. The following year, after the baseball season was over and during our annual Kiwanis/Sparky Anderson Golf Tournament, I had a chance to speak with him for a few minutes. He smiled broadly as I came up to him (he liked talking about the Tigers, and I was the only one who really knew what I was talking about on that subject) and in his usual ebullient way, told me that he'd checked on my story and that it was completely true, even down to the names of the players I had mentioned on Detroit's team that year! Well, that was a wonderful reminder of that incredible summer of 1938!

~

For the next couple of years, life went on rather normally, with school at Trinity, a new neighborhood where I quickly found new friends and kids who loved sports. This was in East Muskegon, a somewhat looked-down-upon part of town, but it was right at the edge of the city and thus close to many open fields, trees, and a wonderful park right across the street from our house on Isabella Avenue. Actually, my going to a parochial school across town in the Lakeside section of Muskegon (five miles away) provided me with a double set of good friends: my friends at school, with whom I remained good friends for many years past parochial school, and my good friends in the East Muskegon neighborhood. The fact that I attended a church school across town didn't seem to make any difference to my friends, and I cannot ever remember any negative comments or teasing about it. To be quite honest, as I look back now on that time of my life, I believe that my active and skilled interest in sports was a big factor in my acceptance and recognition among the boys in the neighborhood and nearby areas. My younger brother, really just a tagalong kid when it came to sports, never found the same comfortableness, camaraderie, and acceptance that I did.

It was at this time that I made friends with a boy who would be one of my best friends until this very day. His name is Fred, and we became very good friends and a terrific baseball combination in those earlier years. We were like members of each other's families, from lunch times together, to overnights, to TV (he had it at his house but I didn't at mine, even after I came home from the Navy and we renewed our close friendship), to almost every phase of our lives, including many double dates. But most of all, Fred was my number one "baseball buddy," and we connected this way for a number of years: when we were kids, when we were high school age, and when I was in college and home for the summers after both of us had spent some years in military service. Most of the time, he was the pitcher (a good one) and I was his catcher.

If the "Summer of 1938" was my defining moment in my love affair with baseball, the spring of 1941 was my defining moment in terms of skill and ability. Up through the first eight grades of school in those days, the only baseball you played was what was called "sandlot" – rather unorganized and unstructured, and with no involvement of parents, umpires, or schedules. We just played whenever a few or many of us got together, and simply played for the pure fun of it. It was wonderful! Around the end of 7th grade and into 8th grade, some kids started thinking about playing American Legion ball (open only to kids in junior high and high school). I didn't even know of such a league at that time.

However, in the late spring of 1941, when I was nearing the end of 8th grade, a number of us in East Muskegon had formed a pretty loosely organized team, and were playing a few other sandlot-type teams from other parts of town. Late that spring of 1941, we were challenged to a game with a team in another part of town. They even agreed to come to East Muskegon to play on a Friday afternoon after school on a baseball lot near where I got off from my ride from school. By that time I had earned a bit of a "reputation" as a player, so this would be a real test. Some of my buddies kind of "bragged me up," and that just added to the flavor of the competitiveness of the "big game." The game was played on a vacant baseball lot with a long building of car garages being the left field and left-center field "wall." It was over 200 feet from home plate, which at that time in our baseball size and ability was impossible to hit over or even reach. I was our first baseman (à la Hank Greenberg, my idol!) and at that time in my life I was as tall or taller than most kids my age. Unfortunately, the game (which even had umpires) was scheduled to start before I could get there from school. Nonetheless, the game began and I didn't arrive until almost the 3rd inning in what would be a seven-inning game (if it didn't get too dark before then). When I got out of the car, my team greeted me with cheers and optimism. After all, I had been hailed as our team's best hitter and I'd finally made it to the game, in which we were already behind. Well, that was almost a big bust! The first two times at bat that day, facing a really good pitcher of abilities beyond what I had experienced up to that time, I struck out ignominiously. Wow! Did I have a lot to learn! Well, the game went on until the bottom of the 7th inning, with agreement that it would be the last inning, even in case of a tie (it was getting dark). By whatever circumstances of the game, we managed to get three men on base that last inning, with the score 7-4 against us. There were two outs, and I came up to bat. Not to make this sound too melodramatic (because at the time it didn't seem that way), but it was a tense situation. I have no idea how many or what type of pitches were thrown to me at that time, but I remember only one thing – I hit one that kept climbing and climbing toward left field, and went high over the left field "garage" wall! None of us had ever been able to do this, even in practice, and everyone but me, just stood and watched the ball disappear over the wall. It astounded me because I've never been what you would call a home run hitter. But I sure hit one that day! Wow! Talk about being a hero! I was that day, even if I didn't fully appreciate it at the time. I don't even remember saying much to my mom about it then. It just wasn't one of those things you dwelled on in the manner of many professional ball players of today who give the impression that their home run is just about the greatest thing in all the world! For many years, I didn't think back very much to that day, because it wasn't really that impressive to me. We were just kids playing a game of baseball.

However, along with other indications, that home run may have triggered a lot of interest in me as a ball player. For example, I was asked to play with an American Legion team (9th- and 10th-graders) that following summer. We formed a team that was sponsored by Star Mattress Company there in East Muskegon, and I think we won the championship that summer. I don't really remember, because just playing on that level was wonderful enough for me. Yes, I played first base and did very well, although I really don't remember much about the season, even though I was and still am very competitive. Mostly, it was just fun!

The next summer found me playing on a team sponsored by the Eagles Lodge, and managed by one of the very best baseball men in the area. Even though I discovered I was in a bit "over my head" with a group of very good players (most of them a year older than me), I knew I'd learn a lot and thought it would be a good season. It wasn't a good season, neither for me nor for the team. Just before the season began, our manager had a health problem and could not coach us. His assistant took over, and that was not so good. He wasn't much of a coach or teacher, and he was quite biased toward several players, to the exclusion of others. The good "chemistry" we started with deteriorated as the season went along and we wound up a flop. I did all right, but not as well as I expected. I also discovered something else that summer – I wasn't growing any taller. In fact, I was just average height by then, and certainly not built to be a first baseman, even though I was an excellent fielder.

One of my great thrills as I got into organized baseball was buying my first baseball mitt – a first baseman's! I remember how I saved up for it for a long time, and the joy of finally having the $3.60 needed to buy the one I had already picked out. What a great moment after I'd walked several miles (with my friend, Fred, of course) to the sports store and bought it! I had that mitt for many years, and used it even after I didn't play first base anymore. Recently, my buddy, Fred, reminded me that I probably was "ahead of my time" when I used my first baseman's mitt as a catcher's mitt, much in the style of catcher's mitts today, in contrast to the older-style "pillow" catcher's mitts.

When I realized that playing first base wasn't going to work out for me, I began learning other positions. And that turned out very well, especially since I learned or had the natural ability to play almost any other position. With my high school team, I was an outfielder because I could run fast, had a good throwing arm, and could hit well. However, the summer after the aforementioned "bad" baseball summer, Fred and I and a number of other kids we knew formed our own team, found a sponsor, and had a great baseball summer! Fred was our best pitcher with a devastating curveball, and I became his catcher. I had simply reasoned to myself that catching would be easy: if the batter missed the pitch, you just caught it, and if he hit the pitch you didn't have to worry about catching it! Not particularly great logic, but it worked and I became a very good catcher. And I enjoyed catching more than any of the other positions in baseball. That summer, however, I had developed a one-fingered, roundhouse curveball which served both as a good curve and as a changeup, to go with my good fastball. So Fred and I wound up as our two main pitchers, although I also played third base a few times. But I always caught Fred, and he was really good. My pitching exploits were pretty good (I had a 6-2 record) and I had a lot of fun pitching. In one game I pitched a one-hitter, the one hit being a ground ball early in the game that was hit past me and which I should have fielded. The best game I pitched was a 2-1 win, in which I gave up a run in the 1st inning, and then stopped them the rest of the way with a fastball I could barely control. For the last six innings (a seven-inning game of course), I threw nothing but fastballs. About the 3rd inning, my catcher – a little guy with more courage than ability – came out and asked why I kept shaking off his signs for curveballs. I said to him, "Bobby, my fastball is moving all over the place and those guys can't come near it. Just sit back and call fastballs, because that's all I'm going to throw!"

My only negative as a pitcher came early in one game, when the score was still close. I wound up and let fly one of my fastballs that "took off" inside to a right-handed hitter. As sometimes happens in such situations, the ball began moving high and toward the batter's upper body, and then toward his head. When I realized (after releasing the pitch) where it was going, I hollered, "Watch out!" But it was too late, since the batter simply "froze" and didn't move to avoid the pitch. It hit him in the head with a sound no one playing baseball ever wants to hear. In those days, there were no such things as plastic batting helmets, and all you had on to protect your head was a baseball cap! The batter never lost consciousness and he seemed to be all right, including a checkup at the hospital. However, he didn't play anymore that summer. I knew him fairly well and his brother was a friend of mine in high school. When I talked to him some time later, he told me it really wasn't my fault because he saw the ball coming and knew what was happening, but he just couldn't move. He claimed that he had time to duck, but just couldn't. As for that game itself, I went the rest of the way without them getting a hit. That beaning scared them, and I could have thrown up "lollipops" and they couldn't have hit them because their knees had turned into jelly!

Except for that bad incident, 1943 was a great and most successful baseball summer. Our team finished the season in first place, and Fred, Walt (the slugger on our team), and I all made the all-star team. With that kind of impetus, I figured I would do well in high school ball the next year since I'd played with or against most of the guys already in American Legion baseball. And remember, Muskegon Senior High School was very large and had what was then regarded as the best high school baseball program in the state. Going into my junior year in high school, our team was undefeated and it remained that way during the season of 1944. We were good! So, it was with great anticipation that I looked forward to that next year in high school baseball. After all, I was reasonably well-known and it was expected that I would do well. I had a lot of confidence. But that soon changed! My high school coach, a good man but a guy who never seemed to exhibit much warmth, sensitivity, or concern for his players, didn't show much confidence in me that spring in practice. He already had such a great lineup of very good players that he certainly didn't really need me. You should also know that there were no such things as freshman teams or junior varsity teams in baseball those years. And there was only one coach for the whole program!

After managing baseball in the summer of 1944, and not being able to play football in the fall, I set my goal on baseball in the spring of 1945. To indicate how good these baseball players were, my friend and locker partner during high school was a guy named Bob Ludwig, who eventually made it to the top of Triple A in the high minor leagues and had a good shot at the majors with the

Chicago Cubs. He never quite made it, and when I saw him some years later and asked him about it and why he didn't stay with baseball, he replied, "I had made up my mind that if I didn't make the major leagues in six years, I would stop and go into teaching, for which I'd been educated at Western Michigan University." As it turned out, he became a teaching colleague of my mother at Bunker School in Muskegon for many years after that.

Essentially, my high school baseball career ended with our team winning its 50th straight game, early in the season of 1945. I was our starting center fielder or left fielder. We did well as we began the season, but things didn't always go that well for me. In that 50th straight victory, which we won 3-1, I made a couple of terrible mental mistakes (inexcusable in any sport or profession) and was now on my coach's "list." Although it was very painful at the time, I really learned a lot from that game, and I doubt if I ever made a mental error again after that. Later, after school was out in the early summer of 1945 (before I went into the Navy that summer), I was playing for two different teams in two different leagues (which meant a game almost every evening – which I loved!). I played in a game in which I must have done very well (three hits, three RBIs, two stolen bases, and a good defensive game in left field). After the game, my old high school baseball coach (who had seen the whole game) came up to me and complimented me on what a great game I had played, and encouraged me to keep up the good playing. I accepted his compliment with a wry smile as I thought to myself, *Why didn't you ever give me something positive when I was playing for you in high school? It would have helped!* This was the coach who had even criticized our best player and pitcher, my friend Bob, after we ended our consecutive win streak at 55 games, by saying that Bob hadn't worked hard enough! I won't repeat some of the things Bob told me some years later when I talked to him about those days of baseball at Muskegon High School. Besides being probably the best high school baseball player in the state of Michigan that year, he had also been voted as All-State running back the previous fall in football! By the way, Bob was also from East Muskegon. He was the best baseball player I ever played with or against.

After high school graduation, I joined the U.S. Navy in the summer of 1945. I didn't have much chance to play baseball the first year or so in the Navy, although we did play a bit when I was in New York the spring and summer of 1946 at the U.S. Naval Hospital on Long Island. What real playing I got to do for the next couple of years took place when I was attached to the U.S. Marines at Camp Lejeune in North Carolina. This was a more stable situation, except when we were on training exercises in the Caribbean Sea or on six-month cruises in the Mediterranean Sea. I got to play with some very good ex-high school and ex-college players, and discovered that I had matured enough as a player to compete on an even level with any of them. That was really enjoyable, and we had many good games with other battalions or regiments that had baseball teams. When I went anywhere in the Navy or Marines and announced that I was a catcher and was able to play any other position, I was warmly welcomed, especially since I could also hit well and was a fast runner. I don't remember too much about those games, except that we had a good time and I did very well. The one incident I remember most clearly was the time I pulled off an unassisted double play. As usual, I was catching. The other team had runners on first and third with only one out. Because our pitcher had a rather slow pitching motion to the plate, the runner on third decided to try to steal home. About two thirds of the way toward home, he realized he couldn't make it and began to retreat back to third. That was his mistake! As I came out of my catching crouch, I noticed what he was doing, so I began to run him down. His second mistake was that he didn't realize how fast I could run, and I tagged him out halfway back to third base. Instinctively, I immediately turned to cut across the diamond toward second base, because I knew the runner from first base would be rounding the bag at second and heading for third base. Well, I caught him in "no man's land" between bases and easily tagged him out, almost before he knew what had happened. At that time, I also realized that I could hit just about any pitcher, as long as I remained aggressive and confident. During this time, I began switch-hitting. I had experimented with this before, so it wasn't new to me and I could do quite well. My last experience in military baseball was the summer of 1949, before I was discharged in late summer.

At this point in my life, I had finally become serious about what I wanted to do, and that was to become a high school teacher and baseball coach. That decision affected two important areas of my life. First of all, I had a very definite and clear goal to pursue in college, and nothing else was as important. Secondly, that meant a decision *not* to play college baseball (which I know I certainly could have done), and definitely not college football (which I'm not sure I could have done). That wasn't always an easy decision, especially in the early spring when baseball was "in the air." As much as I would have loved to compete at that level, I was just more focused on my academics. (Remember, I was not a great mental wizard. But I did wind up my college years with a 3.50 grade point average, and was on the Dean's List almost every year.) Some years later, when I was in my very late 20s and early 30s, I would compete on the college level, and very successfully. That story will come a little later.

After I got out of the Navy in late summer / early fall of 1949, I took it easy for a few months before starting college at Valparaiso University in Indiana. To this day, I tell people that this was one of the best decisions of my life, and I loved my years at Valpo and what they did for me. During the first two summers of college life, I came back to my parents' home in Twin Lake, Michigan (ten miles from Muskegon). I got a job for those two summers at a local brewery, which gave me the little bit of extra money I needed to get all the way through college on the G.I. Bill and with what I had saved up during my years in the service. Those two summers were among my most enjoyable times in baseball. I worked in a brewery eight hours a day, played baseball three or four evenings a week on a good Industrial League team with my good friend, Fred, and had wonderful girlfriend(s) both summers! What a life!

The baseball was even better than the brewery or the girls. Fred and I teamed up for some great games together. I was always the catcher, and in the service (maybe even before then) I knew I could bat both right- and left-handed. Those summers in the Industrial League, I batted both ways very successfully.

There are several memories of those two summers of baseball that fill my mind. Perhaps two that I was most proud of are described here. I was always a good hitter, so I won't go into that. However, what I like to remember were my base running exploits, including the fact that I was a good slider. I recall that in one game I was on base and got all the way around to third. I watched the pitcher carefully, and when I came back to the dugout I announced to the players on my team that I could steal home on their pitcher. By the way, I had done this a number of times when I played American Legion ball, so it was nothing new to me. My guys kind of laughed at my "boast," and kind of let it go at that. A couple of innings later, after hitting safely and moving around to third base, I found myself facing some loud and subtle challenges to my previous boast. So, I stole home! And I think I never received more applause than I did that day from my teammates and fans!

Fred and I had a great time those summers. Between playing baseball and dating girls, we "had it made!" The second memory happened when, as usual, I was catching Fred. As a catcher, I had been warned about a 6' 3", 230-pound All-State football player who was also a good baseball player and first baseman for the other team. He loved to "bowl over" opposing catchers on close plays at home plate. As you might expect, late in a close game he came roaring around third base, determined to score as he headed home. I braced myself as the ball came toward me and he came straight at me with no intention to slide. I got the ball a split second before he got there, and instantly I dropped to my knees, put my forearms out in front of me, caught him across his legs below the knees, lifted him up (his own momentum providing the loft), and he went sailing over my head, landed hard (spraining his ankle), and was called out! After the game I talked to him for a moment, concerned about his injury. He reported that he was all right, but still upset that he hadn't scored the run. I cryptically responded, "Sometimes it's better to slide." He just walked away muttering to himself, to my quiet satisfaction. Such is my competitive nature.

Those were halcyon years in many ways, but not the most important. My four teaching years at Cleveland Lutheran High School were some of the greatest years of my life. This was not only because of the teaching, but also because of the preparation it gave me for the Holy Spirit's prompting to go into the Holy Ministry of the LCMS. Those four years at Cleveland Lutheran High are another whole story, but I just want to emphasize how very important those years were to me. I was assistant football coach for two years, and head baseball coach for the last two years I was in Cleveland. It, too, was a wonderful time, especially because of the kids I worked with and coached.

As far as baseball was concerned, I had figured that it was about over. Of course, I played on our church's softball team for years in Cleveland, and that was fun. And I would do the same in the churches where I pastored years later. However, when I went to the seminary in Springfield, Illinois (the campus was later moved to Fort Wayne, Indiana), I discovered to my surprise that they played intercollegiate baseball with a full 15-18 game schedule against small colleges in central and southern Illinois, as well as our teachers college in River Forest and our sister seminary in St. Louis. Before I could get too excited about playing in the spring of 1958, I was asked to coach the baseball team instead (although I could also play). The regular coach had resigned in February and left things in a bit of a mess. Even though I carried a full academic load, had a small part-time job, and was married, I accepted the request to coach. I'm sure my high school coaching experience was the reason they asked me. That and they were somewhat desperate. The job was bigger than it was presented to me, since I also had to schedule umpires and playing fields for our home games (we didn't have a field at the Sem). All that in addition to organizing and choosing a team, and everything that goes with that! Somehow we got through it all right, and I made myself the major playing "substitute" on the team, whenever that was necessary.

One particularly enjoyable incident occurred when I coached against the St. Louis Sem and their interim coach for a year, the retired shortstop and ex-manager of the St. Louis Cardinals, Marty Marion. We had some interesting chats around the two games we played against each other (I won one, he won one).

The season ended quite well, but one thing left a bad taste in my mouth. When the season was over and we had our awards banquet, there was no recognition or thanks expressed to me by the Dean (who had asked me to do the job in the first place) or anyone else in the administration, except for a couple faculty members. The President of the sem had expressed his appreciation a couple of times during the season, and that was good enough for me. In fact, one of his warmest expressions came when I went into his office on a Monday following a Saturday game in which our team had made several mental errors and I'd blurted out a four-letter word that starts with a "d." He smilingly accepted my apology and said, "The way some of those guys were playing, I probably would have said the same thing!"

So much for my college level coaching career. The next year, with a good, bona fide coach, I did quite well until I pulled a hamstring and finally just couldn't play the last couple of games. The next year, 1959-1960, I didn't play baseball because it was my year of vicarage, doing campus ministry in Los Angeles.

My final year at the sem, 1960-1961, turned out to be a terrific year in many wonderful ways, including baseball. We had been told that the spring of 1961 would be the Sem's last year of intercollegiate competition, since it was getting too costly, etc. Those of us who really wanted to play baseball decided to make a very strong effort to get into good condition (something we usually hadn't done previously) and make it a great, lasting experience. And we did! Beginning in February, we began working out in the gym. And by the time we could go outside to begin practice, we were almost ready to play. Some of us were on the "older" side of things, that is, in our late 20s or 30s (including one guy who was 38 and another who was 39 – while neither of them played that much, they were a great part of the team). I was going on 34, had lost much of my former speed, and couldn't throw as hard as I had before. However, I still could hit well and had lots of baseball "moxie." The coach didn't quite know where to play me, since I was a bit slow for the outfield and he had some good infielders and an excellent catcher. I solved the problem for him! We had a guy playing first base who really was no taller than me at 5' 9", but an outstanding baseball player. Bobby Hoeft had played in the minor leagues a few years for the Detroit Tigers, but never went any further. (His first cousin was an outstanding left-handed pitcher for the Tigers some years previously, named Billy Hoeft.) Our main weakness on the field was at second base. One day, I was teasing Bobby in the gym (it was raining outside) as we worked out as best we could, since the season was about to begin. For one of the few times (if ever) in my life that I would not be in the starting lineup, I still needed to prove something. At any rate, Bobby, who had a short fuse, finally got disgusted with my kidding and threw the first baseman's mitt at me with the challenge, "See if you can do any better!" You may recall the story from *Uncle Remus*, where Brer Rabbit begs not to be thrown into the briar patch, but that was his plan and it worked for him. Well, in a way, that's what I did that day, because I had already figured out that Bobby could play a good second base, and then I'd be the first baseman! Well, we were throwing ground balls to the infielders and they threw back to the first baseman. This went on for a little while and then there was Bobby's challenge. Of course, I was totally comfortable taking over as the first baseman. Then Bobby, becoming a bit angry by this time, began throwing every ball as bad as he could in order to make me look bad. I realized what he was doing, and being a bit cocky myself, I began to show off and made every good play with flair, no matter what was thrown at me. It became a game with the other guys, and we all had a great time! Suddenly, Bobby looked at me with this expression of wonderment and respect, and announced loudly, "I'm going to talk to Coach Wilbert! You should be our first baseman!" And he did. And I became our team's first baseman the rest of the season. The only thing I told our infielders was simply, "Don't throw it too high, but if you keep it low, I can catch anything." And it worked out that way, and I went the whole season without an error. To show you how competitive I was, when I was playing first base in one of our games, the batter belted a vicious, low line drive that landed a few feet in front of me. Instead of trying to field it with my mitt (which would have been difficult), I just dropped to my knees and let the ball hit me in the chest. And then I was able to pick up the ball and make an easy out at first base. When I came into the dugout, the coach gave me this look of amazement and said, "Are you trying to get killed?" All I said in reply was, "I got the guy out. What more do you want? That's the only way I know how to play!" He just grinned, because he had seen me make some "wild" and successful slides on the bases, which indicated that I really was quite fearless when I played sports.

All in all, it was a wonderful and fulfilling way to end my playing career in baseball. I was the second leading hitter on the team with a .350 average (Bobby, of course, was our best hitter), and lots of good memories. We were a team, we were good, we won most of our games, and we truly enjoyed each other in this unique situation in which most of us would never see each other again this side of eternity. Believe me, that alone made every moment of that season very special, and I still thank God for that! And thank you, Coach Wilbert!

Chapter 7

The Women in My Life

In a very real way, this section of my life story will be an egotistical, self-serving, interesting-mostly-to-myself section. But it is important to me to record it anyway. Fortunately, it includes more than just a descriptive recitation of romantic successes, failures, and "close calls" over the years. In my mind, I hope this section is viewed as a compliment and a grateful tribute to a number of women who gave special meaning and joy to my life.

No such section of my story could begin without the special recognition and loving consideration of the first and eternally important woman in my life – my mother! I have written more about her in other sections of my story, except to say at this point that she was my model of true womanhood, and it was she who gave me a very good and balanced view, opinion, feeling, and appreciation of women for all of my life. In fact, it was such a good grounding for a boy growing up that I can look back on *all* of my experiences and relationships with girls/women and say, very honestly, "Every one of them whom I knew in any romantic or friendship way was a truly good person and I appreciated them in just that way." I hope that what I'm trying to say here doesn't sound condescending, chauvinistic, or ingratiating, because that's not the way I am. I just want to "tell it like it is" in this life that God has so graciously given me.

Before I continue any further, I want to make two things very clear. First, I never viewed my romantic experiences with women as a "victor-conqueror" kind of thing, or some kind of "win-lose" situation. No relationship should be viewed that way, particularly between a boy and girl, man and woman. Of course, there were disappointments for me and for them in the sense that things didn't "work out" romantically with some with whom I wanted to be romantic, but that's just the way it was. However, I never considered such encounters or experiences as "all or nothing at all" experiences. They were good, wholesome, enjoyable times, and that's the way I perceived them. Therefore, I have no negative feelings or regrets about any of these times in my life. It even seems to me that such a positive attitude on my part (learned from God and my mother) made my choice and God's choice of Betty and Nancy in my life even more remarkable and amazing. In all of my relationships with girls/women (and there were quite a few, as you'll soon discover), one thing was always true – each one of them contributed a special joy, a special role, a special good experience in preparation for my life with Betty and Nancy.

Second, whoever reads this account must know something else very important about me. I always played it "straight" or "honorable" in a sexual way. When I married Betty in 1956, I spent a few moments by myself on our wedding night in a special prayer in which I simply said to God, "Lord, I thank You for the privilege of Betty in my life, and I thank You for giving me the strength, patience, and spiritual good sense to keep myself just for this, my wife, on our wedding night!" We gave each other something very special that first night together, and I can only thank God, not myself. I never viewed girls/women as potential "conquests" or as persons to be "exploited." In my mind, there is no joy or sense of accomplishment in that! And I believe that was true in their attitude toward me along those lines (most of the time, at least!).

~

So, now to begin. And I begin with Yvonne! What a beautiful name with which to begin one's romantic life. Actually, she has always been known as Vonnie, a playful-sounding name by which she is still affectionately known. When I was an 8th-grader at Trinity Lutheran School in Muskegon, Michigan in 1940, Vonnie was a 7th-grader. Like most girls, she was a bit ahead of her age group, maturity-wise. Up to that time, girls were pretty much a real nuisance in the life of boys. I was a bit shy and "slow" then, but it didn't take long to discover the most remarkable of all God's creation: girls! Somehow, our friendship and feelings expressed themselves in the early months of 1941. When Valentine's Day came, I received something wonderful – a Valentine from Vonnie with a picture of a sailboat, which sent me into ecstasies of joy because it said:

> My ship is afloat, my sail is set;
> I love you, and I'll get you yet!

Such was my introduction to the world of romance, and I never looked back nor did I regret it. What a world! A boy remembers that first "crush" like it happened yesterday! And he remembers all the details of it, as well as everything about the girl. For instance, I remember that Vonnie lived on Estes Street in Lakeside, near our church on the other side of town from me. Her birthday is December 4th. And, yes, I do very clearly remember our first date together. I suppose by most standards, it was not such a terrific date, but it was my first one and it was with Vonnie! Somehow, in the very early summer of 1941, I asked her for a date. She accepted, and we agreed to meet downtown in Muskegon where all the buses met at the main connecting bus terminal for the whole city. From there, we could walk to any of the downtown movie theaters. We met each other that evening in early June, and we went to a movie (I think it was at the Regent Theater). During the movie, I tried at one point to put my arm around her by way of the back of the movie seat, but suddenly got shy and withdrew it at the appropriate moment before she would catch me at it! She probably never realized it. After the movie, we walked to the bus terminal and said "Goodnight" to each other and went home, each in our own direction. Big deal? But, oh, did I enjoy my first date! During the rest of the summer of 1941, I would ride my bike across town from East Muskegon to Lakeside (about five miles), both to see my buddies from Trinity School, such as George, Louis, Benny, and Carl, and with the oft-expected and joyful hope of seeing and spending time with Vonnie (which happened often). Somehow, as the summer progressed, the whole romantic thing began to unravel, and the summer ended that way. It may have ended, for all practical purposes, with a very romantic letter I wrote to Vonnie from Boy Scout Camp that summer, which her father somehow got hold of and read. It devastated me when I found out. Her father was a very wonderful man, but in the eyes of a 13-year-old boy, he was scary! After all, Vonnie was his only child, and she was only 12 years old when this 13-year-old kid was trying to make it with her. How would you feel if you had been her father? Almost needless to say, the summer ended, romantically-speaking, in a downward direction and that was that. And it made me very "gun shy" for the next couple of years as far as girls were concerned.

After that, I would see Vonnie from time to time, in high school, at church, and even casually once in a while as two friends. I did "carry a torch" for her for quite a while into my teens. Fortunately, we were always friends, and when I came home on leave in the Navy several years later, we dated a time or two very enjoyably. Eventually, the old feelings weren't there anymore, and we simply enjoyed being good friends. That friendship has continued down through the years to this day, and we've kept in touch through the years. For a "first love," she set a very high standard for all the girls/women who followed in my life.

But Vonnie will always be very special to me!

~

For the next few years of my teens, before entering the U.S. Navy in the summer of 1945, I didn't really "date" many girls in the more formal sense of the word. I think I was a bit gun shy by then and exhibited quite a bit of one-on-one reticence with girls. Informally, there were the "Walther League group dates" at church. Not much happened in a romantic sense, but they were healthy, social, and safe interaction times for a shy teenager basically afraid of girls. There were a couple of dates with a tall redhead in the group, Marian, whose brother was a good buddy of mine. Another girl, a year or two older than me, but part of our group that was doing a church play, was Leona (who later preferred to be called Lee). Again, not much happened, other than some lovely long walks home to her place after play practice. After I went into the Navy and came home on leave, we had some very enjoyable times together. However, during my high school days, I seemed to back off the romantic stuff. I did date a girl, whom I'll call "Betty 1," who lived near my uncle's home in Muskegon Heights. The most memorable thing about her was a conversation with my grandmother, Oma, at my uncle's house one Saturday morning after a Friday night date with Betty 1 – a good Dutch Reformed Christian girl. Oma "lectured" me for a few minutes about going out with a girl who wasn't Lutheran. All I recall was my reaction of surprise and laughing about the whole thing in front of her and commenting, "Don't worry, Oma, I'm not going to marry her!"

~

The summer of 1945 was a great transition time for me romantically. In a way, it was my "coming out" time when I came out of my shyness shell and discovered that girls sometimes took to me, too. In the spring, I got a crush on a cute little redhead at church who was a couple years younger than me. Because I was a bit older than her, and since I was going into the Navy quite soon, the relationship developed more after I was in the Navy and came home for leaves. Her name was Shirley. We had a few good times together, but nothing more. Being in the Navy really kept me out of the loop back home, and it was difficult to develop anything very worthwhile or lasting (which was just as well).

~

Early in the summer, there was a girl from Detroit named Barbara, who came to stay with her aunt for the summer in the neighborhood. Barbara liked boys, and I was one of them! She introduced me to the joys of "necking," and did we ever! From then on, I enjoyed girls even more, and she was the first girl that I really kissed romantically. It was in the recessed doorway of a nearby school late at night. I was in such a romantic "dither" that I viewed the nearby streetlight as the "moon!" So romantic! From then on, I did my "hugging and kissing" without the expectations of sex and without the physical pawing/fondling on my part. Somewhere along the line, I had picked up this strong sense of morality and ethical behavior, most likely from my mom and my parochial school. For that reason, I played it straight and I really believe that it helped give me many good, enjoyable relationships with girls and women during my pre-marriage years. That doesn't mean there weren't opportunities. It just means that "I did it my way" and it was good, although not always easy! Basically, I believed that girls appreciated my moral standards and my trustworthy actions and treatment of them. In no way am I trying to portray myself as a "goody-goody," because I had all the feelings, thoughts, and desires of any young, virile male. Wow! Did I ever! But I made my choices and, by and large, girls and women treated me very well and with comfortable respect and enjoyableness. Often, our relationships extended beyond the romantic stage and developed into some very good friendships. Quite a few of these friendships have lasted through the years until this very day, and I count them among the very special joys of my life!

~

The next period of what I will call my "romantic life" was really a whole new era, you might say. It was as a young 18 year old that I "blossomed" in my relationships with the opposite sex. And did I ever bloom! Still quite shy by nature, I found myself proceeding with more confidence and self-assurance once I got into the Navy (I'm sure the uniform helped!). The next few pages will describe that time in my life with brief accounts of various relationships with girls during those four years in the U.S. Navy, 1945-49. I quickly discovered that my uniform appeal worked!

~

On one of my first trips into Chicago, when I was still at Great Lakes Naval Training Station and waiting to go to San Diego for Navy Hospital Corps work, I met Florence. She preferred to be called Flo, and she was from nearby Whiting, Indiana. We had several dates and enjoyed each other, the city of Chicago, and long walks in Grant Park. After I left for San Diego, we never saw each other again, but we kept in touch for a year or more. She was a real cutie, and I remember her with real fondness. Out in San Diego, we sailors didn't have much chance to get out of Balboa Park Naval Base and meet girls. We were too busy going to school and doing military stuff. So nothing happened out there, romantically speaking.

~

However, once I hit New York, things really began to happen! Fortunately, I was assigned to a section of the U.S. Naval Hospital in St. Albans, Long Island, which allowed me a greater amount of liberty time than most of the guys. And I really took advantage of that! Since I was not into bar-hopping, my way of meeting girls was usually directed to casual meetings at nearby roller-skating rinks (very popular in those days). The first such "roller rink girl" that I met was "Jeanne 1," from Rockaway Beach, near where John F. Kennedy Airport would be built a few years later. Our meeting developed into one of the most wholesome and enjoyable family relationships of my time in New York – with the family next door! Jeanne and I dated a number of times, and she was a nice, friendly person. (However, her cousins next door turned out to be even more friendly and enjoyable. More about her cousin, Helen, later on.) Jeanne was one of those girls looking for a husband, which I didn't find out until some time later. As my relationship with Jeanne cooled off, my relationship with the family next door increased considerably, especially with Helen. The whole family became a wonderful part of my life in New York, not only that year, but for many years afterwards.

~

Of course, during this time there were other girls that I was meeting and dating. There was Pauline from Jackson Heights, with a figure that could "kill," but also a very good person. When I dated her a couple of years later, after returning from one of our Mediterranean Sea Cruises, I was "blown away" by what a truly beautiful woman she had become. That last date with her was her way of letting me know what I had missed while I was away! Oh, well! During this time, I also met and dated Mary a number of times. She was a very pretty, petite, dark-haired girl from Forest Hills, which at that time was the home of the national and world tennis championships. We also met at a roller-skating rink and while we dated often, it never was very serious (as would be the case with nearly all these girls I met in New York, and even later on). I still remember how impressed her parents were with me, as well as some of her neighbors. But I think Mary was a little bit less impressed! That's the way it goes sometimes.

~

Then there was Denise – right there on Long Island near St. Alban's Naval Hospital. I met her in a strange but "staged" way. My buddy and I came upon these two girls at a bus stop in Jamaica, NY, one evening, and we were immediately attracted to them. At first, they paid no attention to us. So, believe it or not, I pretended to be drunk in order to get their attention. And it worked! They thought I was just another "drunken sailor," and quite harmless and forgetful. Well, I surprised them after we made a date for the following week at a local roller-skating rink, and I actually showed up! I explained to her my "routine" to get her attention the week before, and she thought it was a little crazy and a bit risky. She said she almost didn't show up. Denise was a very interesting person, but quite different from most of the girls I'd met. She was extremely talented, being a classical pianist with a great career ahead of her. I really enjoyed listening to her play in her home when I would come to pick her up for a date. She was a tall, very beautiful, brown-haired girl who was a Conover model in New York. At that time, Conover was a prestigious agency, and they had her in several magazines of that day. But again, it was one of those situations where I was soon out of town and couldn't very well follow up on longer-term relationships. And maybe I didn't really want to!

~

The same thing was true with the next girl that I will write about, only in a different way. I met Ginny, from Freeport, Long Island, at a get-together with a number of people from our Naval Hospital in St. Albans. She totally captivated me at the time. What fun it was to get on the Long Island Railroad and travel out to Freeport to spend a day with her. Actually, she became what I will call my "transition" romance when I moved from New York to North Carolina in late 1946. In fact, I spent most of my Christmas and New Year's leave in New York with either Denise or Ginny. That New Year's Eve led to one of the few times I really got drunk in my life. Ginny stood me up, and left me emotionally in the depths of disappointment (but not in despair!).

~

There is one more girl I would like to write about from my year in New York. Quite honestly, she was the most important and loveliest girl I ever met in New York or anywhere else for many years. Her name was Jeanne (the second girl I'd met in New York with that spelling of her name, but I will not call her "Jeanne 2"). She is simply Jeanne, a truly wonderful and very special person – one of the two most special women in my life, before I met my wife, Betty, some years later. In the best sense of the phrase, she "lit up my life!" I first met Jeanne one evening in the spring of 1946 in Central Park, New York City, during a concert in the Central Park Naumburg Bandshell. I initially spotted her on the big dance area of the band shell. She was with her girlfriend and I had a buddy of mine with me, so I suggested we "look into" the situation. We followed them to the beautiful fountain area of Central Park by the lake. As we followed them, we noticed that a few other sailors and young guys were also interested. Thinking myself very perceptive and innovative (a most questionable assumption!), I realized it might take a special kind of approach to gain their interest, since I noticed that they had turned down several "invitations" of friendship from these other guys. When we approached the fountain, they were sitting on the edge of it, seemingly in an animated conversation and appearing not to notice us. With my buddy next to me, I asked him for a cigarette. He was surprised, because he knew I didn't smoke. As I approached the girls with this cigarette in my fingers, I asked for a light from Jeanne. She quickly replied a bit frostily, "I don't smoke." It was then that I tossed my cigarette into the fountain water and responded, "Neither do I! Let's see what else we have in common to talk about!" Corny? Of course! But it worked! That response led to a wonderful discussion of many things, and we went from there. By the way, I began saying her name as if it were spelled "Jeannie," and she liked that as kind of my pet name for her. Thus began a three and a half year, on-again / off-again relationship which we continued through correspondence and a number of my visits to New York City after I was transferred to North Carolina. Jeannie was a very beautiful, dark-haired, Italian girl who lived on East 95th St. in Manhattan, not far from Central Park. Again, in the best sense of the phrase, she was a "good Catholic girl," but extremely nice, self-effacing, and warm. One of her interesting characteristics was that she refused to let me spend any money on her, by simply saying that she fully enjoyed just being with me. We took long walks in Central Park (it was a safe place in those days), we took time for some long and pleasurable "necking times," and did a lot of walking and talking. She was a real friend, a true confidant, and a totally good person with whom to spend time. We got together many times while I was still in New York, and a number of times after that. With her dark, flashing eyes and beautiful Italian looks and high moral standards, she became a truly special friend as well as a right kind of huggin' and kissin' friend. One time, after I had returned from my second Mediterranean Cruise and had been to see the Pope again, I gave her one of the two medallions which I had received personally from the Pope as he spoke to me in English. Wow! You'd have thought I had given her the Empire State Building! She was so excited and so enthralled and thankful for my gift to her (and it seemed such a small thing to me at the time), that I like to say I could have "taken advantage" of her that night. Of course, that's not a true statement – I wouldn't and she wouldn't. The closure in our relationship came as I left the Navy in the late summer of 1949, and saw her for the last time. It was a beautiful, very sentimental time together (in Central Park, of course), and I'm sure we remain in each other's memories as very special people to each other along the road of life who made a genuine and wonderful impact on each other! I have no idea whatever happened to her, and we never heard from each other again. But to this day, she remains one of the women in my life whom I would most like to see again, just because she was so good and so special to me at a very formative, maturing, and spiritual-growing time of my life! Thank you, Jeannie! And thank you, God!

~

Along with my Navy years in various parts of the country and the world, there were a few things going on back home in Michigan, but not much. By "not much," I mean with respect to romance and numbers of romances. Besides Vonnie, Lee, and Shirley, there was Elise (called Irene by her family), the younger sister of one of my best buddies in Muskegon. Growing up from "kid sister" to a lovely young woman, whom I noticed immediately on one of my early Navy leaves back home, I proceeded to date her a number of times. After my years in the Navy, I got together with her several times when I was a student at Valpo, going to see her in Taylorville, Illinois, where she and her family had moved. Some years later, when I was married and a student at the seminary in Springfield, I saw her again. She and her husband ran a dry-cleaning business in Springfield, and I was able to have some good conversations with her, particularly since I was close to her family, including some of them right there in Springfield. Her brother, Bill, who now lives in Tucson and who was in the Air Force for 20 years, brought me up to date recently. To my surprise, he hadn't even known that I had dated his sister years before!

~

The last girl from my New York era is a girl named Helen. She came into my life at that time and then again briefly many years later in a completely different context. Helen was the next door neighbor and cousin to "Jeanne 1" in Rockaway Beach. After my relationship with Jeanne 1 had faded (mostly because I wasn't serious, marriage-wise, and she was), I continued my friendship with the family next door. That included the youngest of three daughters, a seven-year-old, very gifted child named Danielle, who adopted me as her "big brother," and the rest of the family accepted me as "one of them." Whenever I came to New York, not only did I have a place to stay, but I also had a loving family of very good people who welcomed me and treated me like family. Since Helen was totally with a guy whom she would eventually marry, she became a very good friend. And that is how we continued our relationship through correspondence and visits to New York. I did notice an increasing amount of more-than-friendship feelings on my part toward her, but could expect nothing more in response. When I got out of the Navy in late summer, 1949, I went up to New York for five days before returning to Michigan, and stayed with my "family." During these days, and well before them, I was experiencing these feelings about Helen, but decided that nothing should be done about them. As it turned out, Helen's guy was somewhere off in the Navy, and she and I spent some special times together. I took her to the Broadway show, *Charley's Aunt*, with the incomparable Ray Bolger (the Straw Man of the *Wizard of Oz* movie) in the starring role. We went out several other times after that. Obviously, there was something between us, but she was committed and I was on my way in a very different direction, geographically and career-wise. However, that didn't prevent us from some romantic times together. Many years later, when we met again, she told me about her feelings that last time in New York. I had taken her to her nurse's dorm, where she was in training, and after our final hugs and kisses, she walked away up the stairs to the office and her room. Later, she told me, "As I walked up those stairs and you turned to leave, I asked myself, *Am I making a mistake?*" And that was that. I will return to Helen later.

~

During my years in the Navy, I did have some things going on in North Carolina and back in Michigan. I met and dated a very nice girl in Wilson, North Carolina. Her name was Eunice, and I'd see her from time to time when I went to church in Wilson between my cruises in the Caribbean Sea and the Mediterranean Sea. There was a girl I met in Norfolk, Virginia, in 1947, whom I remember with special affection. Pat (Patricia), just out of high school and barely 19, had accompanied her girlfriend from New York to Norfolk and the sailors there! As it turned out, her friend was there to "lose her virginity in Virginia!" That was not quite Pat's goal, but she was really caught at a difficult time of her life. I'm glad I came along when I did. I'm not sure how I met her in Norfolk (since I wouldn't go to the many bars in town), but it was probably at a roller-skating rink. Anyway, we met and it was quite obvious to me that she really didn't share her friend's "ambitions" in Norfolk with the sailors. After we dated several times, I realized that she didn't agree with her friend in the whole matter, but wasn't sure what to do about it. After several dates, I impressed upon her how important it was for her to return to New York and get on with her life back there. She agreed and promised to go back the next day. While I would have liked her to stay in Norfolk a few more days (my selfish dating desires), I knew that it was imperative that she return to New York immediately or else get caught up in the life of her friend. A day or two after her promise, I was in Norfolk and spotted her in a movie theater with a sailor. Suddenly, I became her protective "older brother" and came down on her very hard. It was obvious that she needed some guidance and support. When I saw her a few days later, by arrangement, we had a very nice time together. But I insisted that she return to New York and get out of this "Norfolk hole." As a guarantee (and I don't know what gave me the audacity of such a request), I demanded that she send me a postcard, postmarked the day she returned to New York, as evidence of her promise to me. And she did it! I had no right to demand such a thing of her, but she did it. The end of this story occurred a couple of years later. She wrote me a long letter, explaining in detail what had happened to her in the intervening year or two, and then told me about her impending marriage to a very good guy! She explained how my time with her and my insistence that she return to New York had totally affected her life. She gave me credit where it really wasn't due, since I would have liked her to remain in Norfolk as long as I was there (about three weeks). But I knew she needed to get out of there as soon as possible, and I insisted that she do so. I'm glad it turned out well for her, but I cannot claim much credit. It was her decision. I only helped her make it. But what a special memory.

~

Once I was discharged from the Navy, I returned home to Muskegon in the early fall of 1949, a little too late to start college in September without being behind at the very beginning. I needed to do some studying in preparation, and my high school grades had not been that good. Remember, I had only taken a general prep high school curriculum, not college prep. So, I didn't begin at Valparaiso University until the Spring Semester (February, 1950). In the meantime, I took a few months off and drew compensation for veterans called "52-20" (up to 52 weeks at $20 per week for any veteran not gainfully employed, and hopefully giving him time to do so).

Girl-wise, it was my re-introduction to the civilian arena of girls in my church and in the community back home, and I dated some very nice ones at that time and the summer months in between college semesters. One was a high school senior in Holland, Michigan (about 40 miles from Muskegon), whom I met at a Youth Rally in Holland that fall. Her name was Renee, a very nice, light-haired girl with an enjoyable personality. Her parents liked me even more than she did – not an uncommon occurrence in my romantic life! Once I began going to Valpo and wasn't around much anymore, the relationship faded. However, going with her provided me with a wonderful story about the Dutch Reformed people, very populous in Western Michigan. A family of Dutch Reformed lived next door to her, and were reputed to be very strict (no alcohol, no activities on Sunday, very pietistic). Late one Sunday evening, as she and I sat on the swing on her front porch, she suggested that we watch the basement lights next door at midnight. Almost literally at the stroke of midnight, we watched the man next door turn on the basement lights, go down the steps into the basement, go over to a cupboard, bring out a jug of whiskey, take a long drink from it several times, then return upstairs. We really laughed about that, but it was also a vivid reminder to me about how easy it is to get caught up in the form and outward show of spirituality, and make that more important than the real basis and heart of Christianity. Perhaps, since I grew up in such a Dutch Reformed area, I have always had a questionable feeling about pious-sounding expressions of the Christian faith without a corresponding feeling of true righteousness, humility, and awareness of my own weakness, sinfulness, and spiritual vulnerability. That is true to this day, as I look at the American religious scene and note all the "religiosity" and sanctimonious pronouncements by certain religious and political leaders trying to turn our nation into another Calvin's Geneva, known as "The City of God," which was a total disaster, both politically and spiritually. You cannot dictate or legislate or pontificate spirituality, or even Christianity, on a nation, a state, a community, or a family! It is the Gospel which saves, not the Law! Well, enough editorializing. Back to more enjoyable subjects – girls and women!

~

Among several girls in our neighborhood, there was Sandy. Some of the guys said that she "put out" – not a nice thing to say about a girl in those days or any other days. Sandy was a redhead whom I knew from years before on my newspaper route. She turned out to be a delightful person. When I dated her a number of times that fall and the next summer, I discovered what I'd suspected – what the guys said was not true. We had some good times together, and she once paid me the compliment, "You're the nicest guy I've ever gone out with!" I realized that what she probably meant was, *You're the nicest guy because you treated me as a good person, and didn't try to "make out!"*

~

There was also a very, very nice girl in Walther League whom I dated several times, and whom I really liked very much, named Jan (Janice). She was a farm girl from a nearby town, and it was just very pleasant to be with her. She eventually met and married one of my very best buddies back in Michigan, and she was a terrific farmer's wife and mother, and a very good person in every sense of the word. And I got to be best man at their wedding in early 1954!

~

At this point, I'm going to spend some time describing a person who, next to Betty and Nancy, was the best woman in my life, both romantically and otherwise. I dislike using numbers to designate girls in my life, but I need to call her "Margie 1" since there is another Margie in my life later on (in Cleveland) who was very significant. All references to "Margie" in this section refer to this first Margie, a remarkable woman! Margie was happily married to a Lutheran pastor who was in retirement in North Carolina. I met Margie in Muskegon shortly after I got out of the Navy, at one of our Youth functions. She was at that time, and still is, somewhat disabled in one hip so as to make her limp rather noticeably. But what a personality! She had come to Muskegon to live with her aunt and to work, since she was a high school graduate from Chicago. Her sweetness, humbleness, and self-effacing personality immediately appealed to me, in spite of her so-called "crippled" condition. Fortunately for me, she lived only a short distance from me in Muskegon, so I found myself at her aunt's home quite often. We did a lot of things together: youth meetings and parties, tobogganing, long rides, and worship services. Our romantic relationship continued on for several years, from those first months in Muskegon and, off and on, through my first three years at Valpo. Shortly after I began school at Valpo (60 miles from Chicago), Margie moved back to Chicago to live with her parents on the Northside of Chicago for a better job. That was great for me because I could visit her on weekends very regularly, as I did those three years at Valpo. It was a tremendous time for me, to be with her family those many times, since they seemed to care for me immensely. I got along well with her siblings, especially her youngest brother, my little buddy Davey. One of my most memorable times with her was the weekend she came to Valpo with her brand new red convertible! We drove around campus and around the dormitories, and I just acted like the "king" as the guys whistled and cheered as we drove by! I don't know who enjoyed that the most – her or me?

To this very day, we are still the very best of friends, and I still consider her one of the greatest, most beautiful girls that has dated me in my whole life! I love her in a very special way!

~

About the time I started at Valpo in February, 1950, I met an old friend of mine from grade school days named Peggy. She was a year older than me –

very bright and I found her to be a very pretty girl, even in the early days of my life. I vaguely recall taking a liking to her back in the 3rd or 4th grade, but that was it. Over the years I would see her at church or elsewhere, but I never had the courage to do anything since she was too mature for "gun-shy" me in those days when I was a teenager. After I came back from the Navy and started looking around, it didn't take me long to notice her, and she was still unattached. I was assisted in my pursuit of her by my beautiful step-cousin, June, and her husband, Barth. My esteemed uncle, Harry Knuth, had remarried after my beloved aunt's death, so June was now my step-cousin. Anyway, June and Barth were good friends of Peggy, so it was quite "natural" that they would invite her over for dinner and cards from time to time – me included! We began dating a lot, and had a very good relationship through the summer of 1950 and well into the fall. However, once I got back to Valpo, things seemed to cool off, and I finally "broke it off" a bit hesitantly. She was quite ready for marriage, but I was not, and she needed to find someone to marry her (which she eventually did successfully). But she helped make that summer of 1950 a very wonderful time. I got a fairly well-paying job at a local brewery, played baseball several evenings a week with an Industrial League team, and I had a girlfriend who came to all the games and with whom I had many good times. She, too, would have been a good choice for a wife, except I apparently was just not ready and couldn't move myself to that realm yet. It was also at this point of my life that I began to wonder if I was even capable of sustaining a romantic relationship with a girl for more than four or five months. The next few years would seemingly verify that feeling on my part. It didn't bother me particularly at the time, but it did cause me to think more deeply about what it was about me that seemed to defy a natural progression toward the marital state. Well, the beautiful and curvaceous Peggy disappeared from my romantic life, and I continued on, well aware that I may have passed up a good woman for the rest of my life, just as I did with "Margie 1." But, that's the way it was.

~

During the winter of 1950-51, I had renewed my good friendship with my farmer buddy, Harland. We had met in the context of Walther League after I had returned from the Navy, and we had many good times together. Actually, it was through our many get-togethers as Walther Leaguers in our area that he met and later married Jan, whom I had dated previously. One time at a Zone

Rally in Holland, he and I mistakenly got into the girls' bathroom and couldn't understand the lack of urinals and all the noise outside the door. With a rising crescendo of female voices, we realized what had happened. Well, we had to "face the music," so we opened the door to the shocked surprise of a bunch of girls and I quipped in a smart aleck way, "What's the problem, girls?" When Harland married Jan in February of 1954, I was his best man (and there's another whole story about our trip to the wedding). At any rate, in this whole scenario about Harland, I discovered his very attractive, dark-eyed, dark-haired sister, Corinne, who was a few years younger than me. She gave reality to one of the popular songs of the day, "Beautiful Brown Eyes" (written by Arthur Smith in 1937). Now remember, I had dated Harland's older sister, Lee, some years before; so this was an indication that I knew where the good genes were! Corinne and I had a brief but very enjoyable relationship until it appeared to her parents (and maybe to her) that it was getting too serious. They didn't know me very well, but it put a damper on the relationship, and that was that. We continued as friends, and it was a special joy many years later to meet her again at Harland and Jan's home as part of a big get-together of "old" Walther Leaguers. I found out how well she had done in life, and what a great guy she had as a husband. By the way, have you begun to notice in these writings how well many of these girls have done in life after my time with them? I'm not sure what that says, but I'm glad for them and for me!

~

During my days at Valpo, I dated a number of girls, but most of my serious relationships were back home in Michigan (Margie, Peggy, Corinne, etc.). However, there was Chris in the summer of 1952 (when I took some courses at Valpo) who did something to a halter top and shorts that shouldn't happen without a fire extinguisher nearby (as one of my St. Louis Sem buddies said one day when he saw her walking along with me across campus on a very warm day!). And there was June, whom I met in one of my classes and we dated a number of times that summer. It was never that serious, but imagine my surprise a few years later when I was a teacher at Lutheran High in Cleveland and I walked into our first faculty meeting in 1955 – and there was June sitting with the other new teachers! And then, there was Jean, the vivacious daughter of a vice president of Valpo. She was home for the summer and with nothing more to do than to have a good time. And I had the joy of sharing a lot of that time with her, as well as her family. I became very attached to them (including spending Thanksgiving Day with them, with all the trimmings and the Lions beating Green Bay on TV!). Some years later in Thousand Oaks, I became even closer to them when they were senior mentors at California Lutheran University and were members of my Redeemer congregation.

~

Unfortunately, it seemed, my "six-month romances" continued. I do not record these many stories with any sense of "victories" or "conquests" on my part. I just was not ready and, as it turned out, the Lord had someone else picked out for me – someone I was completely unaware of all this time.

~

After Peggy, there was "Betty 2," a pretty girl with the most gorgeous red hair in the world! At Valpo, she was a year behind me, having transferred from another college before my senior year. She was from the unique German community of Frankenmuth, Michigan, and was the lead drum majorette of the Valpo marching band. She was really good at it, and had won many prizes and awards over the years. I met her one day while driving from the dormitories on the east side of campus to the "old campus." In the summer of 1952, after summer school, I had returned to Muskegon and had purchased a 1928 Model A Ford for $75 from my step-uncle in Grand Haven. The first car of my own! I was very proud of it and really fixed it up attractively. I added new paint to the black body – trimming the car with silver and red striping – and to the wheel spokes to look real "cool." I had seen Betty 2 at some earlier new student function at Valpo, since I was a boys' dorm counselor. Nothing came of that, but one day I did really meet her when I saw her walking toward the old campus from the girls' dorm. I stopped and offered her a ride, which she readily and happily accepted. That was the beginning of a year-long relationship. Later, when I asked her how she seemed to come into my life so coincidentally, she confessed that she had seen me in my cool Model A Ford, and had determined she wanted to meet this guy in the Ford. So, she said, she watched carefully for several days as I drove from the dorms to the old campus and noted my schedule. Then she managed to be walking toward old campus when I would be driving that way, making it apparent that I would notice her. Since it was not unusual for guys driving back and forth between campuses to "pick up" students walking back and forth, it didn't seem unusual for me to stop and offer her a ride. Oh, the wiles of women! Well, it turned out to be a good relationship during my senior year, and even beyond that for a year or so. Several times I was a guest at her parents' home in Frankenmuth during vacation breaks from school. They owned and operated the Frankenmuth Motel on the edge of town. Once again, I became a good friend of the family, including some siblings. Betty 2 was a fun girl, and we had many good times together, including dancing. She was such an excellent dancer that I actually enjoyed dancing – as long as it was with her!

Our relationship cooled off somewhat by late spring of 1953, but we continued to see each other once in a while for the next year or so, after I went to Cleveland to teach. This dancing "business" led to one of the most interesting, amusing, and useful incidents in my life. Late in the fall of 1953, Betty 2 invited me back to Valpo for a big formal dance, put on by her sorority. Naturally, I accepted and went to Valpo for that weekend. Our arrangement was that I would pick her up at her sorority house, then we would pick up another couple and drive to Michigan City for the dance. (Valpo was not allowed to have dances on campus in those days.) When I arrived at the house, I was welcomed in by several of the sorority girls with the announcement that Betty 2 would be a few minutes late. As I sat there waiting, I noticed that the front door doorknob was loose and not in good condition for protection from outside. So, I began to work on it, even bringing in some tools from my car (I had a 1950 Mercury by this time). As I worked on, with my back to the girls in the front room behind me, I would hear a titter of laughter from time to time. I assumed that I must have been saying some funny or humorous things, as I chatted and worked on the doorknob. As I finished and stood up and turned around, there was Betty 2 coming *in* through the open door from outside. She had a very dark look on her face, as I innocently asked her what she was doing out there. She replied with all the sarcasm she could muster, "Three times I have walked past you at the door after coming down the stairway, and you didn't even notice me!" Uh, oh! Was I ever in trouble! And she looked absolutely beautiful in her evening gown. Well, it took me most of the rest of the evening to get back on track with her. But the incident has served me well as one of my favorite sermon illustrations about focusing on the most important things in our spiritual lives, and how easily we are distracted from the true vision by things that are much less important. And she was a vision that evening! We got together a few more times after that, but that was about it. I did see her once more, many years later when I was a pastor in Thousand Oaks and her son came to Cal Lutheran as a student and football player. He showed up one Sunday morning at church, and introduced himself by saying that I knew his mother quite well. One look at his bright red hair and I immediately identified him – much to his surprise! She and her husband came up to Thousand Oaks once to see him play football, and I had a nice visit with them.

~

Joyce came into my life as a result of my practice teaching experience at Hobart High School, about 12 miles from Valpo. Because I had a car, I was asked to practice teach social studies (mostly history) out of town for the whole Spring Semester every morning. As you can imagine, the kids loved to see me drive up in my Model A Ford each day, even when it was very cold and my car had no heater! The car was "cool" and that's what mattered! Joyce was a very cute, dark-haired, blue-eyed, petite senior student in one of my classes. Nothing happened while I was teaching (I never did believe in men teachers fraternizing with female students), but we knew each other well enough that she accepted my offer of a date that summer after graduation (she from high school, and me from Valpo). Her father worked in the steel mills of Gary, Indiana; it was a very solid family, and we got along extremely well. We dated a number of times that summer (Muskegon was only 150 miles from Valpo and Hobart), and several times after I went to Cleveland to teach in the fall of 1953. However, distance does make a difference, and it became another one of my "six-month romances," although we did get together several times over the next year or so. And it did seem a bit serious for a while. Joyce was an extremely sweet person and more than willing to "convert" to Lutheranism because of me. The whole thing didn't work out, but she is one of the few girls that I would have "second thoughts" about from time to time after we stopped seeing each other. I remember her with very special feelings and fondness.

~

The next girl who came into my life was Margie 2, who was a bridesmaid in the wedding of a friend of mine from Muskegon, who worked and lived in Cleveland. Margie was an attractive, vivacious blonde, a senior at Baldwin-Wallace College in Berea, Ohio, just outside of Cleveland. The wedding was in June, right after my graduation from Valpo. I spent that summer in Michigan at home with my parents. Nothing much happened with Margie in June, except it gave the opportunity to renew the acquaintance the following fall when I started teaching in Cleveland. And renew we did! For a few months it went very well, even though she lived on the east side of Cleveland and I lived on the west side. Baldwin-Wallace was closer to where I lived than her home in Cleveland Heights, so it worked out quite well, travel-wise. She came home with me to Michigan at Thanksgiving – probably viewed as a "sure sign" that it was a serious relationship – and it looked pretty serious in reality. However, in the months to follow things began to "come apart" and it became obvious to me that this wasn't "it" for me. Since she was a good friend of Jan, the wife of my buddy, Otto, I would talk with them quite a bit about Margie. When Margie and I went our separate ways, sometime around Easter that next spring, Jan was the least surprised. It was then that she informed me that Margie was really "husband hunting," and that I would be the one. When I challenged Jan with the question, "Why didn't you warn me?" she replied, "I figured you would make the right decision when the time came!" My "tip off" about Margie's feelings should have come at Christmas when I gave her a very nice present, and then found out later from Jan that Margie was expecting an engagement ring! *Whew! That was a close call!* I remember thinking to myself at the time.

My story about Margie didn't quite end there. Later that spring, after we had parted ways, my high school principal called me into his office and inquired about my relationship with Margie, and was wondering if it could be salvaged. When I chuckled about his seriously-asked question, he informed me that Margie had been in to see him and was hoping that something could still be done about "us!" I responded in a rather cavalier way that he really didn't have to bother himself about my romantic life, and that nothing was going to bring us back together anyway. I felt somewhat less "guilty" when I heard later the next year that Margie had met and married a guy she had met right after she and I had broken up. But, lest what I've said about Margie sounds negative, let me say that she was a very good person and a wonderful part of my first year in Cleveland, and I will always be grateful to her and her wonderful parents, who made me feel comfortable and at home all the time. They were good people.

~

Somewhere in my days between Valpo and Cleveland that first year, I met Trudy, who had friends and relatives in Michigan, near Muskegon. I can't remember exactly how we met – most likely on a bus when I was returning to Muskegon from Cleveland, where I had been visiting my Valpo buddy, Dave, in Rocky River. Anyway, Trudy and I dated a number of times in Michigan over the holidays before I returned to Valpo. Dave then went into the Army, but I kept in contact with Trudy. While still at Valpo, I was able to be in Cleveland for about five days during a vacation and spent most of it with Trudy, while staying with Dave's parents. Dave's mom even loaned me her car for my dates with Trudy! She was a very nice Lutheran girl, and it was good being with her. After those five days in Cleveland, we both went our different ways. However, I mention this particular time in my "romantic life" because it coincides with, and is a part of, a very important and pivotal time in my life. It was through my friendship with Dave Brueggemann and his family that I was first put into contact with Cleveland Lutheran High School and its principal, Dr. Sagehorn, a very close friend of Dave's parents. Not only that, but Dave's father was Chairman of the Board of Directors of the high school and was one of the people who made sure that Cleveland Lutheran High made it through some very difficult financial times. R.F. Brueggemann was a real gift of God to his congregation and the high school!

~

One other girl remains for me to include in this whole part of my life before I met Betty Brasch. Janet was a home economics teacher at Cleveland Lutheran High. She started teaching the same year I did – in 1953. I knew her that first year as a teaching colleague only. As my second year of teaching began, I found myself taking more notice of Janet, and she was well worth it! She was an attractive, blue-eyed blonde with a very winsome manner. We began dating the fall of 1954, and continued through the spring of 1955. Two things characterized our relationship those months: we kept it pretty much away from school and school activities (as one former student told me years later with surprise, "You and Miss B. were dating? We kids never knew that!"); and it was another one of those relationships that didn't make it past six months. As usual, it started out pretty well in the fall and winter, but then faded.

~

I am now skipping across the next five years of my "romantic" life through the age of 28, and the three years between Betty and Nancy. These years were characterized by much dating, many "romances," and a number of more serious "six-month romances," which were painful at times! However, these six-month romances served as an excellent prelude to my meeting Betty Brasch, THE Betty of my life!

~

It began this way: Several girls in my class at Lutheran High came to me one day in the late spring of 1955 and asked me what I would be doing that coming summer. After my somewhat nebulous reply, they suggested that I might like to come to Camp Pioneer as a counselor or program director. Camp Pioneer was a Lutheran Laymen's League camp on Lake Erie – just south of Buffalo, near Angola, New York. It was run by a former teacher, Hap Schroeder, and my students had been there before as camp workers. They assured me that it would be fun, that I was the right kind of person to be part of the program, and that they would really like me to be there. In one of the momentous decisions of my life, I replied, "I have already applied to work for Gates Rubber Company out of Denver (as I'd done the summer before). Of course, I'd love to be with all of you at Camp Pioneer, and I will apply for a job there for this summer, but it will depend on who answers my application first." A couple of weeks after I had applied at Camp Pioneer, I received an acceptance from the camp director to be on staff as counselor and assistant program director. That was on a Friday. I immediately responded that I was accepting the offer, and would be with them as soon as school was out in early June. The following Monday, I received a reply from Gates Rubber Company, indicating that I had been approved to work for them again in the summer ahead. Interestingly, the reply from Gates was postmarked the day before the postmarked date of the response from Camp Pioneer! Due to the difference in time and distance, the Gates reply had arrived later than the Camp Pioneer reply. In God's own wisdom, He must have planned it that way, unbeknownst to me. To this day, I thank God for that wonderful "turn in my life!"

Now, for the first part of my story about BETTY. While there were a couple of "Bettys" previously, this one is MY Betty – THE ONE! I am overwhelmed by the prospect of trying to describe this first part of our life together for 36 years, since she was the full essence of my life after the summer of 1955. I will try to describe what happened from the very beginning of our 36-year "love affair." It begins with my feelings that late spring of 1955, when I was somewhat depressed by the chain of events of the "six-month romances" for the past two years or more. It really bothered me, as a person and as a Christian. When I agreed to go to Camp Pioneer, I had my own "agenda" for the summer: no dates and no romances. I just wanted to get away from that whole scene for a few months, and Camp Pioneer seemed a good way to do that. That resolve, or "vow" to myself, lasted exactly two weeks! When I got to Camp Pioneer, after the usual introductions and procedures, I found myself mostly in the company of a last-year seminary student, Ken Frerking, with whom I would be working. He was engaged to be married later that summer, so I thought that by sticking to him I would be able to stay away from females and be "safe" for the summer. I had not counted on meeting Betty Brasch! She had come to Camp Pioneer as the camp nurse for the summer, at the suggestion of her good friend, whose mother ran the kitchen at the camp. She and Betty had known each other for a long time before. Betty had graduated from Lutheran Deaconess Hospital in Buffalo in the spring of 1955. She and a nurse friend had gone to Texas and Florida for six months of nursing work, but were now on their way back to Buffalo. Before beginning her nursing work in Buffalo, Betty had decided to come to Camp Pioneer for the summer. So, you see, I am convinced that the two of us were drawn together by "forces" unknown to us at the time, but known to God.

At first, I tried not to pay much attention to Betty, since she seemed to have a good relationship with everyone there. She was a very pretty woman of 22, with green-gray eyes that sparkled, with a wonderful personality and the most beautiful smile in the world! I was captivated, but I resisted stoutly. In fact, the first words I ever really spoke to her almost got me in trouble. The first weekend at camp before the regular camping season was a Lutheran Laymen's League retreat. Everyone on staff took part in feeding and entertaining them, including the camp nurse, counselors, and program directors. I was one of the "runners," bringing huge plates full of sandwiches to them on the large veranda of the main meeting building. As I passed through the kitchen, there was Betty, stirring a large kettle of soup, looking tired and perspiring freely in the hot kitchen, no makeup left on her face, hair stringing down – thoroughly "unpresentable" and probably not in a very good mood. In my smart-aleck way, as I went past her with my tray of sandwiches, I exclaimed, "Hi, Beautiful!" What I didn't realize at the time – she had a big soup ladle in her hand. Later, she told me she almost hit me with it! Such was my "introduction" to the love of my life for the next 36 years! I can't explain it, but something began to happen in the next couple of weeks. As a staff, we all ate our meals together. I can remember feeling some twinges of jealousy one time when one of the guys put his arm on the back of her chair, like they had something going on. And I hadn't even dated her yet! But it did get my competitive juices running, I guess, because I sure began to take a more serious interest in her. Well, after only two weeks, I broke my resolve and asked Betty for a date to see a movie in Buffalo. After that, it was just one great experience after another, as we grew to know each other and as we became more and more aware of something special between us. Before the summer was over, I knew that I was in love with her in a far different way than with any other girl in my life until then, and I also knew by summer's end that I wanted to marry her. She didn't quite know that yet, but it would come soon. What a truly marvelous summer that was: swimming at night in warm and clean Lake Erie, walking for miles together, spending many hours in conversation and sharing, and just simply enjoying each other. Betty's father was a Lutheran minister in Buffalo, and I soon realized that she carried a distinct and deep spiritual dimension to her life and our relationship. We believed together as one! That was an extremely important thing to me, and I truly rejoiced in such a special spiritual oneness with her in our relationship and in our growing love for each other.

However, for the first time in my life (and it would happen only one other time), I found myself questioning whether I was good enough for this beautiful woman. While I never really doubted that most of the girls I went out with were my equal or better than me in many ways, I also seemed to feel that I could relate to them positively and that I was maybe "good enough" for them. If that sounds like a contradictory statement, so be it. At any rate, I realized that I wanted more than anything in the world to convince this very special woman that I was the man in her life. To that end, I began the long courtship of her that would result in our wedding the following August 25th, 1956. The biggest problem I had was not with her or her wonderful parents or anything else about her. My biggest problem was with myself and my typical six-month "in-love / out-of-love" history. And yet, as with no other woman I had ever met until that time, I simply knew that Betty was "it!" With that realization, I returned to Cleveland for my third year of teaching, with regular trips to Buffalo every other weekend (usually following a Friday night football game, since I was an assistant football coach). Those were some interesting trips in my 1954 Nash Metropolitan car and its little English Austin engine. The road at that time between Cleveland and Buffalo was bad, and there was the wild winter weather off of Lake Erie. Later that same winter, Betty's father took a call to a small congregation in Pittsburgh, and so I made that trip from Cleveland regularly, about the same distance as to Buffalo. During this time, I went through some serious "mood swings" to the extent that Betty's mother was somewhat worried about this guy who was seeing her daughter so often. My mood swings had nothing to do with Betty, but with me. Once I passed the six-month "wall," I knew even more than ever that God had reserved this special woman for me, and that I had better wake up to that reality and do something about it. So, on Easter of 1956, I proposed to Betty in front of the fireplace in her parents' home (late at night, and after I had asked her parents' permission), standing below a large painting of Christ. To me, that was the most appropriate place to do that. And she accepted my proposal! Hallelujah!

By the way, during that year, Betty would come to Cleveland once in a while and stay at the home of my teaching colleague, Bud Dewitt, and his family. I was renting a room from them that year in Euclid, Ohio, on the east side of Cleveland. Almost needless to say, those, too, were very special weekends and I will always be grateful to the DeWitts for warm hospitality and love.

I finished my third year of teaching in Cleveland, and got a summer job as a mailman (or, as now called, "letter carrier"), beginning in the "Flats" of Cleveland. After a few weeks, they needed a substitute for a carrier who had badly injured his ankle in Euclid (where I lived), and would be out for the rest of the summer. I became his substitute and enjoyed my route, the daily walking and my contact with people, including my pastor and his wife. Since they lived two houses from the end of one street, I would deliver mail to the end of the street and then double back for coffee, a donut, and wonderful conversation before continuing on to the next street! I didn't do this every day, of course, but several times a week. Their teenage daughter, Dorcas, was one of my students who had first suggested I come to Camp Pioneer, where I met my Betty! Dorcas was a very special person, and when Betty and I got married in Pittsburgh, Dorcas was the soloist.

While Betty pretty much planned the wedding, I made the trip back and forth all summer long until the week before the wedding. It was not a large wedding party, in that we used only a maid of honor and a best man (my brother, Dave). Betty's father officiated and it was a very beautiful, worshipful, celebrating wedding, with the reception held on the large lawn area next to the church, Emmanuel Lutheran in Squirrel Hill. Some friends of mine came from Michigan, some of Betty's friends attended, along with a number of Lutheran High students of mine who came from Cleveland. Of course, Betty's brother, Jim, and his wife, Delores, were there, plus a few of Betty's relatives from Canada. By most standards, it was not a large or expensive wedding (we didn't even have a professional photographer), but nonetheless it was a beautiful wedding and we both enjoyed it immensely!

We took a very brief honeymoon (overnight in an old downtown hotel in Beaver Falls, PA, which I thought would be a modern hotel when I made the reservation!). Then we returned to Cleveland on Sunday. Football practice for Cleveland Lutheran High began that following Monday, and I was again an assistant football coach. And Betty was to begin work at a small hospital on the east side of Cleveland. We had an old, upstairs apartment in East Cleveland, whose floors sloped decidedly downhill. In fact, in all the places we lived in the early years of our marriage, we always wound up in an upstairs apartment (five, all total) until the church in Ithaca (my first parish) bought a one-level parsonage in 1963.

There is so much more I could write about these years of our life together, but I think I'll leave it for now and pick up my time with Betty as it intersects with my life in many other ways during the 35 years we were married. Suffice it to say at this point, Betty was the greatest woman in my life until then. Now, there are two "best" women! How blessed I am!

I'm not sure where to go next in this part of my life story, except to move across 35 years. After 35 years of a terrific marriage and the birth and life of three sons, Betty joined her Lord in eternity on December 19th, 1991. Those wonderful, exciting, event-filled, and adventurous 35 years are another whole story, which I will pick up later.

In this section of my life story, entitled "The Women of My Life," I must continue on with what happened after Betty died. Reflecting back on that time, this is not easy to do. However, women continued to play an important part in my life, and affected me in some almost strange and blessed ways, especially when God brought Nancy into my life. Betty, in her usual wise and yet loving way, had carefully indicated to me that if women were to come into my life after she was "gone," that was perfectly all right. She said this to me in several different ways during the four and a half years of her terminal cancer illness. She said it most clearly one day as we were driving together on the freeway and discussing what my life would be like after her. Of course, I didn't really want to have such a discussion, but Betty, in her loving and practical way, found it quite comfortable to speak of such things. Amazing woman! At one point in the discussion (which I was not enjoying and had objected to), she made the prophetic comment, "I'll give you one to two years, Jim!" What she meant, of course, was that I would find another woman for my life within that time span after she was gone. I vehemently objected to her prediction and the whole tone and direction of our discussion, but she turned out to be close to right, within a year or so. However, in her insightful way and with a wisdom always beyond mine, she knew me so very well and she knew how important her words were for me. And she was very secure and strong in the relationship that we had for 35 years. Therefore, she could say something like that and laugh lovingly at my objections to her words! She realized then, as I did not, that my love for her would never be diminished or lessened or reduced in importance and depth by the presence of another woman in my life later on. At the time, I did not accept her premise or prediction, because it was not something I could even begin to think about. However, she knew me better than I knew myself, and she was, in her own sweet way, giving me a truly amazing gift: "Permission" to love again as a husband and special friend to a woman whom God might send into my life later on! Wow! There are no words to convey the depth or meaning of that gift of hers to me. It would take some time after her death for me to begin to realize and comprehend what she was really talking about. But now I know for certain the greatness of that gift she gave me and what special blessing such a gift would be for me and for many other people, particularly a woman named Nancy! I have been blessed beyond all measure all my life! This "proved" it even more!

~

What would my life now be like in regards to "women in my life" after Betty? To begin with, I must say that it was probably the strangest time of my life, ever. I had my work as a full-time pastor (and I decided, along with my congregation's happy approval, to stay on past the retirement age of 65, which turned out to be two more years). I had my three sons, two daughters-in-law, and one grandson, all living in Ventura County. But I also had this tremendous void in my life which nothing could replace. I had some wonderful people around me, including my supportive congregation, my friends, my family counselor and friend, Rev. Ron Rehrer, and others.

At a time like this in my life, memories flooded my mind constantly. Sometimes I found myself feeling down and terribly lonely. Then, along came a gift in the person of Betty's best friend, Joanne Stone. As Joanne said to me one time, "You've lost your wife and your best friend. Well, I've also lost my best friend."

I don't recall how it began, but we found ourselves getting together, "just to talk." Her coming over became almost a ritual each time to which I found myself looking forward. We shared many times together with thoughts and words about Betty. In a kind of bizarre way, I found myself feeling much solace and encouragement, almost pleasantness. She built up my self-esteem, shared some tears from time to time, and helped me put my life into a realistic perspective. It especially helped me when I experienced some seeming "flirtations" or strange "coincidences" in other relationships. At the time, I viewed such experiences with curiosity and a peculiar kind of revulsion – and yet they piqued my male ego.

I suppose there might have been some inkling of a romance between Joanne and me, but it didn't progress. Her loving, constructive handling of the whole situation helped in a grieving, strengthening way – but that was it. To this day, I credit Joanne with not only keeping me on a good, healthy tract while I grieved Betty's death, but she allowed me to open up to someone in many ways that I could not have done with anyone else at the time, because of her closeness to Betty. When I speak of "women in my life," I also mean a few of them in some very special ways, and Joanne was one of the most very special. I will always "owe" her, and it will always be a special joy of mine to keep in touch with her and her life. A little later in my writing, I will tell you about one other way in which she touched my life.

~

At this point, I should interject a brief paragraph on some interesting and somewhat humorous aspects of my life as a mature (?), adult, single male in relative control of his life and faculties, who was once again "loose" in the world! There was the woman whom I had counseled on several occasions in a tough post-divorce situation who sent me a most inviting picture of herself in a Christmas card with some warm words of inviting "encouragement!" There was the ex-wife of a California Lutheran University professor who "suddenly" started showing up at my worship services on Sunday morning in Ventura, even though she lived in Thousand Oaks. Then there was the widowed mother of a young woman I had married. I had befriended the mother particularly at the wedding rehearsal and reception because she always seemed to be alone. She sent me a nice card after the wedding with a most friendly invitation to drop by and visit her sometime when I was in Thousand Oaks. There was the widowed administrative assistant to the president of California Lutheran University whom I knew very well. Her husband had been on the Department of Religion faculty and was a good friend of mine before he died. Sometime later, when I told her of my coming marriage, she congratulated me and said, "I wish I hadn't decided not to remarry, then I might have had a chance at you, Jim!" I just smiled ignominiously. Then there were the rumors at Los Robles Hospital. These rumors all suggested that Joanne and I would be a "natural" to get together. This bothered her very much and it bothered me somewhat, although I was also flattered a bit by it all. Then there were suggestions that it would be nice if a certain very lovely widow in my former congregation in Thousand Oaks and I would get together (a suggestion which I never seriously considered, and which probably would have embarrassed her, had she known of it). There were some other little things that happened along these lines, not worth mentioning. By the way, while I could have interpreted these events and "coincidences" in my life after Betty as a big boost to my male ego, just remember – in a society where the women outnumber the men in my age range by a 2-to-1 margin, I would have been attractive as a "straw man" or a warm, male body!

~

Before I get into the "romantic" bend to my life at that time, let me mention one other wonderful woman during this period. Her name is Jan, the ex-wife of a Lutheran pastor. I knew him from my seminary days, and I counseled them (the two of them, but mostly her) a number of times some years before. He had a position at California Lutheran University and they finally divorced after much counseling and after they had changed congregations because of his position at Cal Lutheran (an ELCA school). Jan was an 8th-grade teacher in the public schools in Ventura (although still living in Thousand Oaks), and someone whom Betty and I both knew very well. Several months after Betty died, Jan called me up with the invitation for a cup of coffee and talk. After that, we went to some cultural events at Cal Lutheran together (where we were both well-known). We also went to some other events around town, and had some coffee and dessert times at Marie Callender's in Ventura when she was through with school in the afternoon. These times together turned out to be both helpful for me and seemingly enjoyable for her. I suppose we both entertained some romantic thoughts along the way, but never to fruition. As we both realized, it was a very good and comfortable situation in these informal ways, but we really did not have a "romantic leg to stand on." To this day, we are good friends and we treasure that in our lives, but that really is it. As she once told me, "We'd never make it together, Jim, because I knew Betty too well, it's still too soon, and neither of us would be comfortable with that." I was relieved and agreed with her. But I am also indebted to her for her loving, Christian sensitivity and good, common sense. She is a gem!

~

Now, on to some of my "romantic escapades" in my life before I met Nancy. In the summer of 1992, about seven months after Betty, I heard from a former student of mine from Cleveland Lutheran High. She was living in Florida and was interested in keeping the class of 1955 in touch with each other, and this is why I had heard from her from time to time over the last couple of years. Gail is a tall (about 6′) former high school All-Star basketball player in the Cleveland area, who even did some professional women's play for a while. In the late summer of 1992, Gail and I struck up a correspondence which led her to come out to California several times. We began what I considered a bit of a romance and a relationship, which I insisted would not become serious. It finally did – for her. When her seriousness became obvious, we ended that dimension of our relationship, but we continued our friendship. You see, when we first got together, she had been really turned off to the church after her two marriages and divorces. I was catching her on the rebound, as the saying goes, and I knew that. So, in this time together, I was able to help get her back to her "roots" in the church, but even more importantly in her relationship with Christ. To her wonderful and everlasting credit, instead of going back to her life as it had been (even though she was disappointed by the fact that our relationship, romantically speaking, had ended), she stayed with her Lord and His Church down there in Florida. In her work for the church down there, she met and married a wonderful widower and was happier than ever! She and her husband have visited Nancy and me here in Orange, CA, and we all look forward to being together at a future Cleveland Lutheran High reunion.

~

I now need to mention Helen again. You met her a few pages ago when I was stationed in New York in the Navy, and was very much a part of her family. After running into her in Ithaca, New York, in 1986 (the 25th anniversary of my congregation there), she kept me abreast of her family – where they were and what was happening to them. In the fall of 1987, I was invited to preside at the wedding of a good friend of my son, Dave. Andy was a member of my congregation in Thousand Oaks whose mother I had attended the night she died in 1970. I knew Andy and the family well, and had met his wife-to-be, Josephine, previously in T.O. While in Ithaca (where Helen now lived and worked) for the wedding at Anabel Taylor Chapel on the Cornell campus, Helen and I met briefly and recounted earlier times I was in New York. But that was it. Several years later, it was somewhat different. Whether it was in Ithaca, where she came back to the church by joining my first congregation (Trinity Lutheran), or when she came out to California to visit her uncle in Chino, we enjoyed getting together. This went on for almost a year, but it really wasn't for me, even though I had some romantic feelings for a while. I really wasn't that interested, mostly because it was still too soon after Betty's death. It was just a very nice time with a very nice woman, and it turned out even better for both of us the way it all went.

~

And now, a special section on Vera. She is the younger sister of one of the two most influential men in my life, Bill Scheer, my 8th-grade teacher in 1940-41. Vera is a year younger than me and was part of the high school Walther League group at Trinity Lutheran in Muskegon in the early 1940s. While I knew her quite well, mostly due to her residence a short distance from my home in East Muskegon, and her older brother being our youth counselor at Trinity, there was never any romantic interest in those days of Walther League "round-robin-dating." She was in love with one of the guys in our group, and that never changed. She married him as soon as she could at the age of 18. I did not hear or know of Vera for many years, but I did keep up a bit with her over the years through information from other people in the Walther League from time to time. When her husband, Don, died near Christmas of 1990, I didn't know about it. The following year, I found out through a Christmas card from her brother in Fremont, Michigan. I wrote her a long-overdue note of sympathy, but that was it. Then, shortly after Betty died, I got a phone call from her from her sister's house in Palos Verdes, CA, just wanting to thank me for my note the previous Christmas. *What note?* I thought to myself. But I didn't bother to carry it any further. We didn't get together then, but the next time I was in Muskegon (late fall of 1992), I became aware that there was going to be a party of "Old Walther League" people at her home, and that I was the main reason for it! Well, I was staying with my brother, Dave, in Twin Lake (ten miles away), so it was easy to get to this get-together with some good old friends, including her brother and his wife. From the moment I showed up at her door early for that get-together, there was something special about our feelings and we really "hit it off" well. She had a very nice, big house in Muskegon in a fairly plush neighborhood, with a very close access to the shore of Lake Michigan (about a ten-minute walk). Her husband had been a very successful inventor and businessman, and had left her in good financial condition. She had six children, all adults by this time. She is also an accomplished pianist and artist. From that immediate good beginning, we began to spend time together, and it seemed that something very special was happening. We went to church with each other, visited her son and family in Pontiac, MI, visited her brother and wife in Fremont, MI, and just generally enjoyed each other immensely. She has a sister in Palos Verdes, CA, so we had a chance to get together whenever she came out to see her sister, which suddenly became more often! For a while, I really believed this was the "real thing." I got back to Muskegon a few times after that, both to see my brother and family, and to see Vera. It was a very good time. Since one of Vera's four sons (she also has two daughters) lived in Iowa City, and was a maker and repairer of violins and cellos, it was natural for me to go to Iowa, and for me to visit my very dear friends, Kay and Jerry Slocum in Cedar Rapids. Previous to this, Vera had come out to visit her sister in Palos Verdes. She and I had dinner with Joanne, since I valued Joanne's thoughts and feelings about anyone with whom I was romantically involved. Joanne, of course, was the essence of decorum and graciousness, but sometime later she shared with me her real feelings and thoughts (which turned out to be "right on"). While in Cedar Rapids, Kay, Jerry, Vera, and I arranged to attend the Iowa City Concert, where Vera's son, Jim, would be playing the cello. The whole concert program was devoted to music of the 60s, 70s, and 80s, including many songs which were associated in my mind with Betty. Well, during that concert I had the most traumatic "Betty-flashback" I had ever had, and it completely devastated me! I spent the whole 30-minute intermission with Jerry, telling him what was happening to me and how I felt. He must have thought I was crazy. It was like a nightmare! It was at that point that I realized I was not in love with Vera, and never would be. It "crushed" me at the time, but that's the way it was. In retrospect, I think it was still too close to when Betty "left" me, but I didn't know it at the time. When I told Vera that night how I felt and what had happened to me, she was very disappointed, a bit angry, but accepting and understanding. A remarkable woman! We continued our relationship for a while after that, but it was never the same. To this day, Vera remains as one of the most gracious and lovely women in my life, and I owe her more than I can ever repay. Our relationship ended when I met Nancy, but I was somewhat haunted by what seemed to be my "six-month romance" syndrome of earlier years. When Vera matter-of-factly told me the last time we were together, "In you, Jim, I not only lost a love in my life, but I also lost my best friend," I really felt badly. She is a truly wonderful person, and I will always remember her with fondness and gratitude. She was the "bridge" between Betty and Nancy, and played an important role in my life. I hear about her from time to time through her family in Muskegon, and they say she is doing very well and making a good life for herself back east.

~

And now on to the second great part of this "women in my life" scenario – NANCY! Actually, I knew Nancy from many years before, when she was a high school student at Cleveland Lutheran during her junior and senior years. I did not know her well, since she was never in either of my classes in U.S. History or American Problems. But in a high school of 450 students, you got to know most of them to some degree or another, even if you didn't have them in one of your own classes. She graduated in 1955, and after a year's wait went to

Concordia University, River Forest, Illinois, to become a parochial school teacher. After brief teacherages in Chalmette, Louisiana, and Collinsville, Illinois, she continued her teaching career at St. Paul's Lutheran Church and School in Orange, CA. This also put her close to her sister and family in California. It was during this time that she met and married Ken Kilian, the pastor of a congregation in South Phoenix, Arizona. She was there with him for ten years, during which time she gave birth to three sons: Joel, Jason, and Nathan. Her husband then took a call into the ministry of Lutheran Bible Translators, located in Orange, where she again picked up her teaching career at St. Paul's. Ken served in various capacities in LBT and then the Southern California District of the LCMS until his death in 1990 at the age of 53. It was during this period that I got to know Ken somewhat, and liked him very much.

I didn't know about Nancy at the time I was serving at Redeemer Lutheran Church in Thousand Oaks, CA. However, there was a very momentous meeting with her in 1985 (it became "momentous" only in retrospect, and in terms of what happened years later!). At a huge and formal celebration for Dr. Arnold Kuntz as the outgoing district president in a prestigious hotel in downtown Los Angeles, we met again, seemingly inconsequentially. As a large crowd of pastors and wives gathered in a kind of "mob scene" in the foyer of the hotel before the banquet began, I was standing with a small group of people. In the midst of the loud, conversational noise level throughout the foyer, I heard what can only be described as a "wee, small voice" speaking from nearby and behind me: "Mr. Lareva?" I said to the group I was with, "It's a former student!" Over the years, I had learned that the only people who address me that way are former students from Cleveland Lutheran High. This is the only way they remembered me by name as a teacher. I turned around and gazed at a very lovely woman with a beautiful face and a gorgeous smile! I didn't recognize her until she began by saying, "Mr. Lareva, you won't remember me, but I'm Nancy Precker Kilian, and I ..." I immediately interrupted her, "Sure, I remember you! You were the high school girlfriend of Ron Fletcher, the trombone player!" With a look of amazement, she smiled broadly in agreement, and we had a brief 2-3 minute conversation. And that was it. I really didn't give it a lot of thought, because those kind of things happen to me from time to time with former students, and it is always a special enjoyment. However, that evening in

1985 it didn't register very much because of the occasion and the general hubbub that permeated the entire pre-banquet time in the foyer.

My next "contact" with Nancy was not really a contact as much as it was a communication on my part. When her husband died (we pastors in the district knew that he was sick, but I didn't know much more way up in Ventura County), I sent her a card of condolences with a short, personal note. It was a difficult time for her and her sons, but I didn't know how much because of my concern and care for my wife, Betty, who was slowly dying of cancer at the time. I felt for her, but I also was feeling deeply about what was happening to Betty.

Betty died in 1991, and I went my way as pastor at First Lutheran in Ventura and in my relationships with several women, as previously noted. As you know from previous pages, I went through some strange and difficult and perplexing times those years, but I was essentially doing all right and was very pleased with my ministry and my ongoing life at the time. As you also will have noted from previous pages, I had some disappointments and some "downers" in my romantic life, but I was still very much my own man and I felt good about everything. Much credit for that must go to Betty, who had so well prepared me for life after her. I really was not prepared for Nancy in my life, so let's get to what happened.

In late spring of 1993, in the midst of several relationships that would not be going anywhere, and I was still busy and satisfied with my life, a little "coincidence" occurred. I put coincidence in quotation marks because I truly believe that with God there are no coincidences but simply His plans, unknown to us! The occasion was the installation of a friend of mine, Rev. Phil Sipes, who had been a member of First Lutheran for one year after serving ten years in the mission work of our church in Africa. He was then awaiting assignment back here in the States. That process was taking a long time, so he went back to our seminary in Ft. Wayne to study and get some additional theological credits. Then I found out that he had been called to be an associate pastor at St. John's Lutheran Church in Orange, CA, in the early summer of 1993. Since few people knew Phil out here or even knew about his installation, I decided that, in spite of the 105-mile trip on a Sunday afternoon from Ventura to Orange, I would be at his pastoral installation and give my personal support to his new venture in ministry. As I pondered all this, it occurred to me in the deep recesses of my memory that Nancy had mentioned that she taught school in Orange. Since it was not unusual in my experiences to "connect up" with former students from Cleveland Lutheran High (as I had done on numerous occasions in the past), it seemed appropriate to contact Nancy. I found her telephone number in our district directory and gave her a call. My opening words were, "Hi! This is Jim Lareva, and I was wondering if you were going to attend the installation of your new associate pastor in a few weeks?" She sounded a bit confused and didn't quite understand what I was talking about. In the ensuing conversation I must have mentioned St. John's because she quickly replied with a certain amount of sarcasm, "I don't teach at St. John's. I teach at St. Paul's!" *Oops!* I said to myself. *Now what do I do?* I had discovered that I really did want to make at least some kind of contact with her, and this had seemed like a good way to do it. I had never had a thought about her until this occasion, and then the Lord must have put it into my head that there was a "Nancy" out there for me and I'd better do something about it! Recovering quickly, I suggested that maybe I could stop by her place and say, "Hi!" and be on my way. That's when she said warmly, "Well, why don't you just come over for something to eat before you go to the installation?" The installation was set for 6:30 P.M. at St. John's. I indicated that it might be better if I came by after the installation for a cup of coffee and chocolate chip cookies (which she had mentioned) before I went back to Ventura that night. That sounded great, and we talked further on the phone about the impending wedding of her oldest son, Joel, in a week or so, as well as about other items of general interest. What happened next was really bizarre, but what a blessing!

On that Sunday afternoon of the installation in June, 1993, I drove from Ventura to Orange – a nice Sunday afternoon drive. When I got to Orange, I decided to check out exactly where Nancy lived. This procedure was due to a long-standing experience in the pastoral ministry. When you are going to call on someone and you have never been there before, "check it out," that is, find out exactly where they live during the daylight so you can find them at night when you go to call on them. Excellent advice for young pastors. So, I drove into Orange in plenty of time for the installation, drove around and discovered exactly where Nancy lived, and prepared for the installation. Since I was driving such a long way, I had put on my casual clothes, including my totally beat up tennis shoes. My suit and gown were in the back of the car, and my intention was to change into them somewhere in Orange. Around 6 P.M., I found the perfect changing place: McDonald's on Tustin Avenue, less than a mile from St. John's and from Nancy's. I went into McDonald's, changed into my dress suit in the restroom, and prepared to come out and head for St. John's. As is normal with most pastors before a worship service, I made a last, quick stop at the appropriate place in the men's room. As I stood there, I looked straight down and noticed, to my horror, that I still had on my terrible-looking tennis shoes, with all their holes and torn parts and worn-through sections. I had forgotten my dress shoes at home! Old tennis shoes were hardly the appropriate attire for a pastor at an installation! With a liturgical gown on, the only things that people in the congregation will see are the pastor's face and his shoes! What to do? I went outside the restaurant and spotted a couple of stores that might have shoes, but it was 6:10 P.M. on a Sunday evening, and they weren't open. With an inspirational thought, I called Nancy, since she lived less than a mile away. My opening words were, "Do you help out pastors in distress?" Her somewhat guarded reply came back, "Well, it depends on what the distress is!" I explained my situation about the shoes, and wondered if one of her sons still living at home might have a pair of black shoes that would somehow fit me temporarily. I was desperate! Suddenly, she warmed up and said invitingly, "Of course! Come on over and I'll see what I can do. By the way, my parents are here and I'd like you to meet them." Oh, good grief! Here I am meeting her parents, and all I want is a pair of black shoes for a couple of hours. Well, I hurried over to her house, came dashing into the front room and kitchen area to find her working feverishly to shine a pair of old black shoes. I rushed across the room, made my introductions to her parents, scurried over to where she was shining the shoes, and said, "Nancy? It's great to see you again!" I grabbed the now-shined shoes, tried them on (they were much too long for my feet, but just the right width), ran out the door with the parting words to Nancy, "I'll be back to have coffee and cookies with you later!" – and off I went! The look on the faces of her parents simply seemed to say, *Who was that guy and what kind of nut is he?*

After the installation, I came back to Nancy's house for coffee and cookies, and we spent a couple of hours just talking. What a totally pleasant time with her! There was nothing pretentious about her, but there was a genuine, warm, soft gentleness that immediately attracted me to her. Besides that, she was and is a very attractive lady! She has these wonderful, beautiful blue eyes, gorgeous white hair worn in a very becoming way, and a smile that will "knock you out!" At that moment, I was completely engrossed with her and mesmerized by her personality of warmth, optimism, and complete graciousness. Almost immediately I knew her to be someone very special, and someone I wanted to know better and more. But – how to convince her of that? As we conversed that evening, something came up about the Cleveland Indians baseball team. Well, I knew a lot of baseball and we shared some of that. Then she mentioned that she had not seen the Indians play since her days back in Cleveland in the 1950s. I didn't think much about it at the moment, but since we agreed to talk again on the phone that coming week, I put that thought of the Indians in the back of my mind. I might have let it go at that, but when I got home, I checked the Angels' baseball schedule. I noticed that the Cleveland Indians were coming to town to play the California Angels in Anaheim Stadium, a few minutes' drive from her house. Seizing upon any possible opportunity of seeing Nancy again (which I was determined to do, but I also didn't want to "scare her off"), I called her up a few days later and announced to her that her beloved Indians, whom she hadn't seen play since 1954, were going to be in town the next weekend to play the Angels, and that she really ought to do something about that. Namely, let me take her to one of the three games, preferably that coming Friday evening. Well, she thought it was a wonderful idea, and I came to Orange the following Friday and took her to the Angels-Indians game. This was our first "date," and it was wonderful and the Indians won the game. Later, she told me how much she appreciated the game because I explained and enlivened the game for her by telling her so many things about baseball. As we walked down the long ramps leading to the parking lots, we were in animated conversation (as we usually were then, and still are most of the time). I noticed that there was an arm and a hand swinging alongside me, as if they had nothing to do! Well, no truly romantic guy is going to let that opportunity pass, so I seized the moment! I took her hand in mine as naturally, gently, and as inoffensively as possible. And she seemed to like it, even though she told me later that it surprised her and she wasn't sure what it all meant. Me? I knew a good woman and a good thing, and I wasn't about to let the opportunity go without a good try! And that is how it all began with Nancy! What a story!

After that first date, I began to see Nancy on a regular, usually weekly, basis. Often I would come up late in the afternoon and stay until late at night and drive back to Ventura – a 210-mile roundtrip. It seemed to bother her more than me, since she had to be convinced that I'm a "late night" person and I don't doze off while driving, even late at night. There was also some background and reason for her concern. Her husband, Ken, was afflicted with narcolepsy and would sometimes fall asleep while driving, especially at night. She had learned how to detect the first signs of this while riding with him, and for a while applied the same kind of watchfulness with me. In time, she realized two things: dozing off didn't happen to me easily, and when I sensed it I would tell her right away. Anyway, I like to drive, and late-night driving was a breeze on the California freeways. And, as I reminded her often, she was worth it! She told this to her younger sons, Jason and Nathan, who were still living at home. So, I got to know them pretty well. When Nancy suggested on several occasions that I remain overnight at her house if I didn't have to be anywhere right away the next morning (usually a Sunday night with Monday as my "day off"), it didn't raise any eyebrows. And, of course, her two sons were still at home. As with Betty, I knew almost for certain within a very short time (like a few weeks!) that I was truly in love with her and that I wanted to marry her. It simply remained for us to spend good, quality time with each other and discover as much as we could about each other. Incidentally, after our first date or two, her oldest son, Joel (who lived only a few miles away), asked her if what we had done the first time or two was really a "date." I suppose he was feeling a sense of being the head of the Kilian clan, and wanted to protect his mother and make sure that everything was all right. When Nancy told me that, I laughed and told her to say to Joel, "If it sounds like a date, if it feels like a date, and if it looks like a date, it probably is a date!"

Betty and Nancy are the only two women in my life about whom I was certain in my feelings in such an immediate and total way. And they are the only two that I wanted to marry! Speaking of marriage, as our relationship grew, so did the possibility that this relationship would lead to marriage. I became well-acquainted with her school and fellow teachers (whom I liked very much and to whom I related easily), her church and its pastors, and her lifestyle and likes and dislikes. It was fun! One time I even made up a card and sent it to her during the week which said, "Yes, indeedy... yer my sweetie!" By

Thanksgiving, I was ready, and I did propose to her, with the condition that she take plenty of time to give me her answer. I really wanted her to be very sure, because it would mean a tremendous change in her life and in the lives of her three sons and her aging parents (who lived in Seal Beach, about 20 miles away).

In between the time I proposed and her acceptance, we had our first Christmas together and proceeded into the New Year with lots of optimism, excitement, hope, and love! Since I had deliberately asked her to take her time about her decision, she did. It wasn't until well into January that she accepted my proposal of marriage, and then we made it official on Valentine's Day, 1994. By this time, I don't think anyone was surprised, but I was very concerned about the reaction of my boys, as well as her boys. I had become more acquainted with her three sons than she had with mine, since I usually traveled to see her and two of her sons were still living at home. They were in their early and mid-20s at that time, and ready to move on with teaching careers, so our marital timing was perfect. There was amazement on their parts, mixed with joy for their mother – and all three happily approved. Nancy started coming up to Ventura a number of times on a weekend, where I put her up at local motels, including the high class Holiday Inn right on the beach in Ventura. She was impressed! My sons got to know her quite well over the months, and I received nothing but compliments about her and my good choice! It was during this time that I also asked my dear friend, Joanne, to have dinner with us and get to know Nancy better. (I had already told her a lot about Nancy and she was anxious to meet her.) It was some time after this that Joanne confided to me that she believed Nancy was more the right person for me, rather than Vera. I valued her opinion highly, so this meant a lot to me. This was in no way a "put down" of Vera, but rather a verification that God in His wisdom had chosen this woman, Nancy, for me – and me for her. Nancy and I both agreed with God's wisdom!

During the spring and early summer of 1994, Nancy and I planned our wedding, deciding to use the small, beautiful little chapel on the hill at Concordia University in Irvine. It would hold about 100 people, and that was about what we figured. We planned our wedding for July 10th – a Sunday afternoon. We each had just one other person standing up with us: my best friend in the ministry, Art Puls, and Nancy's best friend from high school and college days,

Grace Nickel Nemeth, a parochial school teacher in Whittier. Grace was also a former student of mine at Cleveland Lutheran High. Performing the ceremony was our mutual friend, confidant, and counselor, Rev. Ron Rehrer, a family counselor for pastors and teachers of our district. My grandson, Jonathan, was our shy ringbearer. All six of our sons participated in the ceremony. Her youngest son, Nathan, and my three sons all read Scripture and/or appropriate readings. Her sons, Joel and Jason (with Jason on the piano) sang a duet – which included the words "doubly blessed" – which Nancy had chosen after hearing it in a religious bookstore. It aptly described what had happened to both of us. When I introduced Nancy to my congregation in Ventura as my wife-to-be (they had already met her over the months on previous weekends), I did it this way: "When a man is blessed with one wonderful woman in his life, that is grace. When he is blessed with a second wonderful woman in his life, that is to be doubly blessed, or, as St. John might say, 'grace upon grace' (John 1:16)!" Our wedding day was truly a beautiful, sunny Sunday afternoon, and the ceremony (even though we did not bother with a rehearsal) went very well, with only one little, easily-corrected glitch. Afterwards, the reception was held in the backyard of her very good friends, the Froehlichs, right there in Orange. One of the things which made this occasion even more special was the presence of Betty's brother, Jim, his wife, Delores, and their two daughters, Jennifer and Katherine, from Ontario, Canada. Their presence was their way of giving their blessing to this marriage of the man who had been Betty's husband for 35 years. It is almost impossible to describe what that meant to me at the time, and it still remains as one of the most beautiful experiences of my life. To this day, we are closer than ever, and I have reserved a section of my life's history simply entitled, "The Brasch Family." What a special joy to write about them as a wonderful, ongoing, and *very* important part of my life. I truly treasure all of them!

After the wedding, we settled down to life as a happily married couple in Orange, CA. Now that little statement requires a bit of explanation. When Nancy and I first "got serious" and a marriage was in the offing, it occurred to both of us that some enormous changes would have to take place. First, there was the matter of where we would live. I had a very nice townhouse in Ventura in a very good location, and it would not be easy to move from there. She has this one-level house in Orange which she and her husband had bought in 1976, located in South Orange in a good location in a quiet, normal neighborhood. Although both of us were thinking ahead to what and where we would live after the wedding, I had pretty much decided to move down to Orange with her. After all, I had already exceeded my "retirement age" by two years and was ready to "move on." On the other hand, she had begun imagining what it might be like to live in Ventura. Somewhere along the line before our wedding, I indicated to her that I thought it would be best that I officially retire and move down to Orange with her. Upon the advice of my CPA, tax expert daughter-in-law, Teri, I would retain ownership of my townhouse in Ventura and rent it out. This would accomplish two things. First, it would solve the "housing situation." Second, and more importantly, it would allow Nancy to continue her teaching career at St. Paul's, where she had been for almost 25 years and where she would prefer to continue teaching. It also made it comfortably possible for me to retire away from the area of my ministry in Ventura County of 27 years, and re-establish myself in a new area. I know there was a sense of joy and relief on Nancy's part when I made this "decision" of mine. There was not really a good possibility for her to teach in a parochial school in Ventura County, and even if there were, it would be in an entirely new situation. I have spent most of my life moving around from place to place, either in the 1930s during the Depression, my days in the Navy, my years at Valpo, my teaching in Cleveland, and in my years of ministry at four different congregations in four different parts of the country. So what was the big deal with one more move for me? It was no problem and a great solution for Nancy and her life ahead as my wife and as a teacher at St. Paul's. It worked out great! And all three of my sons lived nearby in Ventura County. Another positive factor was that her two sons at home were beginning their teaching careers and moving out of the house to pursue those careers. Jason started teaching in the public school system of Santa Ana and bought a condo; Nathan had completed his teacher training at Concordia University in Irvine and had taken a call to teach at Pilgrim Lutheran Church and School in Santa Monica. Great timing, right? Sometimes I have been asked about God's perfect timing and my marriage, and I reply with a tongue-in-cheek comment: "I retired on June 30th, 1994, and I was so bored that I got married ten days later on July 10th, 1994!" What a gift from God!

Chapter 8

Seminary Years (1957-1961)

Bursting into our apartment in East Cleveland, I shouted out, "Betty, guess what? We're going to the sem this summer!" This didn't surprise her all that much because we had already decided to go to the sem in a year. That timing was due to the planned move of downtown Cleveland Lutheran High School to a new building in West Cleveland. We had decided to stay for one more year of teaching during the transition to the new high school. Then, on that April day, it was announced at school that nothing would happen with the building program because the state of Ohio had decided to build a super highway right through the existing school property and nothing would be happening for another year. So, we changed our sem plans too.

During the last couple of years of teaching, my experience with students on a spiritual level as well as academic helped me see that the Holy Spirit was calling me more and more into the idea of studying for the pastoral ministry. Betty and I began having many discussions about such a change in our lives. Being a P.K. (preacher's kid) she had many good insights and helpful thoughts about such an important move. She was fully supportive and very positive because she realized this was truly a calling from the Lord. (Later she would kiddingly tell people, "Here I thought I was marrying a teacher and settling down, and now he wants to go off to school and become a preacher!") From the beginning, she was with me all the way.

At this time, April of '57, Betty was working full time as a nurse at a local hospital. I was planning to take a summer job and coach a group of ex-Cleveland Lutheran High School baseball players. This would all change when I found out that over the summer I could take a full academic year of Greek in only ten weeks at Concordia College Milwaukee. In so doing, I would save a whole calendar year at the seminary because I already had a Bachelor of Arts degree with most of the requisite courses that they required. With the Greek course, I could go directly into the next level of seminary training.

Betty and I immediately began to make plans to move to Springfield, Illinois, where Concordia Theological Seminary was located at the time. With the help of my friend, Art Puls, already a seminary student, we found an apartment on the south side of Springfield. Betty quickly found a position as a nurse at Memorial Hospital and began work there with her good friend, Gloria Puls, Art's wife. Since everything was working out to start at the sem in the fall, I went up and registered for my special Greek class at Concordia, Milwaukee. At this point, you need to know Art and Gloria Puls. Gloria was an RN. They were living near the sem, and Art was on the six-year program to complete the program for the ministry. I drove to Springfield with a rented truck with our furniture for our upstairs apartment. Art was there to help me, even though it was late at night and we moved all the furniture in the darkness. We did it so quietly that our landlord didn't know we had moved in until the next morning. They were pleased.

Betty began her full-time work at the local hospital, and I went up to Milwaukee for my class in Greek. There were five members in the class: Carl Hort, Dave Krueger, John Josepait, Dave Belasic, and myself. Our animated professor was Dr. Jennerich.

We lived in dorm rooms like regular students, and our prof kept us very busy with lots of Greek day after day – 10 to 12 hours. As you can imagine, we got to know each other very well since Carl and Dave Krueger had flunked Greek that year and were taking it over. Dave Belasic, John, and I needed the Greek to start off the seminary with our regular level class. Several things characterized our time in Milwaukee. Three or four times that summer, I drove back down to Springfield to see Betty, which made Dave Belasic jealous because he wasn't yet married but had a fiancée in Chicago. Of local interest were occasional visits to the many available breweries, and I attended a number of Milwaukee Braves' baseball games. That team included some outstanding baseball players, the most famous being Hank Aaron. They went on to win the World Series of 1957. I really enjoyed those games!

When I went to see Betty occasionally on weekends, I met a number of sem students, all of whom had working wives, including several nurses. My first weekend in Springfield with them was at the home of Jim and Barbara Roseman, who provided much hospitality, enjoyment, and good humor. That was enhanced by the nearby brewery that sold beer for $1.00 a gallon. Those weekends were a welcome respite from my studies, and I got to know a number of sem students before I started coursework there. So I finished my Greek classes and headed back to Springfield for the next two years. The experiment of a year of Greek in ten weeks worked out very well for us. We came into our fall Greek classes really fresh – more so than the other guys who had the summer off. This was really helpful, thanks to Prof. Jennerich.

First of all, a few comments and observations about the sem. The atmosphere on campus was upbeat, positive, and very spiritual, as best expressed by Prof. Spiegel: "The most important reason you are here is not due to you, but to the Lord, Jesus Christ." It was a great feeling to be on my way for the next four years of pastoral training, including one year of vicarage. The seminary student body was an interesting mixture of married students who lived off campus and single students who lived in the dorms. The ages of the students ranged from early 20s to early 50s, from all walks of life. Besides getting involved with my classes, I became the quarterback for intramural football... Lotsa fun! Financially, Betty was a full-time nurse at Memorial Hospital along with a number of other sem wives; I got a part-time job at a grocery warehouse where I could set my own hours. I soon realized that except for Greek and Hebrew, academics were less demanding than at Valparaiso University. Nonetheless, I really enjoyed my classes, especially the concentrated study of Scripture and homiletics. Because I enjoyed writing, sermon writing was a joy. The toughest part was that we had to present our sermons to be critiqued by the whole class as well as by the professor. A few of us were invited by Prof. Steege to preach Wednesday nights during Advent and Lent at the small "black" congregation that he served.

A crisis occurred in the athletic department of the sem when the coach there who had a physical education program, plus coaching basketball and baseball teams, suddenly resigned in January. Professor Eggold, Dean of Students, had a real problem on his hands. He had played and coached basketball, but not baseball. Then he came up with the idea of asking me to coach the baseball team, "just to help out the sem." Even though I was married and carried a full academic load along with a part-time job, I accepted my new position on campus. The most difficult part was that I was left with scheduling baseball fields, umpires, and other matters pertaining to the baseball program besides coaching. My two years as high school baseball coach held me in good stead for this new role. I had a good group of players, some married like I was and all pressed for time as were all of us. We had a pretty good team with a very short time to get ready for the season, and yet we did quite well. I received very little help from Dean Eggold who seemed to take me for granted. When the season was over, Dean Eggold prepared the award ceremony, and my only job was to hand out the letters, which I gave to all of the players. With a minimal expression of thanks, I felt let down, as did some of the players. After all, in colloquial words, as one player said, "Jim, you saved his butt!" He would have had to coach the team, as he had coaching experience. Also, I saved the seminary a chunk of money since I received no remuneration. Although I liked Dean Eggold and he was a good homiletics prof as I found out the following year, I felt disappointed in him.

That disappointment was more than balanced by a wonderful experience with the president of the seminary, Dr. Walter Baepler. During one of our games where the spectator's seats were arranged right behind the team benches, our team was playing badly and I was very frustrated. At one point in the game, when a mental error was made, I jumped up and shouted, "Damn!" When I turned around, I noticed for the first time that Pres. Baepler and his wife were sitting right behind my bench. I was embarrassed but the game continued on. Before I could speak to them afterwards, they had left. Following that Saturday game, I made an appointment with him the following Monday morning. With some trepidation, I entered his office, sat down, and apologized very humbly. His almost-fatherly-manner reached out to me with a warm and understanding smile, as he said to me, with a kind of twinkle in his eye, "Jim, the way they were playing, I might have said the same thing!" He laughed a bit and we talked baseball for a while, and then he warmly thanked me for taking over that job of coach. That meant a lot to me, and I understood why he was so loved on campus. Years later I had the occasion of talking to his son on the Religion faculty at Valpo, Dr. Richard Baepler. I shared the story with him and he simply laughed and said, "That was my dad!"

By the way, I "pulled one" on Dean Eggold the next semester when I had him as homiletics prof. He stressed a long and complete outline of a sermon before writing it. So I put my sermon together by writing the whole sermon before making an outline. I then turned in a two and a half page outline based on my sermon. I showed it to some of my classmates and told them what I had done. On the following Monday, Prof. Eggold held up my outline for the whole class to see and stated, "This is what I mean by a good outline. Now Jim is ready to write his sermon!" A number of my classmates humorously gave me "the business" after the class was over, much to my delight.

As far as social life was concerned, it was spent mostly with married students, of course, especially with Art and Gloria Puls, but also with many of my other married classmates. And then in the summer we went back to Muskegon for several months. There we spent time at my home congregation where I preached a couple of times. Quite an experience for a son of the congregation! We spent most of our time in Muskegon with old Walther League friends, my brother Dave, his wife Betty, and their two sons, Dick and Jimmy. Lots of special time was spent with my mother. Then we went to Pittsburgh and spent time with Betty's family: her parents, her brother Jim, and his wife Delores. Then we went back to Springfield for the rest of the summer.

~

Second Year at the Sem

After a busy summer with the visits in Muskegon and Pittsburgh, I continued my part-time work at the warehouse in Springfield. I had great enjoyment playing intramural football where I was the quarterback. We had great fun!

At the beginning of the semester, I was elected class president. This was mostly an honor but I became very much involved at the time of President Baepler's sudden death. As class president, I had to organize some of the honorary procedures for his memorial service. It was extra work, but I was honored to do it for him.

During this time, Betty was pregnant with Mark, and it was a difficult pregnancy with her in bed much of the time, bleeding. God answered our prayers, however, and brought her to full term. I was called out of the middle of class to the hospital, to the applause of my classmates. After a long wait at the hospital, until almost midnight, Mark was born on December 3rd, 1958. It was a proud and thankful moment for all of us, even our "landlord grandparents!" I think they were almost as excited as we were! Mark was strong and healthy and a very enjoyable child.

Academically, the year went well. Members of our class began preaching at outlying rural congregations regularly. It was a great experience for all of us. Later in the year, I became part of a program conducted by a local pastor who was in ministry to a state psychiatric facility in Jacksonville, Illinois – 35 miles away. Every Sunday morning, we went to the early service at the church in Springfield, and then a group of us went with the pastor to the State Institute. I did this for a year, and then continued to do it after my vicarage year. Ministering at an institution like that in those days was almost an indescribable experience, that was valuable to later ministry.

Baseball in the spring started off very well. We had a new coach, Warren Wilbert, who taught classes as well as coaching basketball and baseball. I like to call him my successor in baseball coaching at the sem. Coach Wilbert was an excellent baseball coach, and I played very well under him until halfway through the season. I pulled some muscles in my leg and played in pain quite a while. Even though I was hitting very well, I finally had to stop playing because the pain was getting worse.

In late spring came the most exciting part of the whole year – vicarage assignments! Each member of our class was assigned to a congregation or a few special ministries. I was assigned to work in campus ministry at USC and UCLA in Los Angeles. Let me explain the unique assignment. I was to work under the supervision of two pastors: Rev. George T. Fisher of El Monte and Charles Manske, a graduate of the seminary but not yet ordained. My best mentor was a UCLA campus pastor, Rev. Ron Goerss, who was taking a leave of absence for a year of study at USC School of Religion. The assignment was a surprise to me until I realized I was the only one in my class with experience working with young people. They simply needed a fill-in for Pastor Goerss.

~

Vicarage

Once again we were on the move, driving in our red and white Nash Rambler, from Springfield to the West Coast. Mark was only six months old! Nevertheless, we took time to visit some of the great sites along the way. For example, we visited the Black Hills of South Dakota and the monument to the four presidents at Mount Rushmore, we spent long days in the desert, and we stayed at Yellowstone National Park for several days. While there, we stayed in a log cabin. One day a bear started getting into the open trunk of our car as Betty was getting things out of the trunk. Betty dashed away hurriedly, slammed the cabin door closed, and locked it. She announced, "There's a bear trying to get into our trunk!" My instant reply was, "Did you close the trunk?"

Needless to say, Betty did not appreciate my lapse in judgment. That bear caused a great deal of excitement the rest of the evening as he prowled around.

When we arrived in Los Angeles, we were directed to the Hospice House near the USC campus where we stayed for two weeks while we looked for an apartment. (In this case, Hospice meant Hospitality place for people in need of short-term housing, mainly students.) Looking for an apartment in that area was made interesting as Manske cruised in his convertible with Ron Goerss and myself. After discussing several apartments we had visited, they finally agreed on an apartment I had chosen. It was a second floor apartment in a six-apartment building on a nice side street close to Crenshaw Blvd. Although I was there for campus work, I took two graduate courses at the USC School of Religion. One was taught by a brilliant young LCMS professor, Dr. Herman Waetjen, who had the Lutheran Chair at the school. The other class was conducted by Dr. Charles Nielson, a brilliant scholar on Martin Luther. I was thoroughly challenged and deeply appreciated the two courses. The following spring, Ron Goerss and I were ushers for Prof. Waetjen's wedding to a graduating student from UCLA. As ushers we were called "Mutt and Jeff" (from the old comic strip), since I was 5' 9" and Ron was 6' 10".

Charles Manske had finished at the seminary and done some graduate work in St. Louis before being sent to do campus ministry at USC. Since he was not yet ordained, he could not be my official supervisor (but we would work closely together). Later in the year, he was ordained at Mt. Calvary, Beverly Hills, whose pastor was Rev. Ted Schoesow. My official supervising pastor was Rev. George T. Fisher. Pastor Fisher was a marvelous pastor and person, and I learned much from him in my vicarage. Betty and I loved both the Fisher family and the Schoesow family. They took such good care of us in California.

My most interesting times were with Pastor Fisher. We would go to his church in El Monte and spend all day Sunday there. I would preach both sermons and enjoy the marvelous singing voice of Pastor Fisher. He would run from the chancel all the way back to the balcony to sing with the choir and then race back to the chancel to continue the liturgy. I can still remember his gown flowing behind him. He would spend all Sunday afternoon with me making calls of various kinds for my personal pastoral experience, and then conclude the evening with his family around the piano, singing lustily.

My duties as a vicar at USC and UCLA included Bible classes at the UCLA parsonage and the Hospice House, and worship at a little nondenominational chapel on the USC campus. Neither campus had their own Lutheran chapel at that time. Other responsibilities included calling on students in their dorms, fraternities, and sororities, preaching at various churches in the Southern California District, counseling, and enjoying the USC/UCLA football rivalry.

About halfway through the year, three important events occurred. First of all, Betty lost our baby in the fourth month of her pregnancy. This affected us deeply as you can imagine, especially since Mark was only a year old. Our students were a wonderful, supportive group who helped Betty and me so much, and were the best babysitters in the world.

The second important event was the struggle with the city of Los Angeles to make plans for a chapel near UCLA. Since UCLA was located in and near large, exclusive, and expensive neighborhoods, they saw the chapel as a threat to their way of life. After several bitter meetings with the City Planning Commission, the judge ruled against our plans. He explained to us that he was doing it for our own good as these people would never stop with their opposition to us. He was very pleasant and his decision was helpful to working out our own plans. As so often happens, God had better plans for us. A short while later, our Southern California District purchased a piece of property on a steep side of a hill next to the UCLA campus – an excellent location. In accordance with the seller's wishes, the city planning architect basically designed the unique, multi-level chapel with a wonderful worship area at the top. And then, he had our district architect sign the design papers. To this day, it remains one of the most unique and beautiful chapels on any campus, and it is still very actively used.

The third important event of my ministry there involved Rev. Manske writing, directing, and starring in a homemade movie for Gamma Delta, a national campus ministry organization of synod. The movie was called *Time Out!* Quite frankly, I wound up doing most of the campus ministry work at the two universities, while Pastor Manske spent much of his time making the movie. (My only involvement in the movie was as a football coach calling "Time out!" during the game.) This need for me to focus so much attention on campus ministry turned out to be a positive experience for my vicarage training, and I'm glad it happened.

I am indebted to Ron and Betsy Goerss and their family for their support, close friendship, and mentoring from Ron about campus ministry, as he was my primary teacher.

~

Last Year at the Sem

So, it's back across the country to the seminary. There were many enjoyable and emotional farewells from the many wonderful students, professors, and close clergy friends before we left. I decided to send Betty and Mark back by plane to her parents' house in Pittsburgh, where we would stay for the rest of the summer. I drove our reliable red and white Rambler, making very good time across country until the water pump gave out just before I got to Pittsburgh. The drive was made more comfortable with the installation of front seat belts – a gift of the Schoessow family.

After the remaining weeks of summer, we drove to Springfield and settled into the apartment of Art and Gloria Puls, who had just left to go on their vicarage out in La Mesa, California. Their apartment was closer to the sem for me and to the hospital for Betty, where she spent most of the year with full-time work, earning her "PHT," (Put Hubby Through). It was great being back with old classmates as we shared the adventures of the past year's experiences in different places of the country. Little did I know at the time how my vicarage experience would affect the Lord's call for me when I graduated.

How does one describe that last year's experience...? Being on the sem campus was so different from before. It was like the "grad class" was a unique group set apart on campus because of the different experiences we had relative to the other students. There were among us such a variety of pastoral and church experiences that belonged to no one else on campus. We seemed to be looked at differently and with a quiet respect, almost envy. And, of course, there were more married men and children and pregnancies than there were when we had left the year before.

Yes, we went back to our classes, but it was with a renewed focus on our purpose and preparation for the Holy Ministry. I think even the professors enjoyed us more than before. That spirit of being in the last year of the seminary seemed to permeate almost everything we did: our studies, social relationships, sports, and activities on campus. There was a general feeling of anticipation and excitement as we were getting ready to enter a whole new world in God's service. I felt a new excitement among my classmates that was not there before. And that added to the joy of our last months together with a lot of men and families we might never see again on this earth.

Early in the school year, Betty became pregnant and we anticipated our second child in November. Even in this, Betty continued to work almost full time and had no pregnancy problems as she had previously. Dan decided to come into this world on a Tuesday morning, in a not-too-unusual happenstance. Like many students before me, I was called out of the classroom to the hospital to the cheers of my classmates.

In those last ten months in Springfield, many great family relationships developed which will last forever, especially among the married men. A closeness developed, and for years we would look forward to any opportunities to cross paths with a classmate. It was a rare and unique time in my life, which I will deeply treasure through eternity.

Along with my studies, I continued my ministry at the State Institute at Jacksonville in which I, along with a local pastor friend, guided sem students through the experience of ministering at a psychiatric facility.

While on vicarage, the seminary got a new president, Dr. George Beto, a renowned and unique leader in the Missouri Synod. He was an expert in prison ministries (and we used to joke if that's why they sent him to the seminary…). He had a responsible position in the state of Texas in prison ministries, which he conducted with great skill. He was "Texas" all the way, including his hat. This led to an incident at Reformation time at the sem. It actually snowed the night before, and the students on campus awoke to a white-covered campus with big footprints leading away from the statue of Luther and then leading to a nearby tree, where Luther relieved himself. Besides that, someone had found a huge cowboy hat and perched it on Luther's head. President Beto had a good sense of humor, but it did not extend to that incident. We appreciated him very much as a president, a scholar, and a visionary for the seminary. My favorite recollections of him were the once a week "off the cuff" evening meetings he held with the grad students. One example I remember clearly was when he emphasized that we have to know our Bible and what is going on in the lives of our people. He illustrated this by saying, "Think of walking down the street among the people you serve with a Bible in one hand and that day's newspaper in the other." Dr. Beto was a wonderful seminary president with great leadership skills. Several years later, this was recognized in the secular world when he was called to be in charge of the entire prison system in the state of Texas.

There is one major part of that last spring at the seminary that I'd like to describe in more detail than usual. In many ways, it turned out to be my most enjoyable baseball experience of the many years I played baseball. A description can be found in my chapter entitled, "My Life in Sports."

A new feeling seemed to pervade the lives of the 75 vicars who had returned for our last year at the sem. Even our studies seemed to take on greater importance and were more interesting. And as we went through the year, it became increasingly obvious in many subtle ways that our lives were about to be changed dramatically at the end of the academic year. Each day was touched with the reality that we were approaching this dramatic change in our lives. "Call Night" would bring the actual information of where we would be serving the Church after graduation. You can imagine the flood of emotions, feelings, thoughts, and hopes for God's plans ahead of us. As we approached Call Night, you could feel all of this building up to a climax. Finally, Call Night came in early May. The entire student body and faculty were assembled at St. John's Lutheran Church in downtown Springfield. It was the only place large enough to hold all of the students and their families. Following the opening worship service, President Beto addressed the audience expressing his thoughts about the importance of the occasion of announcing the divine calls of 75 graduating students and their immediate families. The call destinations of each of those graduating students were announced, and each student received the formal papers of his call. The calls included every geographical direction and kind of ministry involved. A large majority of the calls were to congregations that were either getting started or were large and needed an assistant pastor. A few of them were overseas missionary calls. Several of them were calls to military chaplaincy. And, finally, several calls were for special ministries such as mine. I was surprised and excited about my call to help form a new congregation in Ithaca, New York, and to do campus ministry at Cornell University and nearby Ithaca College. Now I understood better the focus of my interview with the calling committee of the seminary because of my background and work with youth and college students. As with most events the Lord brought into my life over the years, I looked forward with joy and anticipation to whatever the Lord had in store for me and for our family. I left the Call Night service very happy, satisfied, and ready to go to work! It was a high point in my life! I thank the Lord for what He was doing with my life.

SOLI DEO GLORIA

Chapter 9

My Three Sons

Number One Son, Mark

Mark James Lareva was born on December 3rd, 1958, in Springfield, Illinois where I was studying at Concordia Lutheran Seminary. Betty was working as a registered nurse at Memorial Hospital. Even though I had two and a half years of theological school ahead, Mark was eagerly and lovingly anticipated, and his birth brought great joy to his parents. After serving a one year vicarage in campus ministry in Los Angeles, 1959-1960, we returned to Springfield for my final year at the seminary. I was called to a group of Lutherans who wanted to start a congregation in Ithaca, New York, with campus ministry at Cornell University and Ithaca College, beginning in June, 1961.

When we began to realize that something wasn't quite "right" with Mark, we spent several years attempting to get information and help for him. Our pediatrician finally "enrolled" Mark in Cornell's Family Development Department for observation and a diagnostic work-up. On June 6th, 1964, we received the information from Dr. Dalton that Mark was being diagnosed as a severely autistic child at the age of five and a half years. He would require immediate and intensive therapy, if there was to be any chance to help him.

Thus began a treatment program of intense therapy with both parents involved as well as Mark with Dr. Nina Lambert, child psychologist in Ithaca and connected with Cornell University. It did not seem that she could take Mark as a client, but she would give us a few minutes to talk to Mark privately. After a whole hour of sitting and waiting for them to finish, she came out and announced excitedly, "I want him!" Some time later, she told us why she suddenly wanted Mark as a patient. She said, "It was like Mark was in a deep, deep well and the only rope by which to rescue him was a characteristic of his personality – Mark likes to please people."

Her caring, successful treatment lasted one and a half years, and then we moved to Solon, Ohio, where I served as pastor of Our Redeemer Lutheran Church. This is near Cleveland, and we continued Mark's therapy for two years (1966-1968) at the highly recommended Cleveland Child Guidance Center. In the summer of 1968, I accepted a call to Redeemer Lutheran Church, Thousand Oaks, California, about 45 miles north of Los Angeles. Shortly after we arrived, Mark began therapy with Dr. Peter King, a psychiatrist in Encino. This therapy lasted for about ten years, during which time he attended Dubnoff School of Educational Therapy in North Hollywood for four years.

After attending Ascension Lutheran School in Thousand Oaks for two junior high years, Mark attended Thousand Oaks High School the next four years, taking a decreasing number of special education classes each year, graduating in 1978. He then took some classes at Moorpark College and Oxnard College. During this time, he worked at several jobs, including a job in the art department at Point Mugu Naval Station. For more than 20 years, Mark lived at home all the time. He was never institutionalized or placed on any medication of any kind. He did not drink or smoke. At the age of 20, Mark began a group live-in program called "Training for Independent Living" (TIL), given through the tri-counties of San Luis Obispo, Santa Barbara, and Ventura. He was located in Oxnard, and was part of a group home for one and a half years. Then he was placed on his own, living in an apartment in Oxnard, still under the program of TIL.

During this time, he met Rachel Perez, also a TIL resident. After thorough counseling, they were married in July 1983. They always lived in Ventura, first in apartments and then in a condo I purchased for them in a secure area of Ventura. I was able to do this after I sold my townhouse in Ventura.

To give you an idea of Mark's sense of humor, when I handed him the keys to the house I looked very seriously at him and said, "Mark, I am now your landlord. If you ever miss a rental payment, you're out of here!" I said this with my thumb upraised like a baseball umpire calling someone out. Mark just looked at me and started laughing uproariously.

Mark had his own car and drove since he was a teenager. He loved taking "tours" all over California to view all forms of architecture – especially churches – and he could tell you everything about each place endlessly, if you gave him a chance. Fortunately, he had a good driving record. Of course, Rachel accompanied him. He also exhibited a unique art style, with dozens of acrylic paintings which he displayed publicly several times. He worked part time at several jobs over the years. He worked at Goodwill Industries in Ventura for ten years. He did so well at his job that he was awarded "Worker of the Year" for Goodwill Industries of Ventura, which was written up in the local newspaper. He also worked part time doing odd jobs for a real estate man who is a member of the church I served in Ventura.

Mark lived independently for more than 30 years. He was quite self-sufficient, although he and Rachel benefitted greatly from the support system around them. Mark and Rachel met on a regular basis with a TIL counselor for advice and support. This counselor is an active member of Grace Lutheran Church in Ventura, and he continues to be a very religious, spiritually sensitive, and highly moral human being. He was faithful in taking care of their finances and health needs, which was very helpful as Rachel cannot read or write. Mark kept himself constantly busy and occupied with his favorite projects and activities: architecture, music (primarily classical), and his unique artistic paintings, especially his Christian symbolism.

Years ago, his brothers Dan and Dave, and Dave's wife, Teri, stated our intentions for Mark's future. We all pledged to do everything possible to make sure that Mark continued to live and operate independently. The "James Lareva Trust Fund" was to be used in any way to keep Mark independent and functioning at his present level of satisfaction, happiness, and fulfillment. They have recently displayed the spirit and letter of their promise when Mark became sick with lymphoma. Because Dave works in Ventura, a few blocks from the hospital, he was able to help out the most.

~

The saga of Mark's life continued on much the same plane: regular church, his tours by car to see interesting architecture, and drawing his intricate and beautiful design illustrations. His naturally gregarious and pleasant nature kept him in good terms with whomever he met. This was especially true with his interest in classical music. In his special way, he could find musical presentations even in little known places such as church programs, school concerts, and community concerts. He always made it a point to meet and talk with the conductors and musicians after a performance.

Then his life took a dramatic turn. He was diagnosed with lymphoma early in 2013. It was the same thing his mother battled for four and a half years before dying on December 19th, 1991. His doctors felt that with many new drugs and procedures, he would have a good chance of recovery. He was in the hospital including ICU from time to time. But not much was working out for him, even with some new experimental drugs. He became a favorite of the nurses with his sweet disposition and the kindness of the medical staff. When he was in a regular hospital room, he would do many of his unique design drawings, and then would offer them to his nurses. Later in 2013, he was in ICU much of the time which bothered him because he couldn't do his drawings and wasn't feeling well. His brother, Dave, a deputy in the Ventura County Sheriff's Department near the hospital would often visit him, usually bringing Rachel. As I lived 105 miles away, Dave would report to me on those days that I was not able to visit.

In late November of 2013, Mark wasn't doing very well and was back in ICU. On Saturday morning, November 30th, 2013, at the age of 55 he had a brain aneurism and died within an hour. Dave was with him as was the doctor and Mark's pastor, Rev. Koch of Grace Lutheran Church, Ventura. Rev. Koch ministered to him very well and tirelessly for months. On that Saturday morning, Nancy and I drove as fast as we could, but we were late by only a few minutes before he quietly died.

His memorial service at Grace Lutheran was a beautiful witness to his faith in Jesus and his love for the church. Along with our immediate families, there was a large attendance by members of Grace and by many members of Redeemer Lutheran, Thousand Oaks, where I had pastored for 17 years, and members of First Lutheran Church where I pastored for nine years before retiring.

Our whole family was also comforted and strengthened by the attendance of many fellow pastors, as well as nurses and staff of Ventura County Hospital. He had made quite an impact in his death as well as his remarkable life.

~

Mark was a special blessing from God. We are rightly proud of what he accomplished over the years. He was a good man of God, and we loved him very much.

~

Number Two Son, Daniel

Daniel Frank Lareva (Frank after his maternal grandfather), was conceived during my last year at the sem. The first "view" of Dan is a picture taken at my ordination and installation service at Anabel Taylor Chapel, Cornell University, on August 25th, 1961, when Betty was six months pregnant. He was born on

Martin Luther's birthday, November 10th. He was a quiet boy much of his growing-up years. However, he did show some "artistic" expressions when he covered the kitchen with white flour when I was supposed to be watching him while Betty was at work at the local hospital. He also expressed this artistic trait when he painted the entire front grill and bumper of my car one day because, as he said, "It looked better that way." He won a few art prizes or honorable mentions when he was young, but never practiced actual art very much.

As Dan was growing up, much attention and therapy was given to Mark and his condition. Dan got along well with Mark. Then the "surprise" of our marriage came with another son, David, born 14 months after Dan. Dan and his younger brother laughed and played a lot together, as Mark was often in his room listening to classical music and doing intricate puzzles. Dan was the middle child and I think he suffered from that, and sometimes withdrew more into his own world – mostly reading and writing. He was gifted and did well in these areas both at school and during his adult years. In high school, he was the editor of and a writer for the school newspaper. His journalistic skills helped him to get grants and scholarships at Pepperdine University in Malibu. This enabled him to spend his entire junior year at Heidelberg University in Germany.

Before high school and during college, he had a couple of uncomfortable and painful surgeries to deal with. By the age of ten, it was obvious that his feet were not growing right. They were turning inward more and more, and would become a terrible detriment to walking, especially as he got older. So he had corrective surgery on both feet at the same time. He was in the hospital for quite a while, using aluminum crutches during the many months of healing. He handled this time very well, with a good attitude and expertise at handling the two crutches for good mobility. In fact, he became "famous" for moving about on his squeaky crutches. He could easily be heard when he went down the aisle of the church. That lead to the refrain by people, "Here comes Dan!"

The second serious surgery took place during his sophomore year in college. He had developed a jaw growth condition which, if left untreated, would lead to a "Dick Tracy" jaw, and trouble with teeth later in life. Dr. Nagel, a member of the congregation and with a good reputation in the medical community as an orthodontist, took out a portion of Dan's jaw on both sides to shorten his jaw line and line up his teeth. This surgery necessitated complete wiring of both jaw and teeth, with just a hole left to put a straw into his mouth for eating and drinking. For his meals at Pepperdine, he would choose the foods he wanted to eat, and they would put the food in a blender so he could use a straw to eat. It worked well and he lost no weight, dealing with it in his usual quiet, non-complaining strength and great attitude. It was a very successful surgery.

While at Pepperdine, he did not follow his main interest, journalism, but continued to major in history. His writing skills showed in his written reports and assignments. He had good grades all four years of college. The academic year at Heidelberg allowed many travel opportunities in Europe. After graduation in 1984, he began work with Pleasant Hawaiian Holidays as a travel agent. He became very good in arrangements for groups, e.g., 500 fans of Oregon State football, and Concordia University's choir a couple of times. To this day, he continues that employment. For several years, he shared rooming at his brother-in-law's house in Moorpark. Later, Dan rented a room in Camarillo, which gave him more flexibility in his lifestyle.

Dan has been active in the church all his life, both at Redeemer and Ascension Lutheran. His strong personal faith is seen in his work with Ascension library, Stephen Ministries, and in assisting with their contemporary worship services. He and other members of Redeemer joined Ascension after I left Thousand Oaks to serve in Ventura. The group at Ascension, whom I have named "Little Redeemer," came there due to my successor, a very conservative pastor, and Redeemer had always had a special relationship with Ascension – between pastors, the school, and many members.

In his quiet way, Dan continues to fulfill his life in other ways, particularly fiction writing. He likes to come for visits to our home in Orange. He and Nancy have a special relationship, and we always enjoy seeing him. He brings honor to our family, and we love and appreciate him.

~

Number Three Son, David

God had another great surprise for us – the birth of David Jonathan, January 18th, 1963. Betty's pregnancy with Dave was somewhat with the dismay and then the joy of her doctor who had cautioned her not to get pregnant for a while. Like Dan, he was born at the hospital in Ithaca where Betty was working at that time. He was the largest of the three boys at birth, and that continued on in his growth pattern – rising to a solid 6′ 2″ by college. More than the first two boys, Dave was outgoing and "a handful" those early years. However, he did not paint Dad's car like Dan did! Dave matured rather quickly and exhibited good athletic skills early.

As the boys grew, I noticed that I was seemingly always with two or three of them at the same time, with not enough one-on-one time. So, when they were old enough to appreciate it, I took one of them out to lunch every Saturday noon at the restaurant of their choice. I had no trouble remembering whose turn it was each Saturday. They kept track of it themselves, very well! These were wonderful times for me as much as it was for each of them. This "program" lasted all the way through high school, and once in a while we did it later on. Besides that, I got each of them into Indian Guides, a YMCA program where each father hosted and worked with his own son on different projects, meetings, and outdoor activities. I liked it better than Boy Scouts because of the required one-on-one experiences with father and son together, and that was a good thing for me too. All three boys attended Ascension Lutheran Elementary School before they spent four years at Thousand Oaks High School. I was very proud of each of their academic achievements, especially when Mark "mainlined" in a regular school program after his years at Dubnoff School of Educational Therapy in North Hollywood.

Early on, Dave showed a good aptitude for sports, especially basketball. Since we lived on a cul-de-sac, I got him a movable basketball backboard that could be used in the street against the curb. We stored it next to the garage, and he carried it out every time he wanted to use it. A real plus was the location of a street light in front of our house. He often practiced even when it got dark, and I'm sure it helped develop his basketball skills in his early years. The summer when he was ten years old, he was given a special scholarship to attend for one week Coach John Wooden's basketball camp at Cal Lutheran. He was given the highest award during his week as "Mr. Hustle." He would continue to play that way for years ahead. At home, I would play against him one-on-one quite often. Years later, he liked to say that I stopped playing against him as soon as he beat me one time when he was around 12.

About that time, he was getting ready for high school after several years on a "traveling team" made up of the best basketball kids within a grade level. He played very well all through high school and was selected "Most Valuable

Player" of his team and an All Star in the league. He still holds the Thousand Oaks High School record for highest percentage of shots made – 63%! In high school, he actually played football his freshman year as a defensive end, which he was good at. One day before the end of the football season, the freshman basketball team began tryouts in the gym nearby. His coach noticed Dave wasn't always concentrating and commented that Dave seemed distracted during football practice. When he asked him about it, Dave answered, "Once I heard the sound of basketballs on the gym floor, I knew I wanted to be there instead of football practice." From then on, it was always basketball, even though his understanding coach told him that he would be good at football, too.

My favorite story about Dave and basketball those early years, went this way. One Saturday afternoon, when I was putting the finishing touches on my sermon for the next day, he came to me with a basketball in hand and asked if I'd come over to a nearby school with basketball courts and play with him. I kind of brushed him off by saying, "I just can't Dave. I've got this work to finish." In his understanding way, he went out bouncing his basketball. A few minutes later, I came to myself with the realization that my son had just invited me for some time with his dad – and I turned him down. So I got up, told Mark and Dan where I was going, and promptly walked quickly to spend some special time with Dave. Later Dave told me, "When I saw you crossing over toward me, I got such a totally warm feeling of special joy... My dad is here." It was interesting a few years later when Dave was taking a public speaking coarse at CLU from Dr. Bouman – who called us to come over to CLU for something special. When Betty and I got there, Dr. Bouman took us into a room, turned on the TV, and there was Dave. The students in class were asked to write and speak about a special moment in their childhood which would be recorded on TV. There was Dave, speaking very clearly and telling the story of that incident in his life and how it made him feel. There I was, listening and watching him, and it was my turn to have a wonderful, special feeling. He remembered that incident better than I did. Betty and I felt very proud of him. It was the same feeling I got from reading some of Dan's term papers. Being an historian, I really appreciated Dan's writings as well as Dave's. They were both good at that, and also had good reading skills.

During Dave's high school days, he did well academically and began to think about college. His high school coach, Ed Chevalier, advised him to go to a smaller college because, as good as he was, he wasn't big enough to play power forward in a large college program. So Dave, who already was leaning toward Cal Lutheran as a smaller college with a good athletic program, saw the possibility of a small basketball scholarship. Also, he had quite a bit of experience with Cal Lutheran during his high school years. He continued his excellent playing by starting 105 straight games – beginning with his first game as a freshman – and missing only a few games in his senior year with a knee injury. When he came back after his injury, there were ten games yet to play. He seemed tentative, and his playing was not up to his normal level. That situation led to a difficult lunch I had with him. I never tried to "coach" him during his years of playing, but simply encouraged and supported his efforts with enthusiasm and pride. However, because of my own experience in sports and in coaching, I recognized his problem. He was favoring his injury, and not putting out his usual hustle and tough play. At that lunch I told him, "I'm not coming to watch you play if you're going to play that way. You are suffering a typical affliction of someone after an injury. You're letting up because you fear you will reinjure your knee. I know what you need to do. Start playing again the way you always did. You need to play at your usual level – going all out, all the time. If your game isn't strong enough, you will know it. But if it is strong enough, then forget the knee and play hard the way you always do. That's the Dave I want to see again, and I believe you can do it." His eyes welled up because this was different kind of talk from Dad. Then he gave me a look. "You're right, Dad. I'll do it!" That advice worked well, and he played his last ten games as he had always played. They turned out to be some of his best ones ever, especially with his strong rebounding and scoring. I was so proud of him – not so much for his good playing, but for his trust in me and his resolve to do his best. Because Dave was a local high school star followed by an outstanding career at Cal Lutheran, he drew a lot of attention from the local daily newspaper. A "Local Boy Makes Good" kind of thing. During his four years at Cal Lutheran, he was selected three times for the league All Star Team, and he was selected by his teammates as MVP for two years.

In 1985, Dave had two life-changing events. In May, he graduated from California Lutheran University with a B.A. in law enforcement. He began that role with attendance at the Ventura County Police Academy in July. The second great change began on July 21st when he married his high school and college sweetheart, Teri Lallo, a beautiful, tall, dark-haired girl. Her parents are Matt and Teresa, and she has two brothers: Joe (with whom Dave played basketball in high school) and Mike, a photographer.

After his graduation from the police academy, Dave became a deputy sheriff in the Ventura County Sheriff's Department, where he is still employed. Along with all his duties, he was a SWAT leader and a deputy with a variety of responsibilities. In 2015, he and Teri celebrated their marriage of 30 years. That marriage produced three children: Jonathan, Kristal, and Greg (the latecomer, 13 years after Kristal). Teri continues her work in a successful tax business, most of it done at home in her office. Dave has taken a very active role in the church, primarily as a Bible class leader in Bible Study Fellowship, where he has advanced to the role of leader of the weekly leadership classes.

Several incidents help to give a picture of his profession as a deputy sheriff. Early in his career, he was called into a situation where a man had exposed himself to two young girls on their way to school, a traumatic experience for them. The school principal wrote a letter to the sheriff commending Dave's handling of the situation. The principal described how the 6' 2", 230-pound peace officer sat with the girls in a gentle, private, non-threatening manner, talked with them in a kindly, sympathetic way to allay their fears and nervousness. Another incident showed his tender sense of humor. He had stopped a woman driver for speeding. The woman complained appealingly to him that she was only "going with the flow." Dave, with a bit of a smile, said, "Ma'am, you *are* the flow!" and handed her the ticket. His work as a deputy sheriff is long, worthwhile, and contributes to bringing his Christian life into the sometimes threatening world of maintaining the peace. He has done this while being a good husband and father at home.

And finally, Dave became especially helpful when Mark was struggling with lymphoma. Dave was always there. When all the details and necessary decisions were needed, he and Teri and Dan were there. When the 105 mile distance from Ventura made it difficult for me to be there, he was there. When I needed to speak about Mark, he and Teri and Dan were there. When I needed a special person to lean on, he was there, along with many others. When it was important for me to know details of what was going on and decisions that had to be made, he was there. Perhaps the strongest manifestation of this occurred when he, Teri, and her father, Matt, a builder himself, completely renovated the condo for Rachel. The condo really needed refurbishing of the floors, rugs, curtains, kitchen, bathroom, and the two bedrooms. This would be for Rachel as long as she lived. Working furiously for the next month and a half, Matt directed the whole process as well as Teri's brother, Mike, who also helped a great deal. When they were finished, Rachel had a brand new condo.

~

Each son has brought me very special joys, each in his own unique way, and I have been blessed in very special ways because of them. How proud Betty would be of them. Our three sons! Thank you, Lord! Blessed be the name of the Lord!

Chapter 10

Congregations I Served in My Ministry

Trinity Lutheran Church, Ithaca, New York, 1961-1966

On a cool evening in April, 1961, the sanctuary of Trinity Lutheran Church in downtown Springfield, Illinois was fast filling up. Voices were somewhat muted and there was a quiet sense of optimistic anticipation. It was "Call Night" for 75 graduating seminary students of Concordia Seminary. Many of the graduates were already married and had their wife and children with them, waiting for the moment they would find out where they would be sent as pastors. Although the atmosphere seemed to be one of quiet, nervous anticipation, an excitement was present as well because, collectively, they were ready to go where the Holy Spirit would direct them. The general attitude of each of them was, *Wherever I'm sent, I'm ready to go.* As one of the graduating students, I was feeling the same way.

The worship service was upbeat and filled with joy and praise to our God. After the sermon by the president of the seminary, came the announcement of the calls. Each one of us heard our name spoken and the name of the place to which we were being sent. My thoughts went back to my interview with the professor whose first question was, "Is there any place you could not go for health reasons or any other viable reason?" I remember answering him, "I really don't care where you send me, except if you send me down South I might get in trouble." (The Civil Rights Movement was in full swing, and I had strong feelings of support.)

The anticipation and excitement rose in me as each name called came closer to mine. And then I heard, "James Lareva, Ithaca, New York." My mind quickly went geographical. I knew that Ithaca is located in upstate New York, and is the home of Cornell University. I was somewhat surprised because I realized the call might include campus ministry. The call was to work as pastor with a small group who wanted to begin a congregation in Ithaca. I assumed correctly that the call included campus ministry at Cornell and Ithaca College. I also discovered that I was to serve part time in a small congregation in Interlaken, 25 miles north of Ithaca, named Christ Lutheran. To put it succinctly, it was really a three-fold call. My wife, Betty, was amazed but very supportive, and anxious to get going. As a registered nurse, she hoped to work at least part time in a local hospital.

As I sat there, I remembered that in the interview for my call I stated that while my vicarage was in campus ministry at USC and UCLA in Los Angeles, I would prefer experience in a regular parish. I rather humorously said to the professor, "This call process reminds me of an incident in the US Navy where I served four years. After Medical Corps School in San Diego I was asked, 'Which area of operation would you prefer: the Pacific Ocean or the Atlantic Ocean, and what type of ship: large or small?' I told him the Pacific on a small ship, but," I quipped to the professor with a smile, "I wound up in the Atlantic Ocean on the biggest ship in the navy, the USS Midway." As it turned out, God's Spirit made the right "Call," and I'm glad He did!

Our preparations to move to Ithaca included visits with my family in Michigan, and Betty's in Pittsburgh. Then we headed to Ithaca, where an upstairs apartment had been rented for us by the church.

Ithaca is a town of many winding, twisting roads, many hills, and seven waterfalls. The population of the city was about the same as the students plus staff of Cornell University: about 30,000. A beautiful area of upstate New York, we quickly fell in love with the city and the university. The main business of Ithaca was Cornell University, of course, but several other industries were located in Ithaca, like National Cash Register Company and the Ithaca Gun Company. We soon became acclimated to the city and university and the four beautiful seasons of the year. Shortly after we moved there, Betty got a part-time nursing position at the local hospital where both Dan and Dave were born. We were in the apartment for two years, but an upstairs apartment for a family with three rambunctious boys necessitated buying a home. The congregation bought a parsonage which we moved into with much help from many of the students of Cornell. It was a beautiful location on the west side of campus, near the sheep and pig barns – which gave us some special smells once in a while. As the boys got older, we would often walk up the road from the house to see newly born piglets and lambs. This part of Cornell was the agricultural school, drawing students mainly from the farmlands of western New York and Pennsylvania. Although Cornell is mostly known as an Ivy League school, part of it became an agricultural school through the 1865 Land Grant Act to help recovery from the Civil War. Most of the time, Land Grant

Colleges were simply known as State Colleges. The students at Cornell were classified either "Artsies" or "Aggies," which explains the lower tuition in the College of Agriculture and Life Sciences for students who are New York state residents. There was a lot of good-natured competition between the two groups.

Our first place of worship was simply called, "The Little Red Schoolhouse," and was located about two miles outside of town where much of the new housing was being built. The congregation chose the name "Trinity" for the church. The small group that comprised the first congregation cleaned up, painted, and fixed up the schoolhouse and made it a very worshipful little building. However, it had no running water which made using the restroom interesting in the middle of winter, according to mothers of small children. Even the students enjoyed coming to church in The Little Red Schoolhouse, and felt as loyal to it as did the regular members. To this day, the schoolhouse is part of the fond memories of the first members and students of Trinity.

In addition to my assignment at Trinity, Ithaca, and campus work, I was to be part-time pastor at Christ Lutheran Church in Interlaken, 25 miles north of Ithaca on Cayuga Lake. Surrounding the small town of Interlaken were a number of people who were Finnish and Norwegian, with a few Germans thrown in. The parish also included the small city of Lodi, with the state psychiatric facility nearby. Lodi is also known for its "Three Bears" court houses, each one larger than the one before it, built of red brick and each the same style. I would serve Christ Lutheran Church with the first worship service on Sunday, and then back to Ithaca for the second service. I also spent at least one day a week at Interlaken for meetings, calling, and counseling. This arrangement lasted only a year and a half as the workload in Ithaca increased and another pastor was assigned to Interlaken.

Many of my visits to Interlaken included calling on some of the farmers, and they would indulge me with large amounts of food and coffee. On those weekdays at Interlaken, I usually came home to Ithaca with no appetite – a frustration for Betty. Christ Lutheran Church also had no running water. One Sunday morning in the wintertime, an Elder forgot to bring warm water for a baptism, so we went down to the shore of Cayuga Lake, broke through the ice, and used that. The baby did not appreciate it! Once in a while, the Interlaken people would get together with the Ithaca congregation for activities or meetings. Close to Interlaken, on the lake was the summer home of Rod Serling of *Twilight Zone* fame. He wasn't around much, and I never met him. A memorable Sunday morning one summer, the interior of the church was filled with flies which were dying and falling down on everyone, including me. It was an interesting sermon. All in all, Interlaken was an enjoyable part of my ministry.

The arrangement with the Eastern District and the seminary made for a little confusion since I was technically not a called pastor, but a "Pastor at Large." Once Trinity was officially received into membership of the Lutheran Church, Missouri Synod, my status and responsibilities changed. I was officially called and formally installed on August 25th, to be the pastor of Trinity Lutheran Church, Ithaca, and campus pastor at Cornell and Ithaca College.

I worked out an unusual arrangement in which a Missouri Synod pastor worked hand-in-hand with the existing Lutheran Campus Ministry program. Cornell University allowed each denomination to be represented as one group. In a very important decision of my ministry, I prayerfully decided to work with the existing Lutheran program to all Lutheran students. This arrangement gave me access to office space and worship opportunities in the large religious center on the Cornell campus, Anabel Taylor Hall – where I had been ordained on June 25th, 1961. I arranged to have lunch with the current pastor, John Vannorsdall, of the Lutheran program to tell him I would not insist on a Missouri Synod program but wanted to minister with him. He was extremely happy with the suggestion, since many of his leading students were Missouri Synod and he thought he might lose some of them if I started a separate program. We successfully worked together for more than a year when he took a call and a new pastor came on the scene for the Lutheran Campus Ministry program. We followed the same arrangement. I really treasured John and learned a lot about campus ministry from him. I had communion services at Anabel Taylor Chapel most weeks, as well as Sunday evening Bible study and worship. We also took turns teaching some non-credit classes for the students. In addition, we had a number of students who worshipped with us in The Little Red School House, many of whom were picked up every Sunday on the Cornell campus by a rental bus. I truly enjoyed ministering in this situation, even though it was frowned upon in many quarters of the synod. Fortunately, I had understanding leaders in the Eastern District of our synod, especially Mission Board Chairman for Special Ministries, Rev. Herman Frincke. I found out several years later that he had "protected" my work in Ithaca and Cornell when some of the Mission Board questioned what I was doing. He said to them, "We called Jim to do a job in Ithaca and Cornell, and he's doing it. So leave him alone!" A few years later, Pastor Frincke would become president of the Eastern District. He was a real friend, and I admire him to this day. By the way, I had the full support of Trinity congregation in carrying out my student ministry, not only from the many Cornell profs and grad students but also from the many non-university members. This was illustrated when a farmer was taking instruction from me for membership, and he asked a good member friend of mine, "How do you get along so well with all these university people?" My friend replied, "Just remember, Bob, when they get up in the morning, they have to put their pants on just like you and I – one leg at a time." All in all, it was a wonderful, spiritually motivated mix of professors, students (mostly graduate students), and townspeople. And they were a blessing to me in my ministry.

The three part arrangement necessitated making many calls, some of them very interesting. One morning, around 10:00, I had been somewhere near a wonderful family, so I decided to stop for a minute and probably get a cup of coffee and good conversation. To my surprise, the wife appeared at the door still dressed in her nightgown, and this was very embarrassing for her. She was gracious. We had coffee together, but I learned something ... always call ahead, even when you're making a short or simple call! Another time, one of my favorite men in the congregation called me at 10:00 P.M. Christmas, asking fervently if we could get together. He needed to talk about his deteriorating marriage. We met soon after at The Little Red Schoolhouse, and talked until midnight. Another time, Doris, one of my members, called to tell me about a problem. Her husband John was out of town, the kids were in school, and she just heard that her mother, 40 or 50 miles away, was sick and needed to see her. I decided to help by driving her to her mother's house. She hesitated at first, but realized that I was serious and we went to her mother's. It was a good decision. Another time, I had an urgent call in the evening for an emergency situation in Interlaken, 25 miles away. That turned out to be several hours long. Another time, I had traveled by car for a meeting at our district office in Buffalo, 150 miles away. While I was there, I contacted one of our Trinity students attending State University of New York at Buffalo (UB). She was just a freshman and had been a leader in my youth group, so I took her out to dinner, which she really appreciated. Most of my calls were necessary and interesting, such as the afternoon when I had been making calls at the hospital. Afterwards, I decided to stop at the home of our church organist to discuss the next Sunday's service. When she came to the door, her eyes were filled with tears as she announced to me, "I just heard on the radio that President Kennedy has been shot and is dying." That was a good time to be there with her, until her kids came home from school. I'm glad I was there. There were many, many calls, as would be true of my ministry to other congregations. One comment I received when I left each of my four congregations was simply, "You were always there!"

The congregation grew quite fast, especially as more students attended worship services and church functions. Besides the active involvement of the many professors, the grad students were a special delight, even if they didn't have much money. I even traveled to Worchester, Massachusetts to marry two of them. I remember that especially because on the night of the wedding, Ted Kennedy was seriously hurt in an airplane crash at the local airport.

As the congregation grew, it soon became apparent that we needed to plan for building a new church. We chose property a few miles southeast of campus, on the rise of a hill, overlooking a beautiful valley. The congregation wanted to build a church building unique enough to be a good fit for a college town. We chose an excellent Building Committee chairman, Harry Weart, an engineer teaching at Cornell who knew something about building. We chose a local architect who had previously designed a beautiful Catholic church. As is the case whenever a new church building is being planned, there were many meetings, sometimes involving also the district office in Buffalo, from which we would get a loan. Being very pleased with the new design, we went ahead with plans to build. Our ground-breaking took place in early winter with joyful anticipation.

With many connections with my involvement in the Eastern District, I felt a need for a Board of Special Ministries, separate from the Mission Board. Special Ministries included hospital chaplaincy, deaf ministry, and campus ministry in the district. One of the professors in my congregation, Ralph Krenzin, was very strong in promoting the idea, and worked with me to finally get a separate board at a convention of the Eastern District. This lead to the establishment of a full-time campus ministry that was pan-Lutheran at UB. This brought about a criticism from the pastors of Pittsburgh churches who didn't get along very well with each other. When some of them came to me protesting that they should have been given consideration for the next full-time campus pastor in the district, namely at University of Pittsburgh, I replied, "When you guys get your act together in Pittsburgh, we'll give it some serious thought." My comment was based on my experience with working with some of the pastors in the Pittsburgh area previously. The campus work at UB turned out to be very successful when we called and installed a full-time campus pastor.

We began work on building the new church with its rather unique design with a special, extra loan amount from the district. At that time, the usual limit on the loan amount to new churches was $75,000. However, because of the district's recognition of our special situation, They expanded the limit to $86,000. In light of the cost of building today, this may not seem like very much – but it was at the time. Something else unique about the church was the building of a small organ by one of our grad students, John Brombaugh, who had been in Germany and suddenly developed an avid interest in organ-building. Ours was his first organ. It has been added onto since then, and is still serving the congregation very well. Today, John Brombaugh & Associates is well known in the organ-building business. The joy of my ministry there progressed with the growth of the congregation as we watched the church building grow, and everyone seemed pleased with its design.

During this time, the other Lutheran pastor at Cornell with whom I had worked for over a year was called to be president of Gettysburg College. This lead to additional ministry work for me until a new pastor came. I was consulted by the Call Committee of the National Lutheran Council because of my previous involvement with Lutheran Campus Ministry. Within a couple of months, a pastor was called who had no experience in campus ministry but was a very bright and engaging person, and soon became well-liked by the students and me. Our relationship as the two Lutheran campus pastors at Cornell started out a bit uncomfortably. He had some difficulty accepting my role in campus ministry, probably because I was so much a part of the program and knew the students so well. I think he saw me as a threat to his position. I sensed his discomfort, and in the next few months we came to work together very well. We grew in our relationship and carried on a good ministry to the students. Years later, when I was in Thousand Oaks, California, and working with

California Lutheran University as part of my total ministry in Thousand Oaks, he came to Cal Lutheran as a speaker. We had a wonderful time being together briefly while he was there.

Another thing that characterized my ministry in Ithaca was the Civil Rights Movement. Because of my experience in the South while I was in the Navy and Marines, I had strong feelings and interest in the movement, including the Civil Rights March in Ithaca. The Sunday of the march, I told my youth group that I was going to be in the march and invited any one of them to join me. Several of them joined me – a couple of them to the dismay of their parents – but they came along anyway. Generally, the town and the university were very supportive, and it was a good experience for my young people. No negative incidents occurred during the march. A short time afterward, a noted Lutheran scholar, Martin E. Marty, who was in Ithaca because of his Civil Rights leadership, was a guest in our home. He would be speaking on the issue at Cornell that weekend. He was a delightful guest, especially because he enjoyed our three sons who were the same age as his three sons, whom he missed very much.

In January of 1966, I received a call to Our Redeemer Lutheran Church in Solon, Ohio – near Cleveland. As with any Lutheran pastor who receives a call, I gave it prayerful consideration. Betty and I visited Solon, and met with their Call Committee. The call very much surprised me, but I felt a strong inclination from the Holy Spirit to accept it. Later in Solon, I came to realize the purpose of that inclination, which I will discuss when I describe my ministry there. I saw the Lord's working in moving to the Cleveland area when Betty informed me that our treatment program for Mark's autism would require us to move to a large city for continued treatment.

As we prepared to leave Ithaca in the middle of February, we also prepared a farewell worship service in which our new organ – the one built by John Brombaugh, mentioned above – would be used for the first time. John even stayed up all night tuning the organ so it would be ready. The farewell service was enwrapped with many inches of new snow. We completed the service all right, but on to the next item of interest – how to get all of the cars out of the parking lot! Several of the men stood where the driveway was underneath the snow, to serve as signposts for the cars to leave. Many of the other men helped push the cars out of the parking lot to the street, a curving 100 yards or more. Everyone got out safely, but we decided not to go through with the farewell luncheon that was to be held at a local restaurant. The next day, with most of the main roads cleared and no snow, we packed up and left for Cleveland. What a way to close out my first congregation!

~

Our Redeemer Lutheran Church, Solon, Ohio, 1966-1968

Solon, Ohio was and is a typical suburb of a large city – in this case Cleveland. The church is located on the main highway between East Cleveland and Akron, called SOM Center Road. The church property is on swamp land that had been filled in, but was still a mess when it rained. Like my congregation in Ithaca, it was filled with good members and solid leaders. Our Redeemer was built five years earlier with an outstanding pastor, D. Marshall Begley, a friend of mine from seminary days. As I was to realize later, I was more like a long-serving interim pastor, which would turn out to be two and a half years. It was an important time in my ministry succeeding an outstanding pastor, and the congregation had to go through a lot of changes and feelings of grief.

The city of Solon had a wonderful educational system, where all students from kindergarten to seniors in high school were in one large complex to which buses brought them from all over town. Academically, it was a very good school system. Our two youngest sons, Dan and Dave, attended and Betty was a teacher's aid. We were also blessed with a place for Mark to receive help and therapy – in (what became well known) Cleveland Child Guidance Center, part of the Case Western Reserve University system. He received good care all the time we were in Solon.

The congregation was a blessing to our family, and we were a blessing to the congregation. The church parsonage was located one and a half miles away, and was a very adequate two-story home with lots of room for three little boys who quickly made friends in the neighborhood. We became good friends with the neighbor next door who was a faithful Roman Catholic and a well-known banker in town. He had two children the same ages as Dan and Dave. My favorite memory of that family was being invited over once in a while to watch TV, which we didn't have. This was especially true during the football season, as my neighbor was an avid Notre Dame fan. When Michigan State played Notre Dame, it was one of the big games of the season, and I would go over there and we'd watch and have a few beers during the game. One year, Notre Dame was ranked #1, and Michigan State #2. It should have been an epic battle with one team finally able to claim victory, but the final score turned out to be a 10-10 tie. My neighbor friend was furious because the Notre Dame coach had a chance to try to score near the end of the game but played it conservatively, settling for the tie to ensure they would stay #1.

This was also the time of cats and a dog or two, which we all enjoyed. I also had a good neighbor two doors down – a Cleveland city fireman who loved to golf. And in Solon, all the yards were connected with no fences between. This is when I started up my golfing "career." My fireman friend loved to practice his short game by hitting balls through or over the back yards, with many balls ending up in our back yard. I never got very good at golf, but had lots of fun. A pastor friend from another denomination who lived right down the street had a member who owned the local golf course. So we played for free! We did not talk much theology, and the closest thing to it occurred on Ascension Day (which is always on a Thursday). My friend, Howard, was the type of golfer who took a long time to tee off because he did what many golfers do – wiggle a lot before hitting the ball. On this Ascension Day morning, he prepared to take his first shot. Just as he pulled back his club and started to swing, I yelled out, "Happy Ascension Day, Howard!" He promptly hit the ball way off line and into the trees. He turned to me and asked, "What did you say?" I replied, "Don't you know, Howard, this is Ascension Day?" He proceeded to have a poor game of golf... even I beat him! Of course, he blamed his poor game on it being Ascension Day. Exactly one year later – again on Ascension Day – I did the same thing to him. After I yelled my comment about Ascension Day, he had a bad shot and turned to me and said, "Oh, no, not again!" He then proceeded to have a poor game, and I beat him again. So much for my golfing exploits!

My overall description of my ministry could be summed up with one word – counseling. It seemed that everything that can happen in a small town happened during my ministry there. It ranged from standard marriage counseling to a life-threatening situation when a husband was looking for his wife, and he had a gun. She called me up a bit frantic because he was looking for her. So I told her to meet me at church, hoping that he would not find her there. (He didn't go to church very often, anyway.) He didn't find us, and everything settled down all right, but we were both scared.

During my second year there, I attended a class on counseling at Case Western Reserve University conducted by a psychology professor. The class included three Lutherans, one Presbyterian, and three Catholic priests, and we met once a week for the entire academic year. Our professor told us that he realized how much counseling clergymen do, as his father was a Methodist minister. He told us that he admired his father very much, and wanted to share his counseling background because of his father, so he offered the course non-credit and free of charge. Each week we shared counseling problems in our own churches, and we would discuss and he would offer excellent advice. Because I seemed to have a multitude of unique counseling situations in Solon, I would be greeted by the class, "How are things in Solon Place?" (a take-off on the popular book, movie, and television series of the day, a soap opera called *Peyton Place*). Obviously I learned a lot from him, and appreciated his work with us. My most difficult counseling situation occurred when I helped a mother of a 16-year-old girl place her daughter into a psychiatric hospital because she was such a serious problem, and the dad wouldn't even help. Her stay at the hospital even included shock treatments which was done somewhat commonly those days. In the daughter's case, the six week treatment worked. Years later, when she got her life straightened out, she became head of children's services at Cleveland Child Guidance Center and was happily married!

Sometime during the first year, my mother had a bad fall and broke both of her wrists cushioning her head as she fell on cement steps. Since Betty was a nurse, we suggested that she go and take care of my mother since both arms were in casts past the elbows. She stayed for three weeks until the right arm became usable.

My ministry continued to be interesting and challenging, and I really loved the congregation. Many good things happened, such as a relationship with a new Lutheran church of a different synod that moved into town. We did some things together as two congregations, including Thanksgiving and Lenten services, and a personal friendship with the younger pastor developed. My own congregation was very supportive of these interactions, although, for some people in my synod, that would not have been acceptable.

During the years in Solon, I was able to attend some Cleveland Lutheran High School class reunions, which was very enjoyable. One unique incident resulted when some of the boys kidded me about getting married. Just before I got married in the summer of 1956, a group of the boys had a party for me. We had it at the home of one of our wonderful families, Ma and Pa Puls. During the evening of lots of fun and kidding, several of the boys kidded me about getting married at the "old" age of 29, and a colorful conversation resulted. Finally, I challenged them to a pact among us with a case of beer as the prize. The pact consisted of each of the boys signing their names to a document that I wrote up to the effect that I would owe each who got married at 29 or older a case of beer, and each who got married before 29 would owe me a case of beer. Of course, it was a good bargain on my part, as it turned out that just about all of them were married before they were 29. But only one of them paid off the bet. It happened when I was in Solon one Sunday morning after church. One of the boys and his wife attended the service. While the congregation was still standing around, he went out to his car and pulled out a big box – a case of beer! He announced as he gave it to me in front of my congregation, "Here's the case of beer I owe you," and handed it to me. I did a little explaining to the congregation after that, but they all thought it was funny.

One of the disappointing aspects of my ministry in Solon was when I introduced the idea of women voters at church meetings. I didn't rush it, but I did keep it in mind, and the congregation finally decided to bring it to a vote. There was almost total support for the idea, except for two very active families who were not in favor of it and told the congregation that if they approved having women voters, they would leave the congregation. As soon as the decision was announced, the two families stood up and left. They eventually became members at another Lutheran church not far away. Other than this, the congregation felt good about the decision.

Suddenly one Sunday evening, I got a phone call from the president of Redeemer Lutheran Church, Thousand Oaks, California. He informed me that the congregation had just voted to call me as their pastor. I was totally surprised and gave it a lot of thought and prayer because I realized that, in a sense, my "caretaker" ministry in Solon was coming to an end. I felt very satisfied and had good feelings about my ministry there and the people of Solon. I got very close to them in a short time, and until the call to Thousand Oaks came, I had no thought of leaving Solon. In a real sense, I did not want to leave yet, but the congregation was in good order, growing, and looking ahead to an increasing ministry. I went to the Ohio District President, a good friend of mine, and we talked about the call. He was very good about it, and I appreciated his help. He told me something very important that I've shared with other pastors over the years – "Remember, the decision on a call should not be to leave a place, but to go to a place where God is calling you." I very strongly felt and believed God was calling me to Thousand Oaks, and I'll describe why in the next section. Suffice it to say, Betty was with me all the way. She was a little bit surprised, but she was used to these kinds of surprises. After all, she was a PK (preacher's kid). After I made the decision, she told me that Cleveland Child Guidance Center would not be able to help us with Mark any longer. They had recently told her that they had already extended themselves beyond the standard six months of care, although we didn't know there was a limit to how long they would work with Mark. Therefore, since I had made my decision totally on the basis of the call, it was the Lord calling us to another metropolitan area where we could get continued help for Mark. As it was when we left Ithaca, the move turned out to be a blessing. The same would be true with the call to Thousand Oaks, with even greater blessings.

Our departure from Solon turned out to be quite dramatic. The last Sunday before leaving Solon and Our Redeemer Lutheran Church, I was spending the afternoon with the young people of the congregation in our last get-together – a swimming/games/food kind of thing. Since we were at the home of one of the active leaders of the congregation who had a very large backyard, a game of softball was started. To even things up a bit, the boys were required to bat the opposite of their natural way, which meant that most of them had to bat left-handed, including me. What they didn't know was that I had done some switch-hitting playing baseball over the years. Since the house was several hundred feet away, toward right-center field, there seemed to be no danger of hitting it. So, the father of the family was up on the second story level of the roof, replacing a window. The first time I came up to bat, in my enthusiasm I swung at the ball and caught hold of it just right and arched a long drive to right-center field. I yelled loudly, "Watch out, Stan!" He turned just in time to see the ball fly through his new window. I couldn't believe what had just happened – and neither could the kids – as my hands covered my face in abject embarrassment and apologies. Once the kids got over the initial shock, they had a good laugh and kidded me unmercifully. Good ol' Stan was very good-natured about the whole incident, even though he had to re-putty the whole new window. He was very gracious and kind. For me, it was like they say in the old Western novels, "Time to 'git outta town!"

~

During my last year in Solon and before I left for California, I made a special visit to what had become, for me, a special place of ministry – a Home for the elderly, run by an order of nuns from Hungary. It started this way: One day I received a phone call from a person named Sister Mary (there are a lot of "Sister Mary's" in the Catholic church…) who resided in a Home for elderly people about 15 miles away in the middle of nowhere. In a very pleasant voice, she asked if I would come out to their Home for a pastoral visit. She was in charge of a number of elderly people, part of an order of Hungarians staffed by her and several other nuns. They lived quite detached from civilization. Sister Mary informed me that among the 40 or 50 people in the Home, two were not Roman Catholic, but Lutheran. I recalled reading somewhere that there were a number of Lutheran churches in Hungary, and many of the members fled the country when the Russians took over. She asked if I would come and visit them, especially because the two Lutherans wanted a Lutheran Holy Communion. I told her I would be happy to do that in the little chapel at the Home. She added that she would like all the residents and the staff to be in attendance.

After getting specific directions to the Home, I took off one afternoon a few days later. The Home was really in the "boondocks" but I found it anyway. When I arrived, I was met at the front door by Sister Mary, a lovely looking woman in her middle or late 30s. Sister Mary proceeded to show me around the place, which included a large garden in back that helped in feeding the residents. Then everyone was summoned to the chapel where my two Lutheran men were sitting expectantly in the front row. Then began an interesting experience when I went to the small sacristy and started to gown up for the worship service at which I was the only clergyman. I had asked ahead of time if it would be appropriate for me to be gowned for the communion service. As I prepared to put on my gown, I was amazed to be surrounded by a bevy of nuns, all helping me get into my robe, stole, clergy cross, and whatever other preparations were needed. Their hospitality almost overwhelmed me. Then I realized *they* probably had never seen a formally robed Protestant clergyman, but only their own priests.

We went into the chapel and I prepared to do a communion service Lutheran-style. The little chapel was filled, and all the nuns were in the back totally focused on the proceedings. I'm sure they were surprised and appreciative that I treated the occasion so sacredly. I proceeded to follow a brief Lutheran / Catholic liturgy in which we sang from their hymnal. In preparing for communion, I preached a short sermon on the Gospel of the day, just as in the Catholic Church. As I consecrated the elements, the place became very quiet and devout. Then I took the bread and the wine (with a small chalice which I used for private communion in my own ministry). I then proceeded with the distribution to the two Lutherans. As I was doing this, I happened to glance up briefly and was struck by very close attention being given when I gave the wine from the chalice. I realized then that they probably had never witnessed anyone receiving the wine except the priests. The look of awe on the nun's faces, including Sister Mary's, was magnificent and captivating to me. I thanked God that what I was doing was in His name. As I got ready to leave, I was attended to by the same circle of warm cordiality as I had received when I had robed before the service.

For nearly a year, I visited once a month with my special Lutheran / Catholic communion service for my two Lutheran men. I became a friend of Sister Mary to the extent that she was able to get special permission from her bishop to come to my church for a special program for my LWML (Lutheran Women's Missionary League). She was delighted and was a "Big Hit" with the ladies at Our Redeemer Church. We all smiled with her when she announced that she had to leave by a specific time because of curfew back at the Home. Before I left for California, I decided to visit the Home just to say "goodbye," especially to Sister Mary. When I inquired about her whereabouts, they told me to go out to the garden. There I found her busily working, wearing plain working clothes of a skirt and blouse. This was the first time I got to see her long, beautiful hair cascading down to her shoulders. Then I noticed an apron tied tightly around her small waist, which accentuated her perfect "hourglass" figure. This was a stark contrast to the nun's habit which totally covered everything, including her hair. We spoke delightfully for a few minutes, each of us thanking one another as we said our goodbyes. I shook her hand and turned away toward the Home smiling a bit, as I couldn't help but think to myself, *What a waste of beautiful womanhood.*

Redeemer Lutheran Church, Thousand Oaks, California, 1968-1985

Besides the usual feeling about leaving an enjoyable part of our lives in Solon, Ohio, we looked forward with great anticipation to being in Thousand Oaks. I felt good about my ministry in Solon, and leaving the congregation in good shape for the future. The congregation in Solon continued with successful ministry and growth. Now it was time to move to the next place God had called me. We drove across the country after spending time with family and friends in Michigan and Pittsburgh.

We finally arrived in Thousand Oaks, and started moving into our new home for the next five years. In preparation for my installation that Sunday afternoon, we went to the home of my good pastor friend, Art Puls, his wife, Gloria, and four boys, all in about the same age range as our three boys. Gloria made a big dinner for us which took a long time. Since we were in Santa Paula, we barely got back to Thousand Oaks in time for my installation. The installation went very well, with special music from the choir directed by Kay Slocum, soon to be a close friend of ours. I recognized many members of the congregation at the door when they exited because I knew many by name from the pictorial directory I had studied while coming across the country. The church is located in an upscale part of Thousand Oaks, called Lynn Ranch, where some very faithful members lived. It was a fully completed worship building, education space, and church office. We lived in a parsonage two miles away on a main street. Our youngest son, Dave, began developing his abilities as a basketball player, using half of the backyard as his basketball court ... hard clay with no grass. We lived there for five years before we bought our own home.

At this point, I must describe the congregation and the situation there. I knew my predecessor, who had made a good start with the congregation. I knew him from seminary days, and had high regard for him. However, for the two years before I came, he had involved the congregation heavily in the "charismatic movement." It became a serious, divisive factor in the congregation to the point that he insisted that the congregation go along with his program or he would resign. In a somewhat somber and tearful meeting with the congregation, his ultimatum was voted upon. He lost the vote of confidence from the congregation by a two-to-one margin. The next morning, his letter of resignation was given to the congregation. He left right away to begin a new ministry in Palm Desert. But for a couple of years, he continued to meet from time to time with "his people" from Redeemer. I always treated him in an accommodating, evangelical way. My initial experience with a divided church was characterized by both "sides" trying to influence me.

In my first sermon, I tried to set the tone of my ministry of love, care, and honesty. God's Holy Spirit gave me a wonderful phrase by which to divert attention away from the divisiveness that characterized the situation by saying, "When you speak to me about my predecessor, remember you're speaking to a friend of his." Later in the same sermon, I said (quoting Psalm 100:2 (ESV) and paraphrasing Hebrews 13:17):

> I will seek to "Serve the LORD with gladness" with my personal concern for you. I will do this not only because I want to be very involved with you, but I do this "as one who must watch for your souls, for I must give account to the Lord, that I may do it with gladness, and not with sorrow." You can be assured that I will be very much concerned about what happens to each one of you, and what I can do to help and share the meaning of God's Word in these concerns. I will also strive to serve the Lord in my love for you. There will be times when you will not agree with me; there will be times when I won't agree with you; there will be times when I will make mistakes; there will be times when you will become discouraged or disappointed; and there will be good and joyful times as well as tough and difficult times. But for me you can be sure, by God's grace, I will always love you! When you are sick, I will love you. When we are in disagreement, I will love you. When you face a crisis, I will love you. When you face the daily trials and temptations of life, I will love you. In your triumphs and successes, I will love you. In your failures and difficulties, I will love you. In all of the day-to-day, on-going, living and working we will be doing together in this parish and community, I WILL LOVE YOU!

A good deal of support for my ministry and the congregation came from the pastoral circuit which surrounded us. I continued to be strengthened and blessed by all these circuit pastors. I am indebted to Art Puls, Loren Kramer, Cal Fiege, Norm Swolert, Woody Blanke, and many others. With the power of the Holy Spirit, we began unifying and strengthening the congregation. This required many pastoral calls and meetings with groups. Thus began my 17-year "love affair" with Redeemer congregation. Part of this included going off of district subsidy, a pleasant surprise to the officials of our district, who were not expecting it.

At this time, we became very close friends with Jerry and Kay Slocum. Kay was a talented violinist, even teaching Mark for several years. She had such a good choir at Redeemer that they made a record using soloists and choral selections to tell a story of Christ's crucifixion and resurrection. I still have my copy of the record. The Slocum's moved to the Washington, D.C. area, where Jerry worked for the Federal Reserve Board. After that, they moved to Denver. Over the years, we spent many vacations together in Washington, D.C. and Denver. During this time, Kay developed a serious interest in becoming a Lutheran pastor in the ELCA (Evangelical Lutheran Church in America). She continued her studies at nearby colleges and Luther Seminary in St. Paul, Minnesota. She eventually accepted a call to First Lutheran Church, Cedar Rapids, Iowa, as associate pastor, where she continues to this day, now as visitation pastor. I was privileged to be her "sometimes mentor," "sometimes counselor," and always her special friend. I even participated in her ordination in February of 1992.

It's necessary at this point to describe what was happening to Mark, since he would continue to need special help. First of all, we found a wonderful school named Dubnoff School of Educational Therapy located in North Hollywood. He attended this school for four and a half years, with excellent guidance and education. Having him there each day required driving him into North Hollywood – a distance of about 35 miles through lots of traffic. This put a strain on our family's schedule. We are grateful to one of our members, Paul Steffen, for helping with that trip a number of times, since he worked a short distance from the school. We are indebted to this day to Paul. Along with the Dubnoff School, we began with a highly trained child psychologist, Dr. Peter King, also in the San Fernando Valley. He was a wonderful help with Mark's behavioral training.

This would continue a number of years. The two younger boys attended a nearby public school. After two years, they began to study at Ascension Lutheran School, on the other side of Thousand Oaks, and each continued there through 8th grade.

At about the time Dan and Dave started at Ascension, we decided to "mainline" Mark's school experience by placing him into the 7th grade there. As in other instances, we ran into resistance because autism was not well known and had many negative features. However, Mark did very well in 7th and 8th grade, which enabled him to start as a freshman at Thousand Oaks High School. Again, the resistance factor came into play because they didn't know quite what to do with this unusual boy. Betty solved that dilemma because she had discovered that very recently the state of California required schools to accept special education students. Thousand Oaks High School did not feel prepared to deal with autistic children. She had a hard time convincing the school psychologist that he had to do something. After a number of refusals to meet with Betty, she showed up one morning in the psychologist's office with a lap full of books and announced that she wanted to see the psychologist, and she was prepared to sit there all day until he would see her. Finally, of course, he did see her and became a great help to Mark, to us, and to the school, because Mark was the first autistic student in their program. Mark took special ed. classes along with regular classes for three years. When he began his senior year in high school, he was assigned all regular classes. He graduated with his class, receiving a diploma. We're still very grateful to both Ascension Lutheran and Thousand Oaks High School for their loving care for Mark.

Along with a busy time of acclimating to a new situation in the congregation, I decided to reach out to the local college, California Lutheran College (later to become California Lutheran University). I did this by taking the president of the college, Dr. Ray Olson, out to lunch, beginning a close friendship with him. Even though it was not a Missouri Synod Lutheran school, I considered it part of my parish ministry and decided that I wanted to be involved in a relationship with the school. I had talked to my congregation earlier about this idea, to receive their support to add campus work to my ministry. I was very pleased to get their strong support, especially as there was a large number of Missouri Synod students at the college. As I had done in Ithaca, I now involved myself in a total program of working with other Lutheran churches. The district supported our decision, and over the years this turned out to be a very God blessed and exciting part of Redeemer's history and ministry. Along with the growing connection with Cal Lutheran, I found myself very involved with many other Lutheran leaders, and found that a delightful experience, particularly with the southwestern bishops from Denver to California to Arizona. I was also involved in forming the Center for Theological Studies at Cal Lutheran. Most of my participation was on boards and committees of the university as well as ministering to a large number of Missouri Synod Lutheran students and faculty.

This continued throughout my 17 years as pastor at Redeemer, with great support from the congregation. A good example of my credibility occurred when a close friend of mine, Roger Anderson, was elected bishop of this area for the ELCA. I was asked to represent our own Missouri Synod district at the installation of Roger, and was even placed near the head of the whole line of notable church leaders, even ahead of Archbishop Mahony. To put it simply, I enjoyed and appreciated "mixing" with all kinds of other Lutherans. The final evidence of my role at Cal Lutheran for all those years came in 1985 when I was given the Distinguished Service award of Cal Lutheran over those 17 years. The description on my award was a beautifully written testimony to my ministry at Cal Lutheran.

Another area of my community involvement and interests was becoming a member of the Kiwanis Club of Thousand Oaks. I was sponsored by my own church treasurer, and it turned out to be a great experience for about 14 years because the club provided many services to the community, including putting together the annual Conejo Valley Days parade. My special friend, Harry Stillwell, got the Salvation Army band into the parade. For 22 years, he was the director of the Rose Bowl Salvation Army Band. My relationship with Kiwanis was delightful. I even conducted a number of marriages and several funerals. From the Mayor and City Council on down, I was part of the serving community of Thousand Oaks. Here again, our congregation supported all of my community efforts, including being honored as Distinguished Club President one year. I felt blessed to associate with so many community-serving men, and I will continue to treasure the many friendships in the community, outside the specific congregation of Redeemer.

Meanwhile, "back at the (Redeemer) ranch," I was kept very busy with all the demands and opportunities to serve a growing congregation. This was the heart of my ministry in Thousand Oaks – filled with Bible classes, Sunday sermons, personal counseling in many situations, hospital calls, member visitations, Confirmation classes both young and adult, serving on boards and committees of the district, e.g., Board for Special Ministries (social, deaf, hospital, and campus), and helping to build a strong, Christ-serving laity.

Every pastor experiences a number of special events in his ministry. One of the first of these was calling the Youth Minister several years after I began my ministry at Redeemer. Al Roehl came from the Youth Leadership Training Program at Valparaiso University. He gave us several good years, especially with his musical talents on the guitar. This was the beginning of our contemporary worship service. It was the "guitar era," and Al taught dozens of kids to play the guitar. He was with us for several years, until the downturn of the aerospace industry affected the country economically.

Regrettably, we had to release Al of his position. A short time later, I came up with the idea of working with the Religion Department of Cal Lutheran to use some of their pre-seminary students to work with our congregation on a part-time, paid basis of 20 hours per week. The university was very happy to provide our congregation in this way. Each one that was chosen worked for two years at a time. We used this system very successfully with four pre-seminary students, giving them experience for when they would become pastors.

My connection and relationship with Cal Lutheran was encouraged by the congregation, including faculty members at Redeemer. This connection with Cal Lutheran provided several interesting events. First of all, Cal Lutheran for six weeks each summer was home to the Dallas Cowboys football team, with its wonderful Christian coach, Tom Landry. This was brought about by one of my own members, Don Garrison, who was in charge of the summer program. He went to Texas and convinced them that CLU would be a good place for their six week pre-season training. The weather can be hot in Thousand Oaks, but it always cools off nicely in the afternoon. That was ideal for hardworking athletes. It was very popular with the community of Thousand Oaks, as well as with the college. Coach Landry and his staff held their practice sessions two times a day, for six weeks. The practices were wide open to anyone who wished to watch them, which included many townspeople. They were attracted by some of the biggest names in pro football, for example quarterback Roger Staubach, and others. Not only were the practice sessions open to the public, but it brought about a wonderful public relations situation for little boys who would wait anxiously to carry the helmet of a player back to the locker room. Coach Landry was a dedicated Christian who I got to know personally, especially when he had me do chapel devotions early Sunday mornings with at least 25-30 players and coaches attending.

During the summer when Dave was 16 years old, he was given a job to work with the Cowboys and the coaches, which he obviously enjoyed. Sometimes, after their practices, he even got to play one-on-one basketball with some of the football players ... a boy's dream! He earned the trust of Coach Landry by his hard work ethic and willingness to help out in every way. One day Coach Landry asked him, "Do you have a driver's license?" Dave answered, "Yes, I got mine a couple of months ago." He then sent Dave in his big, expensive Cadillac to Los Angeles Airport to pick up the owner and general manager of the football club. Quite an assignment for a 16 year old who had never driven to LAX! Dave told me later, almost casually, "I had no problem." Obviously Coach Landry trusted and liked Dave very much.

Besides Coach Landry and his Cowboy team, the greatest name in college basketball, Coach John Wooden, held weekly summer basketball camps for boys. My son, Dave, at the age of ten, was able to attend one of these weekly camps by the generosity of Coach Wooden. Dave won the most important award of the week, the "Mister Hustle Award." All in all, it was a great summer for Dave, and he did a lot of growing up with the many stories he could tell.

The connection with Cal Lutheran and the summer program provided the background for two interesting events. The first of these occurred when Don Garrison, the head of the summer program, was struck with a debilitating disease, Guillain-Barré syndrome (GBS, sometimes referred to as French polio). One afternoon when I went to the hospital to see Don, as I walked into his room I was met by Coach Landry and Coach Wooden who had come to visit him. We talked for a while, and then when they were beginning to leave Don asked me, "Pastor, will you have a prayer with us?" And, of course, the two Christian coaches joined with Don and me in prayer. Three great humble Christian men joined with me in this beautiful moment with God. Don later told me that he felt God's Spirit in the room that day.

Another great connection with the Dallas Cowboys occurred in the summer of 1976, which I'll simply label "The Debbie Steffen Story."

The Debbie Steffen Story

In that fateful summer of 1976, Debbie Steffen, a 17-year-old girl, spent July 4th weekend visiting relatives in Santa Rosa, California. She was the youngest of four children of Paul and Betty Steffen, strong and faithful members at Redeemer. It was a Saturday evening and the family was gathered together in a large sunroom, with Debbie sitting, listening to the radio next to her which was by a window. Suddenly, there was the crashing sound of broken glass and flying metal. A young man a block or so away had fired a gun aimed at a street light. The bullet crashed through the window and the radio next to Debbie's ear and hit Debbie, rendering her unconscious. While just barely alive, she was rushed to a nearby hospital in critical condition. Her prognosis was poor, with a possibility she would not live long. I was called immediately by the family. Early the next morning, I had Sunday services in the chapel at Cal Lutheran with Coach Landry and a number of players. In my short sermon, I told them what was on my heart and mind, and asked for their special prayers. Coach Landry was so moved that he wrote me a personal letter of encouragement and prayers for Debbie. Dr. Ray Johnson, a dentist and active member of Redeemer, arranged for a small airplane to fly to Santa Rosa that Sunday afternoon. The following day, after she had been stabilized, they flew her back home on a hospital bed, still unconscious. The family, Debbie's boyfriend, and I met her plane at the Camarillo Airport. From there, they took her to Los Robles Hospital in Thousand Oaks. When she regained consciousness, it was discovered that she was completely paralyzed, except for half of her face. After several weeks in the hospital, she was sent to Rancho Los Amigos Rehabilitation Hospital in Duarte, California. Since half of her face was not paralyzed, with a tube in her throat she was able to speak in short sentences. When it became obvious that she would need special transportation to come home for visits, Coach Landry took it upon himself to raise money for a specially equipped van that would cost more than $7,000. To raise that amount, he spoke to his coach friend, Dick Nolan in San Francisco, and they arranged to play a special exhibition football game on Cal Lutheran's football field. With much publicity in the community, the game was played a week later. At the game, Coach Landry had me describe the situation over the loud speaker and then I had a prayer. The effort was very successful as there were several thousand fans in attendance. Debbie had her special van!

After she was moved to Rancho Los Amigos, the family and I and individual friends visited her regularly. Debbie and I had some agonizing discussions, all in short sentences, to help her get through her terrible condition. Since her condition did not change, it was obvious that she might not live long. Nonetheless, she remained in good spirits. Of course, she had up and down times, but she kept to her faith in Christ.

She found the name of the young man who had shot her and dictated a letter to him, sharing their mutual feelings, including her words of forgiveness, and suggesting that he read the Bible which she sent along with the letter.

Several times, Debbie had spoken about not wanting to live. Then, one day seven months after the accident had occurred, I visited her on a Wednesday. We talked some, and then she looked at me with a half smiling face and said, "Pastor ... I'm glad ... to be alive." I kissed her goodbye, thankful to God for her words. The next morning, Thursday, she died quickly, suddenly, almost unexpectedly.

Several days later, the memorial service for her was conducted at Redeemer with hundreds in attendance both inside the church and outside where speakers had been set up. An accompanying newspaper front page article described the service and the beautiful life of Debbie. Over the years, I have remained close to Debbie's family, and there's a special bond between the Steffens and me.

~

I am reminded by the Debbie Steffen story of a poem written by Edith Dibble. Early in my ministry at Redeemer, I had one of the most amazing and profound experiences in my life as a pastor. It involved Edith, a wonderful Christian woman who lived a few blocks from the church with her husband, Ted, and their four children: Polly, Dan, Becky, and Andy. They were all actively involved at Redeemer for a number of years. I married Polly and her husband Chuck, confirmed Becky and Andy, and after I left Redeemer I married Andy and his wife Josephine, coincidentally enough back at my old stomping grounds – Anabel Taylor Chapel on the Cornell campus. I quickly became well-acquainted with Edith, and ministered to her as she was slowly dying of cancer. Ministering to her even included Betty and I taking her by car several times for cancer treatments some miles away, when Ted was out of town and the children were also not available to do this. Those were precious, inspiring, memorable times with her. I was sitting at her bedside those very early morning hours of January 4th, 1970, when her painful four and a half years of struggle ended with the most momentous, dramatic, surprising moment where her life here was changed to there. She was now filled with peace and victory. She was now in the loving presence of her Lord, as she had so beautifully described in her poetic epitaph, that she wrote in late 1969, entitled "Comfort":

> Pity me not,
> I'm in my Master's arms;
> He holds me fast and will not let me go.
>
> Envy my lot!
> I'm in my Lord's embrace.
> With such a lover, who would sigh for change?
>
> Welcome the thought
> That Christ thus cares for me.
> His good and gracious will is done indeed.
>
> Alter naught
> My portion no hair's-breadth.
> Remove no featherweight of burden light.
>
> Cancel no jot,
> No tittle He prescribes.
> The Great Physician knows what cure is best.
>
> Weep now for naught,
> Since no iota, speck,
> Of what the world calls trouble, troubles me.

> What hath God wrought?
> This little season's pain
> He blesses, turns into ecstatic joy!
>
> Perfect the plot
> My Heavenly Bridegroom plans
> Whereby He proves His love. He kisses me!

I conclude this part about Edith with the closing line from John Ylvisaker's hymn, "I Was There to Hear Your Borning Cry":

> When the evening gently closes in,
> And you shut your weary eyes,
> I'll be there as I have always been
> With just one more surprise.

~

The last several years of my ministry at Redeemer were characterized by the need for a second professional on staff, either a second pastor or a Director of Christian Education (DCE), because of the continued growth of the congregation. We discussed whether the new staff member should be another pastor, or a youth and education person. Since the congregation was not acquainted with the DCE program, I suggested that we try to get a DCE for one year. In May, I contacted a friend of mine, the Director of the DCE Program at Concordia University, Nebraska. His name was Bill Karpenko. When I called him and asked him about the situation he answered, "Jim, I have just the one for you! Almost all of the DCE graduates have already been placed, but I have one 3rd-year student who wants very much to do her internship before she comes back for graduation." He talked with me, mostly with a series of questions, about the congregation and the work she would do at Redeemer. The congregation agreed to have her placed at Redeemer for one year. As the pastor who would be working with her for her internship, I was required to go to the Concordia campus in Seward for a two-day orientation program for all the pastors who were getting DCEs. I arranged a flight to Lincoln, Nebraska where I would be met at the airport by the DCE, Sheri Strecker, or a friend of hers. When I got to the airport late the night before the orientation meetings, there was no one there and it was close to midnight when the airport would shut down. I decided to stay somewhere overnight and call Bill in the morning, but I wasn't sure how to do this. The airport was closing down. There was nothing around – no cabs, no transportation – and only a young cleaning woman. When I told her my problem, she offered to drive me to the closest motel about two miles away. I gratefully accepted her generous offer.

When I told the story later, with tongue in cheek, I said, "I met a very nice woman who took me to the motel." She turned out to be a nice Christian woman working two jobs to keep things going. However, she refused to accept any payment for her kindness.

Early the next morning, I called Bill to tell him the situation – that I was stuck in Lincoln and would need transportation to the school 20 miles away. He wasn't too happy about the failure of someone to meet me at the airport since we had the opening orientation meeting after breakfast time. He picked me up and drove me to Seward, dropped me off at a dormitory, showed me my room, and told me where the pastors and DCEs would soon be meeting. As quickly as possible, I went to the meeting room where they had already started. There were about 30 pastors and DCEs in a large circle where Bill was conducting introductions. Most of the DCEs were seated next to their pastor. As they went around the room, each person introduced themselves with a little information about them. It came near where I was seated. The girl next to me introduced herself briefly, describing the dilemma she had caused when she was supposed to meet her pastor at the airport the night before. She said she was looking forward to working with her pastor whom she didn't know up to this point. It was then my turn to introduce myself and I said, "I'm the pastor she's talking about." The rest of the orientation went well for Sheri and me. After that, I suggested that we go out for dinner, where we talked about her arrival in Thousand Oaks which would be in June, a month later. On the way to the dinner, she surprised me by asking, "Can I take my shoes off and walk in my bare feet on the cobblestones?" I smiled and replied, "It's O.K. with me!" – and I knew we would have a good relationship.

On her first Sunday at Redeemer, after church the congregation had a big picnic at the Cal Lutheran campus. Sheri was an instant hit with everyone, with a bubbly personality, sense of humor, and her dedication to serving at Redeemer. This was the beginning of a very interesting, rewarding year for

Redeemer, for Sheri, and for my ministry. We got along well, and she was a good learner with lots of good ideas. I quickly gave her a free hand in her youth work and teaching. At times it seemed almost like a father / daughter relationship. My admiration for her was expressed in my quarterly evaluation reports to Seward. She was delighted one of those times to go to the beach and do our report together there. She knew that Bill would get a kick out of that, and appreciate her diligence to work together with the congregation and with me.

Betty and our three boys loved Sheri and believed that she was the best thing for me and my ministry there. I believed the same. It's difficult to describe how much I appreciated her and the wonderful way that we worked together. I involved her in the worship services in many ways. All in all, it was the best year possible for our congregation. But, of course, the following summer we had to let her go back to Concordia to finish her 4th academic year.

~

By early spring, the congregation and I had to make plans for the next year. To decide the kind of additional professional staff person we would need, after much discussion the congregation liked the idea of having a seminary vicar for a one-year period. This gave us an opportunity to compare and evaluate the kind of position a new staff member would have – pastor vs. DCE. And so we applied for a vicar and received one from St. Louis Seminary by the name of Brad Roberts. If it was a successful vicarage for Brad and for our congregation, we would be able to decide the type of second professional church worker we would need on staff. In the very back cobwebs of my mind, I had this idea that Sheri would be available a year later. This was just a random thought that I shared with no one except Betty. In the Lord's strange way of doing things, we were given a vicar who simply did not measure up. For instance, he didn't really know how to write a sermon, or even how to do an outline. He did not relate very well to the youth and young adults. On New Year's Eve, I asked him to give the sermon. He got into the pulpit, read a few lines of poetry, and said, "Amen!" He did diligently whatever I asked of him but often without a common sense approach. For example, one time I assigned him to make a hospital call on one of our members. When I made a call two days later on that same member in the hospital, she kindly but firmly told me: "He stayed for more than an hour when all I wanted to do was sleep!" I counseled Brad on what I considered the art of calling on members. Several days later, he took my advice and stayed only a half hour on his hospital call. After working with him on how to write a sermon using an outline first, he improved in this area. He was always pleasant and friendly and an easy conversationalist. However, he had one main real goal – to do ministry to the deaf. He already knew how to sign very well, so I connected him with our synod's deaf ministry in Los Angeles. Betty told me at the end of the year, "You should not have passed him! It was the hardest year of your ministry." However, I did pass him, with the reply to Betty, "The Lord has a special place for him somewhere." And He did! After seminary graduation, Brad was called to be pastor in a small congregation in a small town in Northern California. Nearby was a deaf congregation which he could serve. When he stopped to visit me several years later, he brought his deaf wife and her three children from a former marriage and a trained dog for the deaf. He, his family, and dog were seated in the back for our worship service. In the middle of my sermon, a sharp yelp was heard. The look on the faces of the congregation said, *Did I hear a dog?* After the service, I introduced him, his family, and the dog to the congregation, and he gave a brief talk about deaf ministry. Afterward, in the Fellowship Hall, the dog was the most popular thing with the children. So it was with Brad, and I was happy for him and his ministry. God is always right!

~

When it became time, in the early spring, to decide which type of second professional person to call, it was obvious from the experience of the past two years that the congregation felt that a DCE would be best. Like me, I believe that some of them still had Sheri in mind, since she would now be available for a call. The congregation asked me to look into that possibility. Early in the year, before calls would be made, I again called my friend, Bill Karpenko. I told him that God gave us Sheri for one year and then a vicar who was a disappointment. I asked, "What's the possibility of giving Sheri a call to Redeemer? He told me he would keep it in mind and talk to Sheri about it. Shortly afterwards, he called me back and said that it was too early to determine the call list, "... but I will keep you in mind." He also told me that he had spoken to Sheri and her reply was a quick dance of delight, as she said, "I'm a California girl!" So the era of Sheri at Redeemer would continue. The congregation rejoiced with me when I announced in May that Sheri had been given the call and would be happily coming back to Thousand Oaks.

For her installation, we planned to use Cal Lutheran's picnic area with a gazebo in one part of it. We had an outdoor worship service, and during the service we had Sheri installed in the gazebo, surrounded by members of the congregation and friends. Following the service, we had a get-acquainted picnic at which everyone there got to meet Sheri personally. The following year and a half was one of the happiest times of my ministry. Sheri did everything well, and her radiant face gave expression to the joy of her being with us and serving the congregation so well. I noticed a difference in my relationship with her. When she was with us as an intern, I treated her more like a daughter in teaching the many dimensions of congregational work. This time I felt a more professional relationship between us, probably due to her growing maturity. I appreciated her even more. That was my joy of being with her.

In the summer of 1985, I received a call to First Lutheran Church, Ventura, California. Because things were going so well at Redeemer with Sheri and the congregation, my first impulse was to stay. But the reason for wanting to stay at Redeemer was also part of the reason that I could leave Redeemer in good hands. First Lutheran Church was only 35 miles away, and I knew the congregation fairly well from the years of being in the same pastoral circuit. It was a much smaller church with some unique characteristics that God used to challenge me with a decision.

As I pondered and prayed, another event occurred that seemed to bring a fulfillment to my ministry at Redeemer. In the large annual celebration of Cal Lutheran, I was presented with a rare gift: "The Achievement Award for Service," for my part and support in the university and community. I was deeply honored to be the recipient of this award presented to me by the president of the university and the main speaker of the event, the former governor of California, Pete Wilson, along with other dignitaries.

I was moved by the Lord to accept the call because there was a lot of work to do at First Lutheran. I felt compelled by God's Spirit to make this move even though it was a much smaller church. I felt good in my decision and really believed it was God's Call.

First Lutheran Church, Ventura, California, 1985-1994

I followed the advice of a former district president, Dr. Otto Toelke, concerning the pastoral call, when he said, "Be sure you feel completely called TO a congregation, and not seeking to leave your present congregation." First Lutheran Church is a small church at the west end of the seacoast town of Ventura. The town has a lot of history, including one of the missions, Mission San Buenaventura. The Ventura County Government Center includes the county jail. Weather-wise, it is an ideal town, with cool ocean breezes even on the hottest days of summer. It also has the longest pier on the California coast, which gets badly damaged once in a while from winter storms. First Lutheran is located in the older part of town, a few blocks from the ocean.

When I accepted the call to First Lutheran, I had to deal with what we pastors refer to as the "savior complex." That is, taking a call to rescue a congregation in need of a lot of help to sustain itself or even to grow. I suppose every pastor receiving a call from another congregation would have such feelings. When I took the call to Redeemer, Thousand Oaks, and the crisis occurring there, I don't remember feeling that way, nor did I in accepting the call to First Lutheran.

First Lutheran had gone through several short-time pastors and a long intentional interim pastor, Rev. Dr. Walter Moeller, who served very well, and was greatly revered at First Lutheran and throughout the district and our national synod. He had gained a lot of recognition for his six years in the U.S. House of Representatives, especially for his involvement in passing laws dealing with the elderly. When he retired to live in nearby Santa Barbara, he was asked to do a brief interim ministry at First Lutheran. During the several years that he served, he was a blessing. He convinced the seminary that a full-time pastor was most needed. Pastor Robert Crossan was called and installed, and did an excellent job for one year. Actually, things were in good order when I got the call to Ventura with excellent pastoring by Pastor Crossan. His ministry there lasted only one year because he was a Navy Reserve chaplain, and he had been called to active duty. When he left the seminary in St. Louis, he was told it would be four or five years before he would be called up for active duty, so he was sent to First Lutheran. When I was sometimes asked about him and his ministry, I would reply, "He was a good pastor, who 'set the table' for his successor." Beginning my call to First Lutheran, Pastor Crossan was a good help to me, as was Rev. Dr. Moeller. First Lutheran truly required a full-time pastor, and that was the spirit with which I accepted the call there. After my installation in August of 1985, I was ready to go to work.

The beginning of my ministry was quite unique. When I went to the church on Tuesday morning, I found it completely covered with a familiar looking tent used for destroying termites. So much for my first day. Two days later, as I sat in the study, I heard a strange sound by the side door to my office. When I opened the door, there was a very large boa constrictor comfortably curled up on the steps in the warm summer sun. I wasn't about to disturb him, so I observed him for a few minutes wondering what to do. About that time, a small, ten-year-old boy came running from the other side of the street. As he gathered the curled-up snake and cradled it in his arms, he explained, "I was cleaning my room and it got out before I noticed it." We talked about the snake for a few minutes as I gently petted it. Then he went home very happy to have his special pet back safe and sound. He also was happy that I didn't panic or cause alarm. The postscript to this event occurred a couple days later. I had driven to church for an evening meeting with our youth group. As I drove up, I noticed a lot of cars and people and a small fire truck. I asked an onlooker what was going on. He replied, "There's a great, big snake loose in the neighborhood, and everyone is looking for this dangerous animal." Since my youth group was outside with everyone else, we waited and watched for a while. I told them my story with the snake two days earlier. And then we went in for our meeting. They were quite amazed at their new pastor when I told them there was nothing to be afraid of. A few days later, the boy saw me and told me sadly that his parents made him give up his pet.

The sanctuary was a bit old fashioned and somewhat dark, but very worshipful with a beautiful stained glass window above the altar. It lacked a little bit in size, according to its need. To help in that direction, I suggested we look into the idea of building a balcony for more seating and location of the organ. When the question was raised about finances, I asked if the church had any savings. I already knew the answer, but I wanted them to say it out loud, so I could ask, "How long have you had this $15,000?" They said that they'd had it for many years. So I suggested this would be a good time to use some of it. Almost surprisingly, the congregation thought it was a good idea and several men offered to build it. And they built it in very short order. The congregation was very pleased at the addition that made the sanctuary more beautiful and useful. Ken Sharp and Jack Wilson did most of the work, and became two of my most delightful members. Fred Evans, a terrific real estate agent, and Fred Antrim, treasurer, helped with all the financial bookwork and interactions with the City Building Commission. (Later, Fred Evans helped my son, Mark, by giving him part-time work.)

The congregation began to get some "new blood," including children. I was off to a very satisfying nine years as pastor of First Lutheran Church. Much of that good start may have been due to an initial meeting with the congregation while I was considering the call, regarding one of the concerns I knew they had about getting a new pastor. Their concern reflected the short pastorates and long interims in the past. I recognized or sensed what they were feeling, so right off the bat I said to them, "I'm 58 years old and pastors seldom get Calls at that age, so I want to tell you that I plan to be around the next seven years and maybe even more if I accept this call." That really opened up the meeting to many questions and answers as we got to know each other. They were surprised when one of the "grand old guard" raised his hand to ask a question, and I answered quickly, "I know you! You're Otis Wyneken! I met you at circuit events, and I appreciated your work for the church, and your strong theological stance." I also asked them if they knew my son, Mark. And they all nodded and smiled. Everyone knew Mark!

At this point, I want to mention Fred Antrim, his wife Carina, their daughter Yvette, and Fred's wonderful mother, Millie. Our friendship has continued all these years, mainly through Yvette, a teacher at St. John's Lutheran School, Orange. I even got to marry her to Dave Steuwe. All in all, it was a happy, active, loving congregation. There was much pastoring to do of course, and I thoroughly enjoyed and appreciated my last congregation as pastor.

~

That love expressed itself even more when my wife, Betty, was diagnosed with an incurable form of lymphoma, cancer of the lymph nodes, in 1986. She "fought the good fight" until late 1991. Here I must describe those strangely wonderful four and a half years as she suffered the ups and downs of therapy and treatment. During almost all of this time, she continued working 20 hours a week as a pediatric nurse at Los Robles Hospital in Thousand Oaks. As in my previous congregations, she was beloved deeply by everyone, and I was always so proud of her strong, humble spirit and faith. During this time, her best friend, Joanne Stone – a nurse at Los Robles, was a great support and help to her. It helped that Joanne lived in Ventura also. Her doctor in Thousand Oaks was very special, too. One time during the last ten days of her life, when she was at home in a special bed, he did an amazing thing. On a Saturday evening a few days before she died, he was to attend a big social gathering in Ventura. He phoned Betty just before this event and asked if he and his wife could stop by and see her briefly. There they were, the doctor in his formal-cut tuxedo, his very pleasant wife in a long, beautiful evening gown, and Betty in bed quite alert and talkative. She and her doctor spoke for a little while, sounding like a couple of old friends so glad to see each other. What a scene that was in the front room that evening, each of them knowing she had only a few more days to live. This is a beautiful memory for me. Betty told me afterwards how much that meant to her, and I told her it was the same for me.

During those last ten days, our very good friend, Kay Slocum-Dillan, came and stayed with us most of those days, knowing how very much I loved Betty. Even then, Betty kept her sense of humor. Early one evening as the room was darkening, Kay suggested the idea of lighting a few candles. Betty laughed and said to Kay, "If you do that, you might blow us both to Kingdom Come!" as she pointed at the oxygen tank next to her bed. On Sunday, four days later, we had two memorial services for Betty. In the afternoon, it was at Redeemer Lutheran in Thousand Oaks. Many people besides the congregation were in attendance. We had many ties with Thousand Oaks: the hospital staff, members of my Kiwanis Club, and near-by pastors. Then we had the same service for Betty at First Lutheran, Ventura. Both services were very well attended as we wept and smiled and joyfully praised God for the gift of Betty for 58 years. When I asked my three sons which pastors they would like to conduct the services, they clearly answered, "Pastor Puls and Pastor Blanke." Art Puls's connection goes all the way back to when I taught at Lutheran High School in Cleveland and knew his family very well. Woody Blanke was my closest neighboring pastor across the freeway in Newbury Park. They both agreed to the unusual situation of two services because they realized the special circumstances of the two congregations, only 30 miles apart, that Betty and I had served for 26 years. It was truly a memorable day.

~

Now begins what I call "my interim" – the nearly three years between Betty and Nancy – a strange, unfamiliar interlude in my life. Betty and I had hoped to do some traveling when I retired. As the time approached for me to retire, I asked the congregation if I could stay on for a couple more years. I wanted to fill the vacuum in my life, and I knew the congregation would be happy for me to stay. They were so supportive and loving. I will always have a special place in my heart for them. My ministry continued on until I married Nancy in the little chapel at Concordia University, Irvine. Much of this is contained in a section of my chapter on "The Women in My Life."

~

The Brasch Family

My life with Betty was immensely enhanced by what I will call, "My Canadian Connections," or "My Canadian Family" in Burlington, Ontario, Canada – the Brasch Family. Betty had wonderful parents: Frank, a Lutheran pastor, and his wife, Irene. She also had a brother, Jim, who with his delightful wife, Delores, are two of the most interesting people I have ever known. Over the years we have become very close and loving.

Delores is a super homemaker, an outstanding cook, plays the piano well, and has created some marvelous quilts. She loves opera and art, and has exquisite taste. Being in their home for a visit has always been delightful and enjoyable. A typical day begins with Delores as she prepares breakfast before the others are up. I especially remember having wonderful conversations with her. Mornings that had such fascinating conversations were followed hours later with conversations with Jim.

Jim is a retired professor of English and American Literature, and a well-known Hemingway scholar, who taught at McMaster University in Hamilton. Along with his many gifts, he is an internationally known orchid expert, who built his own greenhouse attached to their house. I admire his amazing knowledge and his ability to share that knowledge with me. This often took place in late night and early morning talks in their basement, and included his political opinions, encouraged by ample amounts of gin and tonic.

How I looked forward to those rare visits to Burlington, Canada! After many years in their home with the greenhouse, they are now living in a seventh-floor seniors' apartment overlooking Lake Ontario. They are parents to supremely enjoyable daughters. Jennifer is the oldest and has made a name for herself in special psychiatric work at a large hospital. She has played violin since she was a child, and loves classical music which she teaches to her children. I married her to Kirt Cushnie in the rain in her parents' front yard. They have four children: Jimmy, Sarah and Beth (twins), and Andrew, all of whom play the violin. The girls love to play hockey, and are excellent at it.

One of my fondest memories of Jennifer was driving her on a five-day trip down the California coastline. Several years after the trip with Jennifer, Katherine, her sister, would say from time to time, "I want to go on that trip, Uncle Jim." So I repeated the trip with her. They both loved every mile of it!

Katherine married later in life to Jim Silburn. I married them in a campus building at McMaster University in Hamilton. They now have a baby named Rachel, a bright light in the life of Rachel's grandparents. Jim and Katherine own and run a "pub" in Fergus, Ontario, about an hour's drive from Burlington. All in all, the primary focus for me was visits to My Canadian Family. I treasure them in my life.

~

In the months after Betty died, I was put on a civil trial for causing injury and damage with my car. It was one of those things where I accidently, very lightly, hit the car in front of me at an exit in Ventura. There was no damage to my car, but some damage to the rear bumper and fender of his car. That happened in August of 1991, three months before Betty died. Almost a year later, in June of 1992, I was served a summons to go on trial for injury and damage I had caused with my driving. The other driver was a young and pleasant Hispanic whose job required him to drive cars from different places to a local auto sales company. A Los Angeles "scam lawyer" got hold of this young man and convinced him he could make a lot of money by suing me for personal injury and car damage to the tune of $25,000 or more. This was typical of the scam where they deliberately cause an accident and then sue the other person. My car insurance was State Farm, and they took over from there. There was a pre-trial meeting of both parties with a retired judge for the purpose of determining whether the case had any merit. When I showed up for that meeting in my clergy collar and black suit, the young man's eyes almost busted out of his head, as if he was saying to himself, *Oh, no! It's a priest!* The judge recommended that the case not go to trial. The plaintiff, nonetheless, insisted on a trial. There were a series of interesting interviews for the jurors. For instance, one prospective juror was asked if she knew me. She answered, "Oh, yes, and then continued to elaborate by telling everyone what a nice guy I was, very responsible and honest." The judge quickly dismissed her lest she prejudice other potential jurors. With a civil case jury of 12, only nine have to agree on the verdict. I was the recipient of an outstanding young lawyer who worked these kinds of cases for State Farm. His name was Kevin McTague, an Ivy League graduate, and was he ever sharp and quick on the draw! It is a very strange, uncomfortable feeling to sit there in a court room knowing that what happens might impact your life in some negative ways. I truly felt they didn't have a good case against me, but one can never be sure with the jury. However, my lawyer basically tore up their case against me, caught them in some lies and trickery, and presented such an excellent defense that it seemed that the jury would make the right decision. After four days, the trial ended late in the morning. I was told to go home and wait for a call about the jury's decision. It's easy to imagine my feeling of trepidation as I walked home, which was just ten minutes from the courthouse. I wondered if the jury saw through the lies and manufactured evidence that my lawyer had so cleverly brought out. We were told it might be several hours. But in less than an hour I was called back. The decision was in my favor. What a relief! Some members of the jury later told me that the decision was 12 - 0. Even the judge, after announcing the decision, muttered softly, "This case should never have come into this court! You are dismissed!" I walked home quietly, rejoicing and thanking God for my excellent lawyer and a good judicial system. But, of course, I missed not having Betty, who always was so supportive of me in my ministry and my life. But I'm sure she rejoiced with God in heaven, and that's good enough for me!

~

During this time, all the activities of the parish continued: worship services, counseling, teaching, making calls, and dealing with all the aspects of congregational life. Pastorally speaking, those last couple of years at First Lutheran were filled with joy and fulfillment. Special events included a double baptism of a grandfather (converted from Judaism) and his newborn granddaughter. It was pictured in the Southern California District newspaper, as well as the baptism of triplets after I moved to Orange at St. Paul's Lutheran Church. One of the things I started when I had a baptism in church was to invite all the kids to come forward and stand around the baptismal font along with the parents and godparents. The Elders and I tried it for the first time with some hesitation about the behavior of all the kids. Well, they did very, very well as they stood around fascinated by the baby and the proceedings of this great sacrament that Jesus gave to His Church. What a joyful experience as I held the baby, leaned down so the kids could really see the baby, and say something to him/her.

As I approached the close of my ministry in Ventura, I was also getting ready to get married to Nancy and move to Orange. The congregation prepared a festive celebration of nine wonderful years together. Special speakers included all three of my sons (mostly humorous), Art Puls, and various others of the congregation and nearby clergy. It turned out to be one of those occasions of mixed feelings – both happy and sad. Here I was, 67 years old, getting ready to get married and move 105 miles away to a new life in Orange with Nancy. But, the district president, Dr. Loren Kramer, wouldn't let a healthy, well-equipped pastor languish in retirement too long. Shortly after moving, he called me up and asked if I would replace the newly vacated position of circuit counselor for the seven churches in the immediate area of St. Paul's in Orange. Along with that new role in my ministry, I became an active preacher throughout the district. The presence in my life of Nancy began with a terrific honeymoon up the beautiful coast of California. What a wonderful way to spend the first years of my retirement.

My ministry with four beautiful congregations might be summed up with the words of this refrain in the Hymn, "Here I Am, Lord," by Dan Schutte:

> Here am I, Lord. Is it I, Lord?
> I have heard you calling in the night.
> I will go, Lord, if you lead me.
> I will hold your people in my heart.

Also from Tri-Pillar Publishing

Timely Reflections

A Minute a Day with Dale Meyer

by Dale A. Meyer

*A minute's worth of reading
for a day's worth of reflection*

Timely Reflections is a collection of 365 inspirational devotions from the long-running and ever-popular Meyer Minute weekday online series. Dr. Meyer aptly uses Scripture – along with his own wisdom and experience – to guide his readers through the joys and pitfalls of daily living. Insightful, uplifting, and sometimes challenging, these daily reflections will provide plenty of spiritual food for thought. Set aside a minute a day to read, reflect, savor, and share each one!

Dr. Dale A. Meyer currently serves as President of Concordia Seminary in St. Louis, MO.

$19.95 – Order online at www.tripillarpublishing.com

MEETING ANANIAS

AND OTHER EYE-OPENING STORIES OF FAITH

by James Tino
Foreword by Dale A. Meyer

Bring your faith back into focus!

Are you finding it harder to keep your faith energized? Why does the Christian life, initially so exciting and full of promise, often become routine and ordinary? It is easy to get overwhelmed by the concerns of life and to focus on the wrong things, which quickly drains the life out of our faith. We need to have our vision adjusted by the Word of God and the Holy Spirit so we can see the hand of God at work in our lives. In Meeting Ananias, our eyes are opened to see what we sometimes miss: the ordinary and extraordinary ways that God makes Himself known to us as we follow Him.

Rev. Dr. James Tino is Director of Global Lutheran Outreach, a Lutheran mission-sending organization.

$11.95 – Order online at www.tripillarpublishing.com

Life As a Mission Trip

Dr. Jacob Youmans

Missional Living 101!

Trips to the mission field always bring new spiritual growth and insight to our lives. What if we could learn to see mission not as an event to take part in, but as a lifestyle to embrace? In *Missional U: Life As a Mission Trip*, that's exactly what Dr. Jacob Youmans teaches us as he shows, through Scripture and by personal example, what missional living is all about! If you're looking for a new way to travel, then come along. Missional U is your ticket to an exciting and fulfilling spiritual adventure – one that's sure to last a lifetime!

Dr. Jacob Youmans, a dynamic conference speaker, is Director of the DCE Program at Concordia University in Austin, Texas.

$14.95 – Order online at www.tripillarpublishing.com

MISSIONAL TOO

The Trip of a Lifetime

Dr. Jacob Youmans

Bon Voyage... Again!

In this second volume of devotions on the joy of missional living, Dr. Jacob Youmans shows us what it means to see the world through redemptive eyes, love the world with an evangelistic heart, and travel the world with the Gospel of peace firmly on our feet. In Missional Too: The Trip of a Lifetime, we discover that when we walk in the footsteps of Jesus, the imprint we leave behind is His, not our own – and that makes all the difference. Our journey here as God's dearly loved people is a Gospel-sharing, disciple-making one.

Dr. Jacob Youmans, a dynamic conference speaker, is Director of the DCE Program at Concordia University in Austin, Texas.

$14.95 – Order online at www.tripillarpublishing.com

Shaking Scripture

Grasping More of God's Word

Rev. Mark Manning

Shaking Scripture was written to help develop a hunger within you for God's Word. You will see how intriguing and interesting the Bible can be. You will be guided through some of the well-known stories we've grown to love and that have, perhaps, gotten stale with familiarity. In addition, you will discover some lesser-known stories that just might surprise you because of their readability and application. In all, there are 12 devotions, each aimed at "Shaking Scripture" in a way that helps us grasp more of God's Word. Several reflective questions per devotion are also provided, making this book ideal for individual or group study.

Rev. Mark Manning serves as the pastor of Searchlight Ministries of Orange County, CA, where he shares his passion for understanding Scripture.

$14.95 – Order online at www.tripillarpublishing.com

Abba Daddy Do

exploration s in child like faith

by Dr. Jacob Youmans

Join the adventure of childlike faith!

When you're a child, every day is an adventure! Each day you see and experience life for the very first time. Reclaim the wonder and excitement meant for followers of Jesus as we explore the gift of childlike faith. Jacob Youmans, father of two, walks us through 40 true-life stories, discovering the spiritual in the everyday moments of childhood. Complete with study questions and scriptural references, this book is perfect for the individual looking to grow and be challenged, as well as a family or Bible study group.

Dr. Jacob Youmans, a dynamic conference speaker, is Director of the DCE Program at Concordia University in Austin, Texas.

$14.95 – Order online at www.tripillarpublishing.com

Powerful Love
An Introduction to Christianity

by Rev. Dr. Lloyd Strelow

*You've got questions -
God's love provides the answers!*

Powerful Love gets to the core of the essence of our Christian faith. The first chapter opens the window to God's love for each of us. It is through that window - guided by the Holy Spirit - that Christians see, believe, and live the rest of God's Word. Throughout Powerful Love, Pastor Strelow uses the inductive method, using our questions to lead us to search God's Word and find His answers for faith and life. Written as a basic guide to the Christian faith, Powerful Love also includes thoughtful study questions and an introductory guide

Rev. Dr. Lloyd Strelow has served six congregations in Michigan and California, including Prince of Peace Lutheran Church (LCMS) in Hemet, CA, where one of his primary emphases was to teach the basics of the Christian faith to all who seek to know the Lord.

$12.95 – Order online at www.tripillarpublishing.com

tALKING PICTURES

How to turn a trip to the movies into a mission trip

by Dr. Jacob Youmans
Foreword by Leonard Sweet

Movies and ministry? What's the story?

Movies are everywhere - at the theater, at home, on our computers, even in our pockets! Our culture's fascination with the power of movies brings us together in a shared experience. But did you ever think that watching the latest action-adventure flick with a friend could provide a truly unique opportunity to witness about your Christian faith? Talking Pictures examines the power of movies in our culture and explores effective ways in which we can use any movie as a way to start conversations about our Christian faith.

Dr. Jacob Youmans, a dynamic conference speaker, is Director of the DCE Program at Concordia University in Austin, Texas.

$14.95 – Order online at www.tripillarpublishing.com

for ordinary people

by Rev. Heath Trampe

What's so special about being ordinary?

In a world which equates "ordinary" with "not good enough," Rev. Heath Trampe uses powerful examples from the Bible to prove that even ordinary people can accomplish amazing things. As you journey through these 12 stories of inspiration and hope, you'll discover that "ordinary" is a pretty amazing thing to be. This 214-page book includes Bible study questions for each chapter, with in-depth answers and commentary. It is ideal for both individual and group study.

INDIE 2010 NEXT GENERATION BOOK AWARDS FINALIST!

Reverend Heath Trampe graduated in May 2010 with a Masters of Divinity from Concordia Theological Seminary in Fort Wayne, Indiana. Heath is currently serving as Associate Pastor of St. Peter's Lutheran Church in Fort Wayne.

$14.95 – Order online at www.tripillarpublishing.com

Peter Dibble, digital artist

Graphic Design
Logos & Branding
Web Design
Video Production
Multimedia

Let us help design banners, brochures, etc.
for your church or organization.

www.peterwjdibble.com

www.ingramcontent.com/pod-product-compliance
Lightning Source LLC
LaVergne TN
LVHW061344060426
835512LV00012B/2561